Defiant Bodies

CRITICAL CARIBBEAN STUDIES

Series Editors
Yolanda Martínez-San Miguel
Carter Mathes
Kathleen López

Editorial Board: Carlos U. Decena, Rutgers University; Alex Dupuy, Wesleyan University; Aisha Khan, New York University; April J. Mayes, Pomona College; Patricia Mohammed, University of West Indies; Martin Munro, Florida State University; F. Nick Nesbitt, Princeton University; Michelle Stephens, Rutgers University; Deborah Thomas, University of Pennsylvania; and Lanny Thompson, University of Puerto Rico

Focused particularly in the twentieth and twenty-first centuries, although attentive to the context of earlier eras, this series encourages interdisciplinary approaches and methods and is open to scholarship in a variety of areas, including anthropology, cultural studies, diaspora and transnational studies, environmental studies, gender and sexuality studies, history, and sociology. The series pays particular attention to the four main research clusters of Critical Caribbean Studies at Rutgers University, where the coeditors serve as members of the executive board: Caribbean Critical Studies Theory and the Disciplines; Archipelagic Studies and Creolization; Caribbean Aesthetics, Poetics, and Politics; and Caribbean Colonialities.

For a list of all the titles in the series, please see the last page of the book.

Defiant Bodies

*Making Queer Community in the
Anglophone Caribbean*

NIKOLI A. ATTAI

RUTGERS UNIVERSITY PRESS
NEW BRUNSWICK, CAMDEN, AND NEWARK, NEW JERSEY
LONDON AND OXFORD

Rutgers University Press is a department of Rutgers, The State University of New Jersey, one of the leading public research universities in the nation. By publishing worldwide, it furthers the University's mission of dedication to excellence in teaching, scholarship, research, and clinical care.

Library of Congress Cataloging-in-Publication Data

Names: Attai, Nikoli Adrian, author.
Title: Defiant bodies : making queer community in the Anglophone Caribbean / Nikoli Adrian Attai.
Description: New Brunswick, NJ : Rutgers University Press, [2023] | Series: Critical Caribbean studies | Includes bibliographical references and index.
Identifiers: LCCN 2022053163 | ISBN 9781978830356 (paperback) | ISBN 9781978830363 (hardcover) | ISBN 9781978830370 (epub) | ISBN 9781978830394 (pdf)
Subjects: LCSH: Sexual minority community—Caribbean, English-speaking. | Gay rights—Caribbean, English-speaking. | Transgender people—Civil rights—Caribbean, English-speaking. | BISAC: SOCIAL SCIENCE / LGBTQ+ Studies / General | SOCIAL SCIENCE / LGBTQ+ Studies / Gay Studies
Classification: LCC HQ73.3.C27 A883 2023 | DDC 307.76/609729—dc23/eng/20230309
LC record available at https://lccn.loc.gov/2022053163

A British Cataloging-in-Publication record for this book is available from the British Library.

Copyright © 2023 by Nikoli A. Attai

All rights reserved

No part of this book may be reproduced or utilized in any form or by any means, electronic or mechanical, or by any information storage and retrieval system, without written permission from the publisher. Please contact Rutgers University Press, 106 Somerset Street, New Brunswick, NJ 08901. The only exception to this prohibition is "fair use" as defined by U.S. copyright law.

References to internet websites (URLs) were accurate at the time of writing. Neither the author nor Rutgers University Press is responsible for URLs that may have expired or changed since the manuscript was prepared.

♾ The paper used in this publication meets the requirements of the American National Standard for Information Sciences—Permanence of Paper for Printed Library Materials, ANSI Z39.48-1992.

rutgersuniversitypress.org

*For all Queer and Trans people who dare to hope
for a better queer Caribbean*

Contents

Introduction: Queer Liberation in the
Anglophone Caribbean?   1

1   Liberating the Queer Caribbean   29

2   On the Ground: Challenging Sexual Politics in
the Region   52

3   Between the Walls: Ruination and New Sexual Worlds
in Barbados   80

4   Queens, Kings, and Kinship Networks: Queer Culture
and Trans(gressive) Community Making   106

5   Rumshops, Nightlife, and the Radical Praxis
of Internal Exile   135

Coda: A Defiant Politics of Hope in the
Queer Caribbean   164

Acknowledgments   169
Notes   173
References   181
Index   193

Defiant Bodies

Introduction

QUEER LIBERATION IN THE ANGLOPHONE CARIBBEAN?

A Deeply Complicated Trans Experience

Sandy is a forty-something-year-old Dougla,[1] Trinidadian, working-class trans woman from East Trinidad. I met her on a few occasions, firstly to interview her at her home, and then at two bars in the suburban center, Arima, located about five miles from where she lived. She describes herself as a "drag queen" who always felt feminine. In her words, "I always know myself as . . . since I small and growing up I know myself as . . . I don't know why, but since I small and grow-ing up I always know myself as so. I don't know why I come so, but . . . Well, I does go out there and lime and dress up." She could not tell what made her "so" but knew it was something she always felt, even though she struggled to articu-late it. She is also an introvert and prefers to go liming (hanging out) on her own in the capital city, Port of Spain, without other trans persons because "some of them does get on too scandalous nah. You know. That does cause too much bac-chanal and drama with them when they start to get on that kind of way. People does start to notice you nah so that is why I does like to move by myself. That is why I does go anywhere by myself, or I does move with a real woman" (Novem-ber 2016). She despised the hypervisibility that came with being in the company of other trans women who might behave too flamboyantly, acting rude and loud.[2]

When I met Sandy in Arima, she wore a mini dress and stood in front of the pub smoking a cigarette and calling out to a few of the men as they passed by. Her strong "manly" physique was barely concealed by her skimpy clothing and rough makeup, and her hyperfeminine gait contrasted with her muscular body. However, she was unfazed by her appearance, as a lot of the mostly middle-aged men knew (about) her and her liming partner,[3] Big Redz, another trans woman partying with her that night. Sandy did domestic work, cleaning houses, but was also a "street girl," doing sex work in Arima and Port of Spain. One night in 2014, while returning home from a job cleaning a house, she was brutally attacked by local police officers. She stared at the silhouette of her right hand under the glare of the dim streetlight and recounted:

SANDY: Watch you see this? The police do me that for nothing inno. I get a steel in my hand now.

NA: Where did that happen?

SANDY: Right in Arima . . . I does clean house. I was doing a house in Quesnel Street and coming back home. I walking on the pavement and they bawl out: "where that macoumé[4] man going?" But I walk straight. They bawl out again "aye bullerman[5] is you I talking to!" Me still eh answer and remain walking . . . Bam! They shout, "stop right dey, yuh eh hear we say 'stop right dey' awa?"[6] They jump out the car with the baton. When he fire the first baton I brakes with my hand and it mash up the bone in my hand. Up to now . . . I went to police complaint and ting and nothing ever come out of that . . . this happen about two years and something now . . .

. . . Boy, let me tell you what dem do me eh . . . afterwards, when dey realize my hand break, they hit me all on my foot; all meh foot did swell up big so [gestures to how large her legs were swollen], they take me in the police station down in the back by the cell. It was a woman in charge eh . . . she say "yuh see dat, me eh meddling in dat nah" . . . they carry me down in the back. I say I want to go by the hospital . . . they take the baton and pushing it in my mouth and saying "yuh like to suck prick, suck dis" . . . and afterwards they do so and drag me back in the van, lift me up and throw me in the van and drop me in the savannah and leave me there. Is a man pass in a car and I stop him. He did know me. I say I will pay him to drop me home. He drop me and my tenant help me inside. When I reach inside, and pain start to take me I tell him call the ambulance and they take me hospital. (November 2016)[7]

The incident occurred in Arima . . . I clean houses and was heading home after working at Quesnel Street. While walking on the pavement the police shouted, "where that macoumé man going?" But I ignored them and continued walking. They shouted again: "aye bullerman" we are speaking to you!" I still did not answer and continued walking . . . Bam! They shouted: "stop right there, didn't you hear we said stop right there, or what?" They jumped out of the car with the baton. When he first hit me, I shielded the lash with my hand and the bone was smashed. Until now . . . I visited the Police Complaints Authority and nothing ever materialized out of this attack. This was approximately two years, or more, ago . . .

. . . Boy, let me tell you what they did to me eh . . . after, when they realized that my hand was broken, they beat me about my legs; all my legs were

INTRODUCTION 3

> *swollen really big [gestures to how large her legs were swollen], then then took me into the cell at the back of the police station. A woman officer was in charge ... she said "you see that, I am not meddling in that, no" ... They took me down to the back of the station. I asked to go to the hospital ... they then took the baton and shoved it into my mouth saying "you like to suck prick, suck this" ... and after, they dragged me back into the van, lifted me in and threw me in and the dropped me in the savannah and left me there. A man drove by in a car, and I stopped him. He knew me. I said that I will pay him to drop me home. He dropped me and my tenant helped me inside. When I reached inside, and the pain started I asked him to call the ambulance to take me to the hospital.*

On hearing this story, I asked Sandy if she approached any of the local organizations for help in getting this incident addressed. She admitted that she was unaware that she could have contacted at least six activist groups in the country for assistance after this attack. In shock, I questioned:

NA: You know any of the groups down here doing work?

SANDY: No ... (Sandy bends her head and rubs her left palm with her thumb finger)

NA: So, you telling me that you never hear about any of them? It have CAISO, Friends for Life, I Am One, Women's Caucus ...

SANDY: Well, if I did know that dem was around maybe I would check them. But then too I get so turned off by how nothing eh come out of it from the Police Complaints Authority. Dem groups you talking about, dey need to look to get help from the elderly gays—like me so, who out there long. Like people who more into dem ting to help out. Because they will have more experience nah! More experience from way back ... I could give you a whole history yuh know ... I could write a whole book! (November 2016).

> *Well, if I knew that they were around maybe I would have contacted them. But then too, I was so turned off when nothing came out of the incident through the Police Complaints Authority. Those groups you are speaking about, they need to get assistance from the elderly gays—like me, who are out here for a long time. Like people who are more into these things to help. Because, they will have more experience. More experience from way back. I could give you a whole history you know ... I could write a whole book!*

Sandy, like many other effeminate working-class Black men and trans women, has little recourse for these harsh realities, especially when "they locking you up for nothing, giving you loitering case after beating you. Stripping you and doing all kind of wickedness" (November 2016). Sandy's visibly Black, trans and gay (when she is not "dressing up") body, then, makes her "hypervisible as a transgressive subject" (Wahab 2012, 493).[8]

4   DEFIANT BODIES

She is ridiculed and targeted because of her effeminacy and her inability to demonstrate moral and cultural legibility, which contravenes the nationalist construction of Black heteropatriarchal masculinity. As noted by Alissa Trotz (2014, 355) regarding a 1993 incident against Colwyn Harding by the Guyanese state, the police baton was used as a device of emasculation. In similar ways, by shoving the phallic baton in Sandy's mouth and pronouncing "yuh like to suck prick, suck dis," the police officers reminded Sandy that "as someone with a penis who at once refuses to chase phallic power . . . she doubly pressures the fragile, cherished fiction of powerfully hypernormative Black male masculinity, and cannot be imagined within such Black masculinist discourse without exploding it" (Tinsley 2010, 170–180). Sandy's experiences with police brutality highlight the state-sanctioned violence and discrimination to which gender-nonconforming persons may be subjected. The policewoman's refusal to stop the violence also exemplifies how women are sometimes implicated in masculinized state violence against subordinate genders. She, a lone woman against a group of incited male officers, acted to preserve her own space and power within the patriarchal structure; she enforced its exclusionary boundaries.

Despite this violence, Sandy demonstrates the resilience and agency trans women use to direct their own lives and actualize their gender identities and sexual desires. My interactions with her changed my outlook on this entire project. I remember leaving her home upset that night and with so many troubling questions regarding trans persons' affect and agency within the heteropatriarchal state, but also regarding the disconnect between formalized activism and on-the-ground experiences. In my field diary, I wrote:

Since meeting with Sandy and liming with her in Arima, I keep wondering how people like her could be written into the equation. I think that groups in Trinidad and Tobago need to be more directly connected to "other" communities that are not urban, not educated, and not "attractive" (based on their physical appeal, their activities, and their lifestyles). But are they really willing to get their hands dirty, which will mean actually moving from their offices into the streets? Are they willing to see how life really unfolds in these working class and rural communities to get a better sense of what really happens on the ground, beyond what they write in fancy grant and policy documents?

I think about these questions in light of recent trends that I see among organizers. On one hand, they've been writing about, presenting, and saying all the nice and flowery things about the potential of their work in order to attract foreign investment/buy-in. On the other hand, many of these organizers are trying to leave the country. . . . These NGO elites are getting opportunities to get out of Trinidad at the expense of those they leave behind. It's like "be good and the big guns on the outside will help you get out." I now

INTRODUCTION 5

feel that all the work being done by these organizations are charged by a politics of escape that only benefits the organizers. (Diary entry, November 30, 2016)[9]

I wondered how such a critique could be used to firstly acknowledge some of these complicated experiences, but also to critically examine international human rights discourse that situated queer realities in the Caribbean as encounters of disease, violence, and death, with escape to safe havens like Canada being viewed as the only viable solution. This is not to say that disease, violence, and death are not in the equation, but such narratives represent just one side of the issue. But, as Sandy's story (and others) will demonstrate throughout this book, there are also realities of agency in self-making and claiming space across the region.

A POLITICS OF HOPE IN THE QUEER CARIBBEAN

I begin this book not with narratives of the "unliving" (McKittrick 2014) nor with an enumeration of the dead, but with a tale of resilience despite state-sanctioned violence. As C. Riley Snorton (2017, iix) notes, "The recurrent practice of enumerating the dead in mass and social media seems to conform to the logics of accumulation that structure racial capitalism, in which the quantified abstraction of Black and trans deaths reveals the calculated value of Black and trans lives through states' grammars of deficit and debt." The Caribbean is implicated in the operation of global racialized capitalism, wherein profits, inclusive of monetary and pleasurable gains, are made off the manifold labors of Black bodies, while at the same time absenting or erasing them, in what McKittrick refers to as the "black absented presence." Building on this, Krystal Ghisyawan (2022) offers the discursive erasure of queer people from the spaces where they legitimately exist and act, as a "queer absented presence." As a dark-skinned trans domestic worker and a sex worker, Sandy transgresses the imaginary public-private divide, laboring in unregulated "private" spaces, where she is not afforded the protection of the state. Yet, while in public, walking on the street, the state employs violence to discipline her transgressive body, an act of erasure attempting to silence her loud, visible transgression. Sandy's gender, sexual orientation, race, class, and location within spaces all collide to render her powerless and worthy of corrective violence and disciplining. Yet she builds community, has friends and kin, enjoys sexual pleasure, and claims safe space. This book addresses this and other juxtapositions of power and vulnerability that queer and trans people contend with, not just in the Caribbean, but within broader transnational queer contexts. I systematically address the erasure of queer people within the Caribbean societies, and of trans people within the queer umbrella, by examining the legal barriers to inclusion, the politics of queer organizing, and the neocolonial impact of dislocating queer bodies from Caribbean spaces, before returning in the final two chapters to reestablish their presence through their agentive practices.

Queer experiences in the Caribbean have been problematically reduced to homophobic violence and death, with countries like Jamaica being posited as more homophobic than others like Barbados, Guyana, and Trinidad and Tobago. Thus, I embarked on this multi-sited ethnographic study to explore queer sexual politics in Barbados, Guyana, Jamaica, Trinidad and Tobago, and Toronto, a city with one of the largest Caribbean diaspora communities in North America. Utilizing transnational feminist, Black feminist, Black queer studies, and Caribbean queer and sexuality studies frameworks, this study explores the ways that queer and trans people negotiate, resist, and disrupt homophobia, transphobia, and discrimination in the Anglophone Caribbean. It draws on their everyday experiences within their communities to understand how they live despite being significantly constrained by dominant heteronormativity, heteropatriarchy, sexism, racism, and classism. Keen attention is given to how working-class queer and trans communities are actively co-opting, reimagining, and rearticulating space in these Caribbean sites, despite the discrimination they face for failing to adhere to dominant expectations of legible gender and sexuality. These embodied practices and ways of transgression include drag pageantry; the use of social media and the creation of virtual communities; "down-low" encounters between men who desire other men; and the co-opting of mainstream bars, clubs, and urban night space.

My positionality as a Trinidadian living in the Caribbean diaspora in Canada and the United States of America yet working closely with the queer community in Trinidad for over a decade affords me a unique perspective to examine queer people's labor in a struggle to create more livable spaces "at home" across the region, through activism and embodied practices. I observe how Caribbean people located in diaspora communities in cities like Toronto, backed by white, queer, neoliberal, and homoimperial agendas, continue to influence queer politics in the region through a "rights talk" agenda (M. Smith 1998, 288; 2005, 84). Such politics drives much of the Euro-American human rights activism that is increasingly influencing the region's visions of queer liberation, via the financial and administrative resources made available to local queer organizations from large diaspora funders and activists. This is despite differences in visions of freedom across regional geographies. I unsettle this problematic politics engaged by queer Caribbean diasporas in Toronto, while also closely observing the efforts of various activists across the Caribbean region, many times in contradiction to the divisive agendas gaining airplay internationally and regionally. These agendas, as human rights scholar Neville Hoad (2007, 69) argues in his critique of Dennis Altman's (2002) Global Gay thesis, "ensure the contaminating Western contingencies . . . and more often than not fail to map onto the

INTRODUCTION

bodily practices or more extensive worldings of the subjects they propose to describe." Activists, queer and trans people in the region, and its diaspora envision various ideas of "queer freedom," but it is critical to be mindful of who gets to talk about the deeply complex queer realities in the region.

Thus, I additionally interrogate how Canadian and international human rights discourse positions the Anglophone Caribbean as a place of queer impossibility, exodus, and exile. Inherited colonial histories and neocolonial liberation narratives are used to justify human rights interventions, reducing queerness to physical and penetrative sex acts, ignoring the diversity of queer-embodied practices and their potential for creating full and fulfilling lives. Neoliberal (often white) international human rights advocates posit that queer people are unable to actualize this fullness of their queerness within the region and thus must leave to survive and embrace their queerness. I disrupt and decenter these mainstream queer exile narratives by highlighting the ways that queer people create communities of exile within the region. Furthermore, I interrogate the ways that social justice movements across the region are shaped by their implications in global funding structures and their understandings of how queer people are affected by multiple forms of oppression. My interactions and involvement with some of the organizations doing work allowed me to critically assess how queer activism engages with the everyday negotiations queer people must confront, including their shortcomings in reaching those most in need of intervention, such as impoverished and working-class trans women whose stories are highlighted in this book. Indeed, some mainstream queer human rights approaches, in the Caribbean and in North America, overlook trans people's experiences and needs, a void this book seeks to fill.

Marquis Bey, author of *Black Trans Feminism*, asserts that when the term "LGBT" is used, it is often in reference to gay or lesbian, and the B and T identities are erased, even when the gender transgression is the more important or relevant aspect of the situation, such as when someone is the victim of a hate crime. It is not so much about the sexual identity but the perceived transgression of gender boundaries. Similarly, "queer" is inadequate and distinct from "trans" as a category. Bey (2021, 197) argues, "Queer theory, in short, has tended to universalize the term transgender, imbuing into transgender subjects a perpetual, dehumanizing ontological gender trouble that queer theory heralded as our salvation," and note queer theory's neglect of the lived experience of transgender persons. According to Heather Love (2014, 172), "Queer and transgender are linked in their activist investments, their dissident methodologies, and their critical interrogation of and resistance to gender and sexual norms." Consequently, I must differentiate my own usage of these two terms, and not conflate them, as they are not synonymous. My discussion of queer organizing highlights the specific and pervasive erasure of trans people and their particular challenges, as seen above in Sandy's unawareness of their existence when she needed assistance.

In 2008, I embarked on a mission to document trans women's experiences in Trinidad and Tobago to better understand their sexual and gendered praxes, and to learn more about how they built community. That project has sparked an enduring commitment to investigate underground and on-the-ground queer culture and the critical role that queer community plays in negotiating and resisting dominant heteronormativity, homophobia, transphobia, and discrimination. Furthermore, I was especially invested in better understanding the various ways that queer people thrive in different racial, economic, social, and cultural geographies. This decision reintroduced me to vibrant queer communities occupied by men, women, trans women, trans men, and other gender-nonconforming people who live, party, and organize in their homelands as they reimagine their belonging. My focus on these queer moments such as drag pageantry; the creation of kinship networks; "down-low" encounters between men who desire other men; and the co-opting of mainstream bars, clubs, and urban night spaces offers a theorization of queer and trans experiences in the Caribbean. It provides a new starting point for thinking critically about how these experiences differ within the region and across various geohistories. Focusing on queer and trans people's everyday negotiations allows for understanding the contours of queerness from multifaceted perspectives that are attentive to race, class, location, and so on.

The trans women in this book reveal how they envision transgressive ways of existing despite the various forms of violence they face. In this project, I draw attention to how these formations, ideas, and gender and sexual praxes not only circulate locally but also extend across regional borders to touch, feel, and embrace queerness in spaces similarly affected by our colonial and present histories, including new colonizing discourses, such as neoliberal queer human rights activism, that focus on narratives of mortality, disease, violence, and a need to seek exile elsewhere. Such narratives are insufficient for understanding queer and trans people's deeply complex experiences in the region.

The book's title, *Defiant Bodies: Making Queer Community in the Anglophone Caribbean*, references how queer and trans Caribbean people live in the region despite prevailing discrimination and violence. As it suggests, this act of queer defiance is a political act that is both personal and communal and goes against the grain of all codifications of heteronormativity. Even when claiming citizenship and belonging is disrupted and punctuated by violence, this work of queer space-making provides hope for something transgressively new in the region. I undertake a response to M. Jacqui Alexander's provocation, which asks what it might mean for queer people to envision home when it is not "immediately understood nor distinctively accessible" (1994, 22). This is especially salient when we consider what it might mean to be gender nonconforming in the Caribbean.

Navigating Multi-sited Ethnography and the Ethics of Fieldwork

Drawing on five years of ethnographic research in Barbados, Guyana, Jamaica, Trinidad and Tobago, and Toronto, and applying a theoretical approach grounded in transnational feminism, Caribbean queer and sexuality studies, and Black queer studies, I use the Anglophone Caribbean as a site of analysis to interrogate the opportunities and limits of queer liberation activism as a strategy for helping people who are understood as being denied their basic human rights. I also disrupt the notion of the Anglophone Caribbean as *only* hostile to queers, thereby exposing the limits of queer human rights as a stand-alone strategy for queer liberation. In this book I examine the ways that queer people enact gendered and sexual agency as another way to seek queer liberation and to exist in and create space in the region. I seek to examine three central questions: How does regional and international human rights activism overemphasize the region as uniformly homophobic, transphobic, and discriminatory toward queer and trans people? How are queer and trans people in the region articulating their own responses to nonhegemonic sexuality and queer human rights in the Caribbean? What potential does queer and trans experiences of transgression, erotic autonomy, and community making hold for reimagining the look and feel of queerness in the region? These broad questions frame my discussions throughout this text. Here I explore some of the methodological challenges experienced while undertaking this work, including accessing participants across racial and class boundaries.

Like many Caribbean queers who increasingly move across regional state borders for work and pleasure (among other things), I have enjoyed increased access to various spaces in my research sites through the relationships I have with people in each country and networks of people who keep queer communities alive. Doors were opened to me because of my connections with friends who are activists and community organizers, people who participate in drag queen pageants and other artistic spaces, and others who frequented queer party spaces. For example, I first met my Guyanese interlocutor in Georgetown in December 2015, while on a trip to Guyana and Suriname with friends from Toronto. I shared my research interests and desire to return to Guyana in 2016 to meet and conduct interviews with activists there. We continued to communicate after this trip and upon returning, he scheduled a series of interviews with twelve persons that he deemed important. His gatekeeper credibility helped me to gain access to people and spaces that would have been typically out of reach (Chaudhuri 2017), like the three high-profile foreign diplomats I had the privilege to interview. All but one of these interviews appear in this book because of concerns over the officials' anonymity; however, these interactions provided valuable insight into the landscape of human rights organization in the region.

I was able to make similar connections in Barbados and Jamaica through activist networks. In Trinidad and Tobago (T&T), I was familiar with most activists who were also already aware of my research, having done previous work with the local trans community between 2008 and 2013. I privilege Trinidad and Tobago as my site of entry for thinking about these questions across the Anglophone Caribbean because of my positionality as a Trinidadian scholar with greater access to financial and research support from Trinidad and Toronto. It is also important to note that, at the time of my data collection, Trinidad and Tobago was making significant strides in activism, and it demonstrated how the local is connected to wider circuits of knowledge production. T&T's legislative changes and activist mobilization exemplified how the space is "constructed out of a particular constellation of social relations, meeting and weaving together at a particular locus" (Massey 1994, 154). When deciding to augment the Sexual Offences Act to account for consensual sex acts conducted in private (2018), Justice Devindra Rampersad cited changes made to India's Penal Code in 2017 that recognized privacy as instrumental in decriminalizing sodomy (Puttaswamy versus Union of India 2017); Rampersad thus recognizes that T&T's legal challenges were occurring at the intersection of global human rights discourses, postcolonial homophobias, and nationalist ideals about inclusivity and decolonization, by removing colonial era legislation enshrined throughout the British empire, wherein my other research sites are implicated.[10] Close relationships have developed between activists and community organizations across the region that have made it possible to engage in rich conversations across borders.

Other boundaries were more difficult to overcome, for instance, race, class, and sociocultural dynamics. While I tried to collect and analyze data reflective of the racial differences in the region, and especially in Guyana and Trinidad and Tobago, my access to spaces occupied by non-Black queer people was limited. This is largely because middle-class queer Afro-Caribbean people dominated organized activism in many of the sites. Apart from interviewing one Indo-Guyanese and one Amerindian trans woman in Georgetown, and one Indo-Trinidadian activist from a group based in South Trinidad, all the other activists I interviewed were middle class Afro-Caribbean and catered mostly to lower- and middle-class people located in urban city centers. Both Barbados and Jamaica have predominantly Black populations, and this was representative of the work being done there. Even the queer people who attended community events where I conducted research were predominantly Afro-Caribbean, except for Guyana. Consequently, this book unintentionally focuses on the experiences of mostly Black Caribbean people in relation to activism, resistance, and community making. Some of these tensions are explored in each of the chapters, where activists and community members acknowledge and confront the various ways that race, class, and gender dynamics impede more wholesome engagement with issues facing queer people. I met all the trans people in this work in the community

INTRODUCTION

spaces they created. Often, these spaces existed "below the radar" of mainstream society and came alive under the cover of darkness.

While still in Toronto, I reached out to contacts around the region. However, when I arrived at the research sites, I still encountered barriers to accessing people who expressed interest. There were even several failed attempts to connect with some of the more prominent activists in Barbados and Trinidad, who were either unavailable or stopped communicating. I found that female activists were more likely to decline meeting with me, even if they had previously agreed. Was it because of our unfamiliarity? Was it because of my status as a Caribbean researcher coming from Canada? Or was it because I was a man seeking to retell lesbian women's stories? Despite my inability to provide an extensive account of lesbian experiences, Black lesbian feminist theory by scholars like M. Jacqui Alexander, Audre Lorde, Rosamond King, and Angelique Nixon, among others, is foundational to my framing of the intersections of race, gender, and sexuality among trans-identified and queer people in this book, even in those moments where I point to the tenuous situations of lesbians within the Anglophone Caribbean. Through such frameworks, it remains important for me to consider this issue of representation and how I strive to convey the stories being told effectively and ethically. For example, while in the field and throughout the writing process, I often reflected upon my location as a middle-class cisgendered man in relation to my participants, who are mostly working class and trans-identified, bearing in mind that I could run the risk of becoming voyeuristic. I also paid keen attention to how I named people in the region (as queer and trans in this project) without replicating prescriptive models used to make them intelligible.

NAMING QUEERNESS IN THE CARIBBEAN

I reference several Caribbean terms throughout this book in locating the social, cultural, and political vernacular of the region. Terms like "bullerman," "battyman," and "antiman," for example, are typically uttered in the pejorative to define homosexuality, or as Makeda Silvera (1992, 42) argues, "dread words. So dread that women [and men] dare not use these words to name themselves." However, research participants and I invoke them to reclaim the sexual and gender praxes that are made to appear threatened by prevailing homophobia, and to call attention to the fact that some Caribbean queers have reclaimed terms like these as markers of endearment to embody their transgressive nonconformity and to negotiate and resist dominant gender and sexual hegemonies over time (King 2014, 94). It also serves as a reminder that despite such long histories of classifying queer Caribbean people negatively, there exists a Caribbean where these terms hold particular resonance for queer people as they actualize various forms of erotic autonomy over time, establish communities, and continue to negotiate and resist prevailing heteronormativity. Or as Audre Lorde (1982) and Gloria Wekker (2006) capture in their work on Zami and Mati, many queer people have moved beyond these negative descriptors to envision other ways of being.[11]

I also refrain from adopting popular medicalized and "NGOised" terms like LGBTIQ and MSM to refer to my research participants and the groups of people I discuss who fall under the Lesbian, Gay, Bisexual, Trans, Intersex, and Queer umbrella, and who are framed as men who have sex with men. Shona Jackson (2016) reminds us in her writings on sexual sovereignty in Guyana that "these terms, which tend to have a more diasporic usage, do not originate in the region and they often work to eclipse our own ways of knowing and naming Caribbean sexualities, both positive and negative." Andil Gosine (2005, 61) argues this succinctly in his analysis of development work for queers in the Caribbean, where he observes:

> While a more appreciative understanding of the complexity of the sexual experiences and arrangements of Third World peoples is emerging in some quarters—no doubt because of the insistence by individuals and communities in the Third World and their allies—and conceptions of sexuality as fluid are gaining favour in the West (especially among queer anti-racist scholars), it is still this universal model that informs National AIDS plans, which remain, in many countries, the only space available for official recognition of sexual dissidents and/or minorities. In most plans, such as those implemented in the English-Caribbean nation-states, MSM are neatly boxed outside the "normal" population and effectively cast as deviants.

Instead, I use the term "queer" to reference sexual and gendered praxes in the region. This is despite the reality that this term may not necessarily resonate with people uniformly in the sites I traverse. Queer as a concept has often been challenged because of its white Euro-American baggage that arguably imposes ideas that are sometimes unrepresentative of nuanced Caribbean realities. Cathy Cohen (1997) argues that while people like Judith Butler, Eve Sedgewick, Teresa de Lauretis, Diana Fuss, and Michael Warner are credited for defining the field of queer theory, "the inability of queer politics to effectively challenge heteronormativity rests, in part, on the fact that despite surrounding discourse which highlights the destabilization and destruction of sexual categories, queer politics has often been built around a simple dichotomy between those deemed queer and those deemed heterosexual" (440). She argues further, "We must reject a queer politics which seems to ignore, in its analysis of the usefulness of traditionally named categories, the roles of identity and community as paths to survival, using shared experiences of oppression and resistance to build indigenous resources, shape consciousness, and act collectively" (480). Jafari Allen (2016, 39) similarly notes that the word "queer" can be sometimes offensive but can be useful because "the radical promise of Black/queer work today is located in schol-

INTRODUCTION

arship, art, and activism that has cellular and psychic connections to resistance to enslavement, which tried but failed to dehumanize our ancestors." On the note of the queer potential that exists within artistic practices in the Caribbean, Angelique Nixon (2016, 103) calls on us to think through the usefulness of "queer" (and "queerness") despite its complications, and how it registers in contemporary artistic contexts. She offers,

> Nevertheless, it can be useful to consider the ways art spaces are queer— meaning spaces that are non-normative and that can be safe or safer for those who are sexual outlaws or gender and sexual minorities (i.e., LGBTI people). The category "queer" then becomes itself a space for difference that represents sexual diversity and perhaps multiplicity. However, it is important to think through the ways "queer" doesn't quite register in many local spaces across the region as an identity category. Yet I find it is being embraced more and more by younger people, especially by those who identify as gender noncon-forming. Therefore, we can ask further what this category "queer" represents, in terms of various artists and their artwork.

With these arguments in mind, I acknowledge that there is not at this moment a specific term or phrase that is common to a region characterized by a multitude of experiences or that can fully classify "queerness" in the Caribbean context. But, in line with these scholars, I appreciate the ways that queer politics creates room for a theorization of unruly, disruptive praxes of nonnormative formations in the region. This points to endless opportunity to further interrogate a politics of naming among queer people in the region. Such reality is, however, not seen as a shortcoming; rather, I understand this as a key characteristic of the heterogeneity of experiences in the sites that refuse to align neatly with and disrupt Euro-American ideas of what queerness, especially in a Caribbean context, means.

David Murray (2002), for example, observes the fluidity and messiness of gender and sexual identity politics, what he calls opacity, in Martinique where straight-passing men, termed "gai men," reinscribe and destabilize popular discourse about gender identity (11). These men, who adopt heterosexual masking as a technique to pass as "acceptable," tend to get married, have children, and follow a heteronormative trajectory (121). In doing so, "this masking contributes towards an ongoing governmental silence and erasure of alter-sexualities, allowing heterosexuality to remain the operative subjectivity defining appropriate, normative citizenship and belonging" (114). However, Murray explains that Carnival festivities offer a site of symbolic tension where, on the one hand, they "further perpetuat[e] the ugly stereotype of the pejorative 'macoumé,'" but on the other they allow gai men "to pursue their 'natural' homosexual desire that is taboo in day-to-day interactions" (146). Beyond the Carnival space, and against this backdrop of obligatory public masking in Martinique, Murray also concludes that gai men "search out enclaves where the duplicity of the mask may be exposed and ridiculed" (114). He finds spaces like private discotheques and secluded beaches operating as "safe spaces" for men to explore their desires.

Caribbean scholars like Gill (2018) and Ghisyawan (2016, 2022), both utilizing the concept of "erotic subjectivities," also make timely contributions to the field of Caribbean queer and sexuality studies; in particular, they offer a nuanced view of the sexual politics at play among gay men and lesbian women in Trinidad and Tobago as they claim space and citizenship through their erotic practices, inclusive of their spiritual, sensual, and political practices. These arguments are particularly instructive as they offer a way to further debunk popular ideas of compulsory heterosexuality, while also expanding discourse on the nuanced ways that queer people negotiate their relationships within national, regional, and international discourses and spaces. This attention to sexual politics in the region is important because, as Allen (2011, 194) notes in his study of queer politics in Cuba, "individuals get on with their lives. They deal with situations in which they are embedded, making choices according to what they view as possibilities."

Research on queerness in Jamaica by Nadia Ellis and Carla Moore has also been foundational in thinking critically about not only how nonhegemonic sexuality and gender performance complicate ideas of virulent homophobia locally and regionally but also how multifaceted queer praxes are in the region. Both scholars examine how queer-identified men claim space in Jamaican dancehall, by maximizing on the inherent queerness within dancehall spaces, while simultaneously pushing against boundaries of respectability, gender, and sexual legitimacy.[12] Ellis's (2011) theorization of a queer performance hermeneutic across Caribbean and Black diasporic culture provides an analytical tool for the investigation of how queer sexual agency disrupts dominant heteronormativity. Regarding fashion, for instance, she notes how queer men "become just risqué enough, just bad enough, to live on the edges of closely guarded rules of masculinity, and in doing so, to demonstrate a certain mastery of those rules" (9). She also positions the drag queen as "one of the purest forms of masculine testing of limits," usefully meditating on how dancehall spaces offer opportunities for "male-male" sexuality under the guise of a "bad man" dancehall aesthetic through clothing, lyrics, and male homosocial choreographed dancing (10). Or, as she puts it, these spaces inform the embodiment of the "dancehall masculine queer" where "crowds and performers enter into an unspoken arrangement that ritualizes and contains queer performances" (15). Moore (2014, 102) pushes Ellis's queer hermeneutic further to interrogate how queer men actualize their queerness within the confines of such hypermasculine and conditionally homophobic arrangements. She learns that "queerness, rather than being marginal, is central to several aspects of the dancehall scene." She continues: "Queerness, or the denial of it, also offers stability to dancehall artists, giving them constant 'creative' fodder. . . . Specifically, queer men are accepted in the dancehall when they provide fashion worthy of imitation, service in the beauty and creative industries, and mock-able figures for 'heterosexual' dancers. Thus, though queerness is permitted, it is allowed within strictly demarcated lines and is valued, it seems, as a characteristic of straight men."

Although the dancehall space encourages hypervigilance in relation to queer identities and performances, Moore contends that contrary to popular belief it is not automatically repulsive toward same-gender-desiring people. Instead, for many men who have sex with men, especially those who are members of the inner-city communities, they become spaces of queer marronage where these men reconfigure the dancehall space through their cultural labor as fashion gurus and choreographers. However, in this context they also negotiate their queerness through the "strategic deployment of heterosexual signifiers in an attempt at misdirection" (ibid., 108). Chapter 6 of this book similarly centers the rumshop as a queer space for strategic trans embodiment. Recounting the experiences of three gay working-class Jamaican men in dancehall, Moore (99) asks: "How might we re-imagine queer possibility if we deliberately center the queer/ MSM dancehall participant as the holder, creator, and conveyer of knowledge and thus as human?"

In line with these scholars, I employ the term "queer" in referring to nonhegemonic people, groups, experiences, and praxes in the region. In this project, I acknowledge these dynamics and seek to continue dislocating queerness from a position of victimhood as it is often envisioned in queer activist discourse. I consider what it means for queer people to *also* negotiate their modes of being despite realities of homophobia, transphobia, and discrimination. I think critically about the ways that queer resistance involves not just an acknowledgment of confinement and unbelonging but also the work of creation and community building.

THINKING DIFFERENTLY ABOUT TRANS EXPERIENCES IN THE CARIBBEAN

As I emphasize throughout the following chapters, gender transgression often occurs beyond the purview of formalized organizing facilitated by large international groups and community activists, highlighting the misalignment between what we understand as differences between "queer" and "trans," with trans experiences being persistently underserved and undertheorized. Following Black trans feminist theorist Marquis Bey (2021, 199), I appreciate that "trans is a political intensity that arises from an antagonistic, subversive relationship to power," so since trans operates on a political register, it marks the tearing of bodies and embodiment from their assignation as gendered. It is, indeed, the introduction of altogether unsanctioned genres of encountering the world order.

As Bey (ibid.) theorizes, "One cannot be trans; it is what we do, how we engage the world and others, yes, politically." In other words, while we might consider "transgender" to refer to "gendered corporeality," transness is "a way of doing things with (our) subjectivity," a praxis "that engenders different ways of making and breaking sociality" (ibid.). Ultimately, "trans" possesses a valence of transgression, disruption, and reconstruction.

Gender and sexually nonconforming people fall into a space of unbelonging and exclusion, where nation-state rhetoric is used to enforce their social, political, and economic exclusion. Trans people are often the most marginalized and punished for their inability to fit neatly into the predetermined gender categories used to organize a given society. Bey describes such "trans" positionality as follows:

> Trans is not to be conflated simply with a purported ontological state of being transgender, the limits of which are nebulous at best and beholden to medicalized discourses of the exact boundaries of "gender dysphoric" embodiment at worst. I hold that trans refers to, following Susan Stryker's etymological uptake of it, "*the movement across a socially imposed boundary away from an unchosen starting place*—rather than any particular destination or mode of transition"; those who "cross over (trans-) the boundaries constructed by their culture to define and contain that gender"; or put in a slightly different register, trans marks "a movement with no clear origin and no point of arrival." (Stryker 2008, 1; emphasis in original; Snorton 2017, 2: as noted in Bey 2021, 194)

In other words, trans identities are not fixed or monolithic but rather refer to an array of transgressive practices. In my earlier work (2013, 132), I noted some of the many ways that multiple trans-identifications materialize in Trinidad and Tobago to influence how bonds of solidarity and community are formed, "especially when they feel that another does not necessarily represent what a true 'trans experience' entails." I noted a group of people who called themselves "drag queens" or "dress-up girls" but identified as gay men. Other trans women saw their involvement in sex work as necessary for economic stability; they may include a third group known as "titty queens," who were "transitioning," taking hormones (mostly birth control pills they get from local pharmacies) to feminize their bodies (softer skin, less facial hair, breasts, etc.). A fourth group comprises trans women who live full-time as women and are less involved [publicly] with trans communities but are well known and respected. Trans women base their concepts of belonging, legitimacy, and authenticity on these different embodied practices of trans personhood, utilizing them to create their own communities of (un)belonging, rendering their space-making practices even more important.

Imposed interpretations of the Caribbean as a place of violence, death, and disease limit the potential of seeing the region as inclusive of trans praxes, desires,

INTRODUCTION

and embodiments. Queer Global North human rights activism has taught us little about these possibilities because of its overreliance on narratives of wanton homophobia and transphobia and a discourse of escape. In the final chapters, I offer a new analysis of the transgressive possibilities actualized by trans people within the region through active negotiation, confrontation, and resistance to the prevailing norms that continue to define gender and sexual (il)legibility. Consequently, I think about how trans experiences not only reflect silence, invisibility, a pervasive sense of fear, instances of violence and the difficulty of transcending historical structures such as gender codes and state power but also reveal their resilience and disruptive agency as they negotiate prevailing transphobia and discrimination. Despite these narratives that categorize the Caribbean as a space of negation for queer and trans embodiments, and a space from which they must flee in order to pursue the actualization of their gendered and sexual selves, the reality is that the region is full of queer people of various races, social classes, transgressive genders and ages, who create space and communities of belonging. Trans women resist this erasure to actively co-opt, reimagine, and rearticulate space in the Caribbean, despite the discrimination they face for failing to adhere to dominant expectations of legible gender and sexuality. Through their transgressive praxes, they utilize their sexual and gendered positionalities to claim visibilities and disrupt the status quo "below the radar" in spaces of exile within the region.

GENDER IN PRACTICE: DISRUPTING NORMATIVE MASCULINITIES

In this work, I explore the praxes of disruption and resistance embodied by queer and trans people that expose the historically, socially, culturally, and politically motivated normativity governing Caribbean societies, examining transgender bodies. I do this understanding trans experience not only as sites of disruption but also as generative sites of creation, in line with what C. Riley Snorton (2017, 2) refers to as "conditions of possibility," in their theorization of negotiating Blackness. Snorton notes how the dominant logic of identity positions "race" and "gender" as fixed and knowable, while considering "trans" to be "a movement with no clear origin and no point of arrival within 'blackness' . . . an enveloping environment and condition of possibility" (ibid.). Thus, they position "trans" and "blackness" as appositional, parallel, and having the same referent. Snorton offers "transitive" as a concept to "provide critical insight into the transubstantiation of things"—namely, how "black" and "trans" are "brought into the same frame by the various ways they have been constituted as fungible, thingified, and interchangeable, particularly within the logics of transatlantic exchange" (6). Consequently, they charge a rethinking of our relationships to things and confronts how they have come to be defined through history. Categories of gender and race in the Caribbean have been defined as they intersect on the sugarcane plantations and persist in structuring everyday life in the region: how we think, how we act, how we see gender being performed across time and place, and how we replicate gender and sexuality among people and across generations (Lewis 2003). Caribbean feminist scholar Patricia Mohammed (2002, xiv) argues, "We are not born men and women, but we do become our gender. We each take our biological script and shape it into something we define as our gender and our sexuality. The essentialist contouring of gender, and its contingent sexuality . . . ensures that there is a reference group with whom as individuals we can work out our similarities and differences and thus our capacities for survival." For instance, family and peer groups are two of the most effective social mechanisms for inculcating attitudes and values in persons as they grow and learn to interact with each other; children internalize the prescribed ways to perform racialized gender norms through imitation and reinforced instruction of the values and associated behaviors (Chevannes 2001; DeShong 2012).

While the construction of masculinity differs between communities, scholars of Caribbean masculinities posit that differing histories influence specific sexual subjectivities; specific patterns are evident in the construction of Caribbean manhood. Sociologist Barry Chevannes (2001, 115) theorizes that men are required to adopt what he terms "markers of manhood" where, in addition to expectations of being physically robust, they are also required to engage in various forms of promiscuous and multiple partnerships and occupy public space by being outdoors, socializing and drinking by rumshops or street corners, playing sports, and gambling. Likewise, Linden Lewis (2003, 115–116) offers the idea of "metaphors of masculinity" to show how Caribbean men must embody particular traits in order to be legitimized, such as "their ability to play certain sports, or to display great devotion to them, indeed, to be the guardians of their history and the collective conscience of masculinity. Accordingly, hegemonic masculinity is heterosexual and decidedly homophobic, priding itself on "its capacity for sexual conquest and ridicules men who define their sexuality in different terms" (108). Chevannes (2001, 220) notices that homosexuality, or nonvirile masculinity, "creates a breach, so to speak, in the male ranks, by directing male sexuality, the principal mediating form of inter-gender relations, to other men," rather than to women. He concludes therefore that homosexual men are forced to maintain "a curtain of privacy around their sexuality" in order to be afforded space (ibid.). Men can confine their "feminine" activities and pastimes to the privacy of the home (Lewis 2003, 117), but still "run the danger of a confused identity—the sissy, the mamaman—unless their confinement inside is focused on activity that is non-female and carries greater values, such as education." Wesley Crichlow (2004, 204) reflects on his own "involvement in competitive sports such as football and cricket was a means of survival" for him growing up as a gay Trinidadian man. He explains: "Sports offered an accepted

INTRODUCTION

arena in which young men could exercise their masculinized personhood and erase same-sex suspicion." These tensions remain relevant today and constantly remind Caribbean men that "the sexual identity of men who stepped outside their traditional masculinized or mannish role was always in question" (ibid., 199).

Forms of Indo-Caribbean masculinities adheres to similar metaphors but simultaneously "represents a cultural contradiction of belonging and nonbelonging—of being a part of all that is the Caribbean yet not wanting to belong so completely as to be overwhelmed by the dominance of the African presence in the Caribbean, which confronts them on all levels" (Ramsaran and Lewis 2018, 1). Existing within a context of competing cultures and patriarchies, Indo-Caribbean men must grapple with, on one hand, "what they often mock as stigmatized 'old time' or 'coolie' values" including being economically tied to agriculture and some vague notions of caste/class endogamy, and on the other, modern, postcolonial constructions of "national" cultural values, also coded as Afro-Saxon and creolized notions of respectability (Sampath 1993, 241). They strive to be integrated within Caribbean society, while at the same time, try to maintain the group's distinct cultural identity. During indenture and the postindenture period (until about 1947), men attempted to create new sexualities free from strict kinship rules that allowed them some privileges, such as marrying out of their caste, having more than one woman, and practicing serial monogamy (Mohammed 2002). At the same time, violence was used as a means of control over women (Sampath 1993; Mohammed 2002). Patriarchal violence in the domestic sphere, virility, and domination of public spaces, like the rumshop, therefore remain markers of Indo-Caribbean masculinity.

The dramatic short *Antiman* (2011), by Guyanese film director Gavin Ramoutar, explores these tensions of masculinity, where Anil, a young cricketer, is ridiculed about his fondness for cross-dressing. Cross-dressing in this context is understood as a cis-gendered man wearing female clothing for pleasure (not necessarily sexual) and to realize his transgressive gender. As Charleston Thomas (2010, 122) argues, "transgressive bodies" are invented within the conventional boundary markers that define sex and gender, yet Anil may not necessarily be considered trans, as such identity practice is insufficient for theorizing gender nonconformity and transgression in the Caribbean. Guided by his older trans friend, he learns quickly that a sure ticket to acceptance will be mastering the art of cricket—read as mastering (Indo-Guyanese) masculinity. Anil's winning the cricket tournament meant he could attend an annual masquerade, meet his secret love, Dano, and gain the acceptance of his community and his father (Ramoutar 2011). This short film exposes the important reality of gendered relations in the region where, as Crichlow (2014, 32) theorizes, "for most young men in the Caribbean, the success and strength of their manhood to a large degree depends on how well they can perform 'normative, straightjacket or dominant masculinity' to obfuscate any form of tenderness or effeminacy." Therefore, boys must quickly learn that once they can successfully embody the metaphors of masculinity, they can benefit from prevailing systems of control.

TRANS EXPERIENCES AND INTERACTION WITH
TRADITIONAL GENDER EXPECTATIONS

Scholarship on trans experiences in the Caribbean has been limited to sex work and HIV studies (Scheim et al. 2016; Miguel 2018; Cabezas 2019), with only few ethnographies exploring identity and self-making.[13] Cultural production in the Anglophone Caribbean offers space for transgressive gender performance, including cross-dressing in Carnival and trans characters in literature, both of which Rosamond S. King discusses in her book *Island Bodies: Transgressive Sexualities in the Caribbean Imagination*. King (2014, 25) argues that in Caribbean fiction, the trans character is accepted as part of Caribbean culture, but "in a backhanded maneuver that keeps them in subservient, marginal roles." She posits that literary pieces like Shani Mootoo's *Cereus Blooms at Night* and Michelle Cliff's *No Telephone to Heaven* position trans characters as central to the narration yet keep them in the margins of the novel as minor characters. "Even when they are telling the story, trans people do not get to tell their *own* story" (ibid., 39; italics in original). She links this kind of treatment to that portrayed in popular Caribbean culture where trans people typically become visible through comedy, drag performances, and erotic entertainment as sex workers, which "avoids exploring how inclusion and acceptance of trans individuals could challenge binary Caribbean gender" (ibid., 43, 61). Much of this potential, she believes, remains largely hidden in the region's literary imagination (ibid.).

Cross-dressing, on the other hand, occurring during the context of Carnival, is employed mainly as parody, which Rosamond King (2014, 52) asserts may have "subversive and positive effects, opening up a space to critique gender norms [. . .] it can also have backhanded, negative aspects, in this case the ridicule of black working-class women and trans practices and people." However, being accepted in the Carnival cultural space emphasizes how taboo cross-dressing is in daily life for every gender but especially for men wearing "women's" clothing (Ghisyawan 2022). These men's effeminacy challenges the patriarchal order wherein gender roles are rigidly defined yet differentiated according to other social factors, like class, race, and religion. Lewis (2003, 517) cautioned, "We should also be fully cognizant of the fact that culture (religion as part of culture) is a very powerful tool for reproducing patriarchy in ways that transcend race, class and age." Consequently, not all men have equal access to power within the society. Men who fail to perform masculinity well are also viewed as sexually transgressive, and thus inferior, warranting their exclusion. This does not mean that there are no queer men in positions of power but rather that overt

INTRODUCTION 21

demonstrations of gender or sexual nonconformity are not tolerated and the interest of queer persons (as it relates to their gender and sexual actualizations) are not necessarily sought.

Additionally, Lewis (2003, 519) recognizes the critical need for addressing men's use of violence against women and subordinated men; he blames the socialization of men for empowering them to act as warriors and defenders of honor, nation, country, and God, all of which are implicated in the normalizing of gender ideals. Afro- and Indo-Caribbean men alike use physical and epistemic violence, the deprivation of rights, and political and corporate marginalization to discipline and enforce conformity and punish transgression (Sampath 1993). Addressing the issue of violence against homosexual men, Lewis (2002) argues, although "rationalized by both men and women on religious grounds or by appeals to nature," cannot be condoned when the same violence against women is condemned. He notes, "We need to be more vocal in our condemnation of the physical and verbal abuse of others, irrespective of gender or sexual orientation. Failure to recognize all forms of violation is tantamount to being disingenuous" (522). But these violations also occur at the state level, are built into state rhetoric and law, and impact the everyday lived experience of queer people in the Caribbean. I discuss this further throughout this text, giving attention to advocacy challenges and changes to legislation and state practices across the region.

Scholars of Caribbean gender and sexuality studies offer insight into how people constantly confront notions of "legitimate" gender and sexuality so that constructions of masculinity in the region marginalize nonhegemonic men, necessitating queer people's contestation and negotiation. However, these works position queer people as threatened, doing less to make sense of queer culture in the region by simply emphasizing an idea that these people are left with little choice but to hide their desires and practices (Crichlow 2004; Kempadoo 2009; King 2014). Essentially, this type of portrayal strips gender and sexual minorities of any agency or autonomy, while reducing them to victims of a heterosexist and patriarchal order.[14] More recent scholarship on queer sexual autonomy has begun to address this shortfall, reclaiming agency, space, and belonging for people with nonhegemonic genders and sexualities (King 2014; Nixon 2015; Gill 2018; Ghisyawan 2022). It is in this field of queer Caribbean sexuality studies, and particularly Caribbean trans studies, that I contribute to examine gender and sexual agency and embodied practices of trans people in the Caribbean.

In my theorization of the connections between race, gender, and class, it is notable that the trans people I interviewed and interacted with were mostly Afro-Caribbean. It is also important to recognize the absence of Indo-Caribbean trans people in the spaces where I examined trans identities: urban bars, clubs and rumshops, drag pageants, Carnival fêtes, and parties. However, I explore trans women's self-making, space-making, and community-making practices that confront traditional and normative relationships between gender and space. I interrogate, for instance, who is allowed to occupy and to thrive in specific geographies within the region. For example, the rumshop juxtaposes pleasure and violence, even today, remaining a central locale within Trinidad and Tobago culture. Although it is male dominated and a forum for the circulation of patriarchies, my research demonstrates how it functions as a space of transformation of gender ideals through trans women's embodied practices.

CONFRONTING THE NUANCES: QUEER EMBODIMENT'S CHALLENGES TO HETERONORMATIVITY

We destabilize that which hegemony has rendered coherent or fixed; reassemble that which appears to be disparate, scattered, or otherwise idiosyncratic; foreground that which is latent and therefore powerful in its apparent absence.
—Alexander 2005, 192

Pioneering scholarship in Black queer studies and transnational feminist analysis led me to this intellectual crossroad where I can interrogate the contentious ways that queer and trans people negotiate and trouble the region's sexual politics. A key analysis taken up in these fields, for instance, is the centrality of the gendered and sexual labor that Black queer people perform, oftentimes with limited agency, to disrupt and resist, on one hand, the inherent minimization of the work, lives, and cultural production of queer people of color, and to acknowledge, on the other, how difference among queer people enables a deeper appreciation for Blackness and queerness as world making (Johnson 2003, 131). My examination of the erotic, economic, and political practices of queer and trans people in the Caribbean rests on these principles, revealing the multiple intersections of labor, experience, and embodiment when it comes to making life in the Caribbean.

A transnational feminist analysis requires us to confront, interrogate, and disrupt the legacies of the colonial empire that continue to control the flows of power that work to define our ways of being and relationships to others. My scholarship responds to this call by actively examining the ways that ideas about legible (hetero)sexuality flow into, out of, and across the Anglophone Caribbean region and its diasporas and exploring the ways that queer people disrupt these very notions of citizenship and belonging to the nation, as M. Jacqui Alexander reminds us in the above epigraph, in contexts where legible sexuality is still enshrined in law. Alexander's theorization of state-sanctioned discrimination against nonheterosexual persons is critical for understanding the ways that heteropatriarchy is framed in nation politics, but more importantly how the queer subject threatens the restrictive legislating of compulsory heterosexuality. While colonial sodomy laws still exist and are rarely enforced, they remind queer people that they are falling short of claims to legality by mere virtue of their aberrant sexual and gendered praxes. Severe social penalties are attached, and it is often the sociocultural policing of sexual desire that perpetuates unfortunate and sometimes deathly circumstances for those who transgress. Alexander makes this clear in her argument that the state's heteronormative conventions of personhood and desire are enshrined in the assumption that identity, sexuality, and gender are fueled by a "natural" affinity to opposite-sex desire and attraction. Thus, the sexual inscriptions placed on some bodies thereby outlaw their very existence: "No nationalism could survive without heterosexuality—criminal, perverse, temporarily imprisoned, incestuous or as abusive as it might be, nationalism needs it. It still remains more conducive to nation-building than same-sex desire, which is downright hostile to it, for women presumably cannot love themselves, love other women, and love the nation simultaneously" (Alexander 1997, 83). These sentiments are laid in concrete terms through the regional laws that replicate colonial ideas about the proper kind of citizen and translate into beliefs about aberrant nonheterosexual practices. She posits further that they inscribe "powerful signifiers about appropriate sexuality, about the kind of sexuality that presumably imperils the nation and about the kind of sexuality that promotes citizenship" (Alexander 1994, 6).

Alexander (2005, 192) offers erotic autonomy, where "unproductive sexuality" embodied by queer people is able to "destabilize that which hegemony has rendered coherent or fixed; reassemble that which appears to be disparate, scattered, or otherwise idiosyncratic; foreground that which is latent and therefore powerful in its apparent absence." She calls on queer people to craft "interstitial spaces beyond the hegemonic where feminism and popular mobilization can reside" (65), to call attention to the various ways that we "construct home when home is not immediately understood nor distinctively accessible" (1994, 22). Claiming nonhegemonic sexual desire and gender identity present an opportunity to actualize bodily pleasure, while implicating one in political power struggle. As I posit in this work, this erotic sense of feeling and doing is often contrary to the dominant heteronormative and homonormative expectations that influence ideas about belonging to the Caribbean nation and the claiming of both sexual and political citizenship in it. Audre Lorde (1984) also provides me with a vocabulary to assert the necessity of the erotic in queer lives and the importance of embodiment and praxis in reinforcing and resisting power discourses intended to control and discipline certain bodies. In my discussions, I think about how it functions to give life to the creative and oftentimes calculated ways that queer people continue to resist, not only through formalized strategies of activist organizing but also through the sometimes less apparent ways of existing in and claiming space across the region.

Thus, embodiment comes to be a central theme in this book. I examine how embodiment of queerness and transness by persons in the Caribbean confront the limits of citizenship, and how we could use the lessons learned from trans people to inform queer activism. The idea of embodied theory offered by Caribbean feminists Angelique Nixon and Rosamond King (2013) is attentive to the complexities of this queer resistance, as it allows for an appreciation of and keen attention to people's situated experiences. They posit that embodied theory "encompasses the importance of community organizing and attention to the local" (2). Such an approach is useful for this undertaking to provide an account of how people's sexual and gendered realities are informed by the social, cultural, and political circumstances that surround them. Embodiment is a means for Caribbean people to actualize their *imagined lives* and the ways in which they envision belonging in the region (Robinson 2011). In adopting an embodied theory approach proposed by these Caribbean feminists, I retell stories using the experiences, language, and ideas of the research participants to capture the tensions, contradictions, and nuances of their realities.

This work represents my journey, not only as a scholar of the queer Caribbean but also as a Trinidadian-born, -raised, and -educated product of the region. It reflects my ideas and theorizations of the nuanced experiences that people, in their same-sex-desiring, gender-transgressing, and fluid gender and sexual praxes have in their countries. It also confronts the complicated relationships between queer Caribbean people and activists within and outside the region and the accompanying power dynamics at the intersections of imperialism, colonialism, and control, all of which are refracted through racist, classist, sexist, and gendered assumptions about the queer people of the region. It also provides some beneficial insight and lessons for activists doing the complicated work of addressing the needs of queer and trans people in the Caribbean. The chapters build on each other as I make space for often-silenced realities, or if I may, other truths about queerness in the Anglophone Caribbean.

In This Book

The book examines the radical shifts in the Caribbean to conceptualize queer citizenship in the contemporary neocolonial global structure. Despite the sociocultural and political circumstances of unintelligibility, queer Caribbean people continue to claim visibility on regional, national, and communal levels as they situate themselves in relation to dominant understandings of belonging. This visibility is an integral characteristic of the issues I interrogate in the Anglophone Caribbean.

The discussion entails three major sections. Firstly, I discuss activist organizations in the Caribbean and their implication within the global industrial NGO complex, paying attention to how funding from North American queer rights groups not only influences the ways in which these local and regional organizations operate but also dominates discourse about the region's queer realities. Secondly, I give attention to the neocolonial influence of the tourism industry, as an extension of the same colonizing discourses and activities that both limit understandings of queerness and provide an opening for the actualization of queer desires. These two sections strategically juxtapose regional activism with other visibility formations by queer and trans people across the Anglophone Caribbean to bring these two areas, always at odds with each other, into closer conversation, and to lend a sharper focus to the need for better understanding how queers negotiate and resist prevailing heteronormativity and homophobia on multiple levels in the Anglophone Caribbean. The final section of the book shifts focus away from colonizing influences to the agentive practices of trans men and women in Trinidad and Guyana. I consider the world-making potential of queerness that moves beyond organizing, to contemplate the ways that queer people claim visibilities and push against boundaries through their unruly and disruptive modes of resistance across the region. Doing so contributes to the bourgeoning discussions of resistance and makes a useful departure from medicalized and pathologizing conceptions of queerness as deviance that, as Caribbean sexuality and art scholar Andil Gosine (2005, 60) argues, "leaves intact development's colonialist-imperialist and patriarchal-paternalist trajectories." It also exposes some of the critical gaps that separate queer activism from queer reality by using firsthand participatory experiences in regional rights organizing and by documenting the oft-excluded lived experiences of trans people.

Chapters 1 and 2 engage with neoliberal human rights activism, which reinscribes "the epistemic erasure of sexual minorities or the pathological representation of queer subjects" (Rowley 2011, 174), while "claim[ing] that protected life is available to all and that premature death comes only to those whose criminal actions and poor choices make them deserve it" (Hong 2015, 17). In reality, development work is embedded with heteronormativity that continues to influence human rights interventions and results in the displacement of gender variant bodies through the imposition of Euro-American understandings and a teleology of sexual becoming (Rowley 2011, 178). Not only does this rhetoric overlook and silence trans experiences but it also occludes the needs of queer communities in the region in favor of the goals prioritized by Global North queer liberation and homonationalist agendas that are spread through global capitalist machinery, such as mass media, corporations, and even aid organizations.

Chapter 1 examines how Canada positions itself as a global "queer liberator," a savior, bringing modern freedoms to today's queers around the world by utilizing racial capital to further the interest of transnational queer organizations. Firstly, this means that Black and brown bodies are mobilized, employed, and used through a rhetoric that legitimizes an oppressive Caribbean and secures Canada's location as the queer haven. Secondly, these international organizations fund projects within the region to further their own aims through the labor of the region's queer and trans bodies. I discuss several examples of queer human rights activism that produce what I conceptualize as notions of conditional queerness in the Anglophone Caribbean that further the stigmatization and pathologizing of the queer Caribbean body through an excessive focus on HIV/AIDS. I show how everyday experiences of queerness and transness end up receiving limited attention from activists. Capital investment is tied to these goals and projects that reproduce trans exclusion and fail to improve the institutional infrastructure of local and grassroots organizations—for instance, by providing financial literacy and other skills training. Through tracing the work of these organizations across international, regional, and ideological boundaries, I examine how capital is controlled and routed through these networks to perpetuate the depiction of queer Caribbean peoples as ill-equipped to solve their own problems and, therefore, in constant need of saving.

Chapter 2 delves further into the work of regional activist organizations and the potential disconnects between activist work and the everyday experiences of the intended target populations. I examine the tensions arising out of two legal cases that were resolved in 2018, both challenging colonial era laws that continue to infringe on the freedom of colonized subjects through their demarcation of acceptable practices for respectable citizenship. Firstly, *Jason Jones v. The Attorney General of Trinidad and Tobago* secured the decriminalization of sodomy among consenting adults and flared up homophobic religious nationalist passions that used panic and scare tactics to incite public outcry against gay marriage and other issues not even at stake in this context. The case also revealed the rift in the goals of regional (such as CAISO: Sex and Gender Justice) versus international advocacy groups (represented by Jones) on what they believed was truly impactful and beneficial to the local queer population. The second case I attend to, *McEwan, Clarke, Fraser, Persaud and SASOD v. Attorney General of Guyana*, challenged cross-dressing laws that stated it was not allowed for "improper purposes" that presumably go against moral codes of legible gender and sexuality. I show the connection between this and other colonial era legislation, like loitering and vagrancy laws, that restrict the mobility and gender expression of people who utilize the public sphere for their economic sustenance, like trans sex workers. These laws were all constructed to create an image of respectable citizenship within the empire, as procreative and heteronormative. Through the chapter, I examine the shifting definitions of queer respectability and queer citizenship, to produce a conditional queerness that exaggerates limited acceptable ways of being queer, while silencing people's deeply complicated realities. I turn to two of CAISO: Sex and Gender Justice's public information campaigns to demonstrate this tenuous belonging that queer people experience within national rhetoric: the "Homosexual Agenda" (2010 and 2015) and the Keep Safe campaign (2018). These campaigns provide insight into the different ways that the group continues to engage ideas of queer belonging in the country.

INTRODUCTION

Neocolonialism and global capitalism further demarcate belonging through its control of economic opportunities in the Caribbean, such as the tourist industry. In chapter 3, I examine how abandoned hotel projects in Barbados are anachronistic artifacts, relics of a past story of territorial appropriation, and at once, are generative spaces where new meaning is given when it is co-opted by queer people, for secret sexual rendezvous. Half-finished hotels, abandoned when international investors ran out of money, lay wasting away in the tropical climate, only to become symbolic of queer absence and simultaneous queer presence. These ruins, silent and abandoned during the day, are haunted by traces of queer life, representing their marginality, while at the same time presenting opportunities for the actualization of queer desire. The graffiti, some warding off the gays, promising them punishment, and others inviting them to fulfill their desires, and debris, like empty rum bottles and discarded condom boxes left in the wake of sexual encounters, tell the stories of what occurs there despite the absence of bodies. The absence of bodies in the space reflects the silence around nonhegemonic sexualities and genders. I draw on Ann Stoler's (2013) reflection on Imperial Debris, wherein scholars use the framework of "ruination" to critique how the processes of empire leave indelible marks on the societies they have touched.[15]

Colonialism has long been at work ruining the Caribbean, evident in economic drain, political rivalries, and the racialized gender systems established by old colonial powers that are exacerbated by neocolonial discursive, economic, and political practices. The abandoned hotel tells the history of colonial empire in the Caribbean: its having been treated as the brothel of Europe; its continued framing as a sexual destination and thus reliance on the tourist industry. Simultaneously, the empty building provides an opening for the contemporary queer co-opting of the space, intended for leisurely use by wealthy foreigners, now a playground for locals. Still, queer praxis occurs in the shadows, not visible, relegated to the margins and having to confront religious homophobia, and discourses of disease and decay. I resist this depiction of queer life in the Caribbean and thus shift the narrative in the book's remaining chapters to populate the Caribbean space with the bodies of actual queer and trans people, demonstrating how they make life happen—make life happy, healthy, pleasurable, and whole (enough)—in the Caribbean.

In chapters 4 and 5, I center the radical ways that trans people in the Caribbean create communities in transgressive spaces of liberation that lie beyond the purview of formalized activism and of "queer" frameworks. Lorde suggests that "without community there is no liberation" from oppression (1984) She reminds us that community must not overlook differences but confront how they separate us and foster various forms of embodiment. Everyone's personal experiences inform their political praxis. As Marlon Bailey (2013, 47–48) argues of the ballroom culture, members "create a minoritarian sphere for those who are excluded from or marginalized within the majoritarian society. This minoritarian sphere enables individuals, houses, and sectors of the community to undertake a process of identity making and remaking, against pervasive notions of identity that are fixed and permanent." Similarly, queer people across the region nurture communities for trans and gender-nonconforming people and gay men and lesbian women in multiple spaces beyond the reach of activism. Chapter 4 details the space of drag pageantry and its potential for creating community and kin networks, while chapter 5 looks at leisure spaces, bars, and nightclubs for their community-making potential. These spaces are charged to unsettle, complicate, and destabilize the status quo.

CHAPTER 1

Liberating the Queer Caribbean

A Homonormative Gaze: Canada's Influence on the Queer Liberation Narrative and Praxis

In the name of saving queer people in the Caribbean, Canada has operationalized multiple forms of control to shape a regional queer politics that rely on and benefit from Canada's long and sordid imperial history there. Despite Canada's self-positioning as an innocent, postracial, multicultural land of freedom, this settler colonial land is maintained by a history of destruction, enslavement, and genocide that casts long shadows over the country and in other places like the Caribbean. Critical race scholar Sherene Razack (1998, 89) reminds us that, indeed, Canada thrives on an ignorance about its role in "saving" the Other: "In the Canadian context, the imperialist as savior of the Third world peoples is an important construct in nation building. Canadians define themselves as unimplicated in the genocide of Native peoples or the enslavement of African peoples, a position of innocence that is especially appealing because it enables Canadians to imagine themselves as distinct from Americans. Canadians also mark themselves as the peacekeepers of the world, as living in a country that welcomes immigrants and as having few imperialist pretensions." Razack's work sets an important foundation for understanding how Canada positions people from the Global South as victims of their oppressive societies who must be rescued by white men and women, where "powerful narratives turn oppressed peoples into objects, to be held in contempt, or to be saved from their fate by more civilized beings" (3). This helping imperative, as development scholar Barbara Heron (2007, 3) argues, is fueled by presenting white middle-class knowledge, values, and ways of doing things as at once preferable and right, since the North, especially Canada, appears orderly, clean, and well managed in comparison to the situations in which it intervenes.

More recently and relevant to my work, David Murray (2016) demonstrates how this very notion of saving the "other," influences the controlling nature of Canadian queer human rights activism and the complicated negotiations that queer asylum seekers need to make to authenticate their queerness when they arrive in Canada on Sexual Orientation and Gender Identity (SOGI) refugee claims. He discovers that few SOGI claimants arrive in Canada thinking of themselves as "refugees," and some do not think of themselves as members of a particular sexual minority or gender identity group or may not even recognize or identify with sexual minority terms as they are defined and organized in Canada. However, in the period leading up to their hearing with the Immigration and Refugee Board (IRB), SOGI refugee claimants must learn relatively quickly how to "be" or at least "occupy" one of these LGBT identity categories authentically, as their hearings are dedicated to assessing the credibility of their claims to be members of a particular social group who have faced persecution in their countries of origin. They are reminded repeatedly by their lawyers, peer support group leaders, and one another that there are several components, characteristics, and assumptions utilized by IRB members to determine the credibility of a SOGI refugee claim. This typically includes recollection of violent attacks against them by family members, the state, or others, and tangible evidence of a need to flee by way of police reports, newspaper articles, and other public documents to help build their cases. Therefore, if they learn and perform these assumptions and characteristics associated with Global South "LGBT" identity politics and integrate them into an appropriate narrative of identity formation and persecution based on that identity, then they stand a better chance of a successful hearing (Murray 2016, 45). They must embody victimhood as constructed through Canada's white savior perspectives that deem them in need of saving.

Canada's white savior positioning extends beyond queer human rights and, in the Caribbean, dates back to the nineteenth century with the insertion of Presbyterian missionaries who entered the region to convert indentured Indians.[1] Historian Brinsley Samaroo (1975, 42, 46) argues that Indian-Caribbean women portrayed in colonial documents were seen by colonizers and missionaries as wicked, and the men ignorant and prejudiced "as a result of long ages of ignorance, mistrust and degradation." Canadian missions therefore saw it necessary to reform their perceived Aryan fellows by "appealing to adults in their own language, providing education in English for the children so that they could become good citizens and, above all, good Christians, and training East Indian teachers and preachers" (47).[2]

Caribbean scholars have established that these missions not only delegitimized the religious ethos of the non-Christian Other but also violently erased aspects of the sacred by "splitting apart mind, body, and spirit into peculiarities of (white) manliness, colonized 'other' and (Christian) religion, respectively" (Alexander 2005, 280). In her novel *The Swinging Bridge*, Caribbean novelist Ramabai Espinet (2003, 64) reflects on these racial tensions in postindenture Trinidad, where "these [Presbyterian] church people from Canada interfered so much with our lives, to me it was very puzzling. Big strong men like Pappy and Mr. Bhim up the road, allow a few white men to rule their lives and tell them who to marry and who to leave. And what about love? Did Pappy love Mama or was the bamboo wife his one true love, like in love songs?" Conversion meant that the church had influence over every aspect of converts' lives, to ensure they properly performed their religion and the civility it endowed. As Makeda Silvera (1992, 42) argues, "Our foreparents gained access to literacy through the Bible when they were being indoctrinated by missionaries. It provided powerful and ancient stories of strength, endurance, hope, which reflected their own fight against oppression; this book has been so powerful that it continues to bind our lives with its racism and misogyny."

Having been "forged in the crucible of a colonial encounter," the region was made susceptible to Canadian influence; it is impossible "to think of the Caribbean without considering the colonial linkages that give it its historically specific imprint" that has opened the door to Canadian intervention (Trotz 2007, 8). For instance, other financial institutions were seizing the opportunity to expand into the region, like American City Bank, which had ninety-five overseas branches in the region by 1920 (P. Hudson 2017, 141), prompting Canadian banking competitors to "quick[ly] seize the region's shifting needs for capital, brought on by both the end to slavery and the emergency of nominally free populations of Africans and Indigenous workers and peasants, and by demands for capital by independent postcolonial states seeking to fund their modernization projects" (6). Trotz (2007, 8) emphasizes the significance of this long Canadian presence in the region:

> Canada is very much a part of this transnational circuit, which historically encompasses 19th century missionary and banking link, trading routes for ships from Halifax bringing cod and timber and returning with sugar and rum, Maroons in Nova Scotia, bauxite ventures, and a Caribbean population in Canada since the 17th century (Bristow et al. 1994; Chodos 1977). Today, those connections include banking interests, mining companies, the involvement of the Canadian state via 'development' work in the region and the central role played most recently in the removal of Jean-Bertrand Aristide from office in Haiti (and the deployment of Canadian police officers during the interim administration of Gerard Latortue).

While queer human rights efforts are positioned as providing necessary relief in times of crisis, it is important to read them against this backdrop of Canada's long history in the region and to consider the deeply complicated relationships that are being maintained between Canada and the Caribbean. This is necessary when queer liberation initiatives in the Anglophone Caribbean have allowed Canada to reenter the region in similar ways to establish itself as a formidable "gay international" force (Massad 2007) through the deployment of human rights interventions that continuously frame the region as salvageable or "underdeveloped on one hand, while reinforcing Canada as manager of global imperialism" on the other (Gordon 2010, 14). Its helping imperative is mobilized through queer rights talk aimed at emphasizing the barbaric nature of the Caribbean region in ways similar to its evangelizing missions, thereby imposing its hegemonic imperialistic agendas to save queers who are at the mercy of "savage" homophobic Others. Queer Canada has invested heavily in Caribbean countries like Jamaica and Barbados, and its homohegemony, as Jamaican sexuality scholar Carla Moore (2014, 52) terms it, enacts a queer liberal hegemony put forth by those who purport to be the holders of queer legitimacy and who justify their intervention of a colonialist development rhetoric. Queer human rights activism therefore emerges within broader understandings of the Caribbean as a region that continues to be plagued by histories of political, social, sexual, gendered, and racialized colonization where there remains a strong desire to "fix" the various countries and their people.

Focusing on Canada's homoimperial positioning of itself globally as the poster child for queer refuge, this chapter provides a discourse analysis of Canadian-led queer activism in the Caribbean. I focus on how such initiatives usher queer people into positions of what I theorize as *conditional queerness,* the performativity of idealized notions of queerness based on Global North, often white, ideals that incite particular dichotomies of queer embodiment between themselves and others elsewhere. This model limits queer people to embodying particular validated models such as being or becoming liberated and free in the Global North versus being vulnerable, at risk, and dying in the Global South. The conditional queerness that people are made to perform in the Anglophone Caribbean, then, limits discourse to exaggerations of impossibility, dismissing the fact that queer people are actively maneuvering the prevailing homophobia, transphobia, and discrimination in radical and truly defiant ways. I also discuss some of the recent human rights work queer organizations and people in Toronto are undertaking, which is spearheaded by mostly white Canadians and queer Caribbean people living in Toronto's Caribbean diaspora. I then explore the human rights discourses that civil service organizations are introducing within the region as they continue to negotiate queer politics and international human rights funding streams available to them. I question what it means for a liberatory human rights agenda (in that moment) to drastically influence the prevailing advocacy and intervention focus.

International Queer Human Rights and a
Culture of Conditional Queerness

Initiatives in the Anglophone Caribbean by Canada and other Global North authorities, like UNAIDS (as I show later), continuously frame the region as readily available for salvaging. Canadian human rights advocates justify their interventions through a colonialist development rhetoric that establishes a homo-hegemony, a queer liberal hegemony that situates Canada as a homoimperial power as the holders of queer legitimacy, in contrast to the impossibilities that exist elsewhere. This exemplifies the experiences of persons from the Anglophone Caribbean (and elsewhere) who have relocated to countries like Canada, the United States, the UK, and the Netherlands and have been positioned within white neoliberal queer discourses as holders of exclusive knowledge of the realities in their countries of origin. Through asylum networks, tales of suffering back in the region reaffirm an image of the Caribbean as extremely oppressive to queers. Additionally, when such narratives are supported by finances from the Global North, they produce a culture of conditional queerness that exaggerates the impossibility of queer life in the Anglophone Caribbean. It diminishes the fact that queer people are actively maneuvering prevailing homophobic, transphobic, and discriminatory conditions that currently define legible gender and sexuality across the region. This is largely because most international funding models do not allow for community-centered engagement that is attentive to the needs of varying queer and trans populations. The current top-down approach to funding queer activism therefore functions to keep in place the homonormative arrangements that influence regional organizing at the risk of a more nuanced and embodied approach to queer liberation. I explore the consequences of such models in the examples that follow.

The Sensitivity Model and Conditional Belonging
in the Queer Caribbean

The queer neoliberal model adopted by the Canada-based advocacy organization AIDS-Free World could be understood as reinforcing ideas of conditional queerness in their attempts to bring about change. AIDS-Free World, an international human rights organization founded in 2007, with offices in Canada, also seeks institutional change through "creative legal approaches and high-level advocacy." To achieve its goals, the organization partnered with Jamaican lawyer and human rights activist Maurice Tomlinson and his white husband Tom Decker in 2011, a former police officer and a pastor who designed programs aimed at "schooling" police in sensitivity toward gays (Charles 2013). On behalf of AIDS-Free World, the couple conducted the training sessions with the Royal Barbados

Police Force, the Royal Saint Lucia Police Force, and the Royal Police Force of Antigua and Barbuda (among other countries), using models adapted from similar sessions provided by Decker in Toronto while he was employed as a police officer with the Toronto Police Service. The training was described as "unique in as much as it combines Maurice's extensive knowledge of local Caribbean culture and International Human Rights Law and Tom's experience as a police officer and program designer" (AIDS-Free World 2013). They reflect: "All these sessions are held at the invitation and with the cooperation of local LGBT groups and police services. . . . *The couple's joint delivery of the sessions allow [sic] participants in the Caribbean to experience first-hand a married same-sex couple who also happen to be accomplished professionals. This experience helps deconstruct some of the deep-seated stereotypes prevailing in the Caribbean about LGBT individuals*" (AIDS-Free World 2013; emphasis mine).

Such a statement reveals their reliance on a white gay homonationalist fantasy of the stable and respectable gay couple as a medium for their message and work. Jasbir Puar's mapping of homonationalism in queer times theorizes this inclusion of homosexuality within national imaginations.[3] This includes an idealization of the stable middle-class nuclear family that this queer couple is invited to mimic when they return to teach the Caribbean about what a same-sex couple could look like. Such positioning recognizes a need for some kind of visibility model for making queer life wholesome.

These sensitivity training workshops also provide prime examples of paternalistic arrangements between Canada and the region. For example, in a review of training done in Suriname, AIDS-Free World highlighted the unsafe nature of many Caribbean societies and the perception that queer people feel threatened. In one of its earliest articles, dated May 30, 2013, the organization places great emphasis on this dynamic:

> Members of the Caribbean LGBT community frequently report that officers are generally unsympathetic to gay victims, and police agencies are slow to respond to crimes motivated by hate. It is also reported that some officers even participate in these homophobic attacks. LGBT individuals are therefore reluctant to report their victimization. Their experiences with the police are typically negative, and there is a perception that police are unaware of the issues facing LGBT communities; or worse, consider them unapprehended criminals. Such a toxic mix of factors results in an exclusion from justice by Caribbean homosexuals and men who have sex with men (MSM). This drives the vulnerable community underground, away from effective HIV prevention, treatment, care and support interventions. It is critical to grasp that the Caribbean has the second highest HIV burden after sub-Saharan Africa (http://www.unaids.org/en/regionscountries/regions/caribbean/), with the MSM community being disproportionately impacted. (AIDS-Free World 2013)

LIBERATING THE QUEER CARIBBEAN

Pushing the discourse of a barbaric Caribbean versus Canada as queer haven even further, AIDS-Free World's narrative is cradled in an incessant trope of crippling homophobia where "Maurice and Tom always prepare themselves for some strong homophobic push-back and verbal attacks" (ibid.). However, the couple has been able to stave off such attacks as "participants appreciate the facilitators' openness to answer personal questions, have been respectful, and have demonstrated an eagerness to learn" (ibid.).

The organization has described Barbados as having "the harshest penalty for homosexual activity in the Western hemisphere on its books, but overall enjoys a culture of tolerance," in contrast to "the savage homophobic attacks of its fellow Caribbean Community country, Jamaica" (Tomlinson 2013). At that time (in 2013), Barbados was positioned as a progressive regional leader with support from politicians who made public statements against discrimination.[4] Additionally, the country is presented as ushering change with the formation of a coalition to address homophobia and discrimination, alongside guidance from Tomlinson and Decker who conducted a one-day sensitization training session with police officers, prison officers, members of the defense force, Ministries of Labor and Health, and the National HIV Commission. With the Canadian HIV/AIDS Legal Network, a second round of training was conducted in Barbados in March 2017, with sixteen police officers and representatives of several local queer advocacy community-based organizations.[5]

In Saint Lucia, Tomlinson and Decker were credited for providing "crucial training for the Royal St. Lucia Police Force" (Charles 2013). However, unlike in Barbados, Saint Lucia was presented as more unreceptive to the idea of human rights training, and especially the concept of LGBTI sensitivity. As Tomlinson (2013) described, "Yesterday the Police Commissioner made it very clear he did not wish to discuss LGBT issues in depth, he wanted to be more general . . . so given that the man at the top is not overly interested in getting to grips with gay issues, how difficult is it to deliver the message of human rights for LGBT to a police force that is used to treating the gay community as criminals?" Decker appeared to be optimistic about the outcome, noting that while the first day focused more on "general human rights issues," they were able to address how "the paradigm shift from a paramilitary organization of policing towards a community-based, strategic policing model" would guide officers in decisions pertaining to their use of force. Yet, in discussions of the trainings in Saint Lucia, Tomlinson (quoted in Charles 2013) still reverts to Jamaica, arguing, "With hate crimes in Jamaica happening at a staggering frequency, and anti-buggery laws under challenge in the JA courts, the handling of homosexual victims within a society where they are criminalized provides a particular challenge." He supports this sentiment by emphasizing that "in Jamaica, one in three MSM (men who have sex with men) is HIV positive—one of the highest prevalence rates in the world. And because they're not out . . . 60% of MSM have sex with women, many to mask their homosexuality, allowing HIV/AIDS to bridge into the general population" (ibid.). Here he purports that many gay men are forced to conceal their sexual identities to remain safe from violent homophobic citizens, from physical violence, and from social stigma, while prioritizing a neoliberal rhetoric of "coming out" based on white North American sexual identity politics that privilege these achievements as markers of queerness.

Drawing on C. Riley Snorton's (2014, 31) recent work on down-low politics in Black American communities, I see how this narrative is "premised on a notion of otherness, which requires (smuggles) Black and brown bodies for its analysis while white sexual norms are established in opposition to an imagined aberrance inherent in Black and brown identities." These Caribbean societies must thus be reshaped to fit the white savior model, whose definitions and embodiments of queerness are deemed legitimate and exemplary. Media coverage of the work of the AIDS-Free World and the Legal Network obscure the multiple and complicated realities that especially working-class queer and trans people navigate—for instance, homelessness, unemployment, and access to safe and appropriate medical care—and how people interface with the sociolegal situations in the various islands where the trainings occurred. Via the positioning of a need to usher state officials, in this instance police officers, into awareness, readers are left with an impression of silenced, fearful queer and trans people in need of critical intervention. This rhetoric is further solidified by the imagery of a happy gay couple who mobilizes a white queer neoliberal politics that prioritizes gay marriage as a symbol of queer legitimacy, while at the same time presenting Tomlinson and Decker as stable and productive, unlike the Caribbean queers they seek to help. This limited space and narrow focus being adopted by the Legal Network unfortunately reinforces what Caribbean scholar Amar Wahab (2012, 27) calls "colonialistic flavor" of the queer Caribbean diaspora in Canada.

ENVISIONING QUEER RIGHTS AND FREEDOM: TELLING THEIR STORIES

The Society Against Sexual Orientation Discrimination (SASOD) was established in 2004 by students attending the University of Guyana who were interested in engaging the student population on issues of human rights infringements against queer people in the country. The organization has since expanded to become one of the more prominent queer advocacy organizations in Guyana and the region, and it has sought to address questions of constitutional, institutional, and societal discrimination.[6] In 2013, SASOD partnered with a Canadian queer human rights initiative titled Envisioning LGBT Human Rights (Nicol et al.),[7] which propelled a similar narrative of rescuing queers in the region. Envisioning explicitly focused on "commonwealth countries that maintain criminal code sanctions against same-sex intimacy, working with partners in selected countries where such laws are currently being challenged (India, Uganda, Kenya,

Botswana, St. Lucia, Jamaica, Belize and Guyana)" (Nicol, Gates, and Mule 2015). The project produced three reports between 2012 and 2014 to explore various issues related to Canada's human rights commitments elsewhere.[8] In this final report, titled "Envisioning LGBT Refugee Rights in Canada: Is Canada a Safe Haven?" (2015), there are many moments where Envisioning succeeds in positioning Canada as a refuge for queer people seeking help. For example, it concludes, "Prior to their arrival in Canada, many of the LGBT refugee claimants in this study lived lives of silence and social isolation due to discrimination and fear of persecution" (21). It also draws heavily on persons' stories of "persecution and violence they had experienced and/or witnessed at home and which had led to their decision to flee their home to seek asylum elsewhere" (24). Statements like these reify discourses of victimhood where Envisioning's publications solidify ideas that countries like Canada have what it takes to save the Caribbean and the rest of the world.

SASOD's partnership with Envisioning enlisted Guyanese artist Ulleli Verbeke to produce a photo essay titled "Capturing Migration from the Caribbean to Canada," which was launched at the Canadian Gay and Lesbian Archives for Toronto's 2014 World Pride. In this piece, Verbeke photographs queer people who resided in the region or left in search of safety or, more precisely, to avoid death. Interestingly, the respondents in the Caribbean remain anonymous through their framing—back toward the camera, heads bent, or ambiguous body parts being shown—while those in Canada are photographed with broad and confident smiles. Each picture is accompanied by a short quote that reinforces Canada's location as a safe haven. For example, Karlene from Jamaica (face shown) says, "I'm out now and living very open again. And I'm even more out than I was before. It's going to be hard to go there [Jamaica] to live. I do miss my friends and my family. I do not miss the lifestyle of Jamaica. I do not miss the homophobia. I probably miss the country, the physical country itself but going back there to live is a no-no. Definitely not. Maybe for a quick visit and that's it" (Verbeke 2013). Similarly, Dood, now living in Canada, shows their face bravely and explains: "I totally empathize with people's plights while they're living there. That's why I can never, ever go back. I have absolutely no desire to" (ibid.). An anonymous contributor from Guyana positions their back toward camera; they blame the government for persistent homophobia, stating, "When we look at the struggles of the huge gay movement in the Global North in terms of the gay revolution it requires a lot of work. And if we are looking to give equal rights to the LGBT community, then a lot more has to be done. And we can only do that with the support of the government" (ibid.).

While much of this discourse on Caribbean queerness, just like that mobilized by AIDS-Free World, centers mortality and rescue, other interventions have also attempted to groom people in the region toward a rainbow modernity, "wherein the 'correct' performance of 'queerness'—usually premised as visible queer resistance—and the acceptance of that performance, become the markers of development and human-ness" (Moore 2014, 4). So, instead of targeting repressive conditions, they have sought to aid grassroots communities who "suffer from isolation and a lack of resources and are particularly in need of documenting human rights violations affecting LGBT people" (Nicol, Gates-Gasse, and Mule 2014, 2). In other words, they are curating these tales of suffering to create a narrative of oppression, in contrast to the rainbow modernity that is purported to exist in the Global North. Toronto's 2014 World Pride was an arena used for the showcasing of queer freedom and for telling these narratives, hence the featuring of Verbeke's photo essay on this forum. Activists from the Caribbean, Africa, and the Middle East are implicated in the retelling of these narratives when they were brought to *Tell* [their] *Stories* at a World Pride Human Rights Conference during Pride, and to exhibit their struggles at the Canadian Lesbian and Gay Archives (CLGA).

At the CLGA, video shorts streamed stories from Botswana, India, Uganda, Saint Lucia, Kenya, Belize, Jamaica, and Guyana. These accounts drew extensively on victims' memories of homophobic violence and the need to escape "homelands" to survive. The Caribbean narrators all spoke, on one end of the spectrum, about being stifled or abandoned and chastised for their sexuality by family, friends, and community. In extreme instances, they reminded the Canadian audience "how it hits home when we lost friends to brutal murders simply because of them living their lives" (Placide 2014). On the other end, they yearn for the opportunity to "be like a regular couple" (Hunte 2014), to "go to school, get an education, work, make a living and be who we are" (Quetzal 2014), and for people to "know us as people first" (Broderick 2014). In these accounts though, very specific victims emerge—like Placide, Quetzal, Hunte, Broderick, and McDoom—whose accounts rely on tropes of despair in framing Caribbean queers as injured and quickly succumbing to the violence of their phobic and restrictive societies. Through these stories, there is an implicit reverence for the "help" received from the already-liberated North America and Europe. Or, as Vincent McDoom reminds us in their reflection, "France gave me something that St. Lucia never gave me. France gave me a voice" (McDoom 2014).

Project lead, Nancy Nicol (2014),[9] explained that these reflections were touted to teach Canadians "about discrimination and violence fueled by state, church, workplace, family, and community. Most importantly, we hear stories of resistance and resilience: building support within family and community, building movements, using media, challenging the laws through legal cases." Yet missing, or overshadowed at the very least, are the various other contours of queerness that define Caribbean people's resistance to the prevailing homophobia and heteronormativity in the region. In these depictions, trans people, and especially working-class trans people, are also sacrificed in the pursuit of producing the dying queer body.[10] At the same time, Envisioning used these narratives to emphasize the "particular challenges for Canada in fulfilling and upholding its international commitments and obligations to protect human rights and to provide a sanctuary for people fleeing persecution due to their sexual orientation, gender identity or gender expression" (Nicol, Gates-Gasse, and Mule 2014, 10). As Nicol goes on to reflect, "This body of work speak[s] to profound discrimination and violence: random violence in public places; police harassment, extortion, custodial rape; 'corrective rape' against lesbians 'to make them straight'; exclusion and violence perpetuated by friends, family and community." These stories were well crafted and moved audiences to sympathize with the struggles activists faced as they "continue the struggle for LGBT rights at home and internationally, despite violence and risk" (Nicol 2014). This dynamic authenticates the queer other's despair and legitimizes Canada's imperative to help the region. The efforts of this Envisioning project then readily cement Canada's vision as a defender of people who need to be freed, but they also expose some glaring gaps between questions of representation and truth telling where particular types of victims emerge in narratives framed by this kind of homonormative rhetoric. In the chapters that follow, I challenge these assumptions using the lived experience of queer and trans people in the Caribbean.

THE JAMAICAN PRIDE MODEL: THE PROBLEM OF TEACHING CARIBBEAN PEOPLE "HOW TO BE QUEER"

Another initiative by Canadians to "modernize" the Anglophone Caribbean is evident in the introduction of North American–themed Pride celebrations to Montego Bay, Jamaica, despite long-standing celebrations of queerness in that country and across the region. Montego Bay Pride was first hosted on October 25, 2015, with a series of events for queer Jamaicans who were purported to have limited access to the island's first official Pride festival hosted in Kingston by the Jamaican Forum for Lesbians Allsexuals and Gays (JFLAG) in August that year. By 2017, this alternative Pride had also garnered increasing technical and financial support from Canadian organizations such as the Canadian HIV/AIDS Legal Network, the AIDS Healthcare Foundation, Toronto P-FLAG, Rainbow Alliance, and the Ontario Public Service Union. By 2017, the Montego Bay Pride expanded to over 850 attendees, and reflections on the event described its social justice project as "revolutionary for LGBTQI Jamaicans," since it attempted to "build bridges with officers" of the Freeport Police Station, "many of whom have been very hostile to members of our community" (Tomlinson 2017).

Although very little was said about these events in local or regional mainstream press, international queer media, like Gay Star News and Daily Xtra, have popularized the image of Black Jamaican queer people dancing, embracing each other, or dressing in drag, free to be queer in Jamaica because of the Canadian organization and their queer liberating infrastructure. For example, following the 2017 event, Gay Star News announced on its website that it is "proud to be global media partner of Montego Bay Pride 2018 in Jamaica":

> The bigger the event gets, the more the Jamaican government has to take them seriously. Gay Star News is honored to stand in solidarity with our LGBTI family for Montego Bay Pride . . . We hope 2018 will be the start of a long-term partnership. We want to empower LGBTI Jamaicans to tell their stories to the world and advocate for change in their country . . . And for those who want to visit the island, what better chance could there be than Montego Bay Pride to enjoy the natural beauty of Jamaica and the warm hospitality of our LGBTI community there? . . . A robust security system helps to ensure the safety of Montego Bay. It has now run for several years with no reported violence. (Protopapa 2017)

This announcement mobilizes a rhetoric of death and danger but also propels a fantasy of a slowly changing Jamaican landscape, where sentiments like "security," "advocate for change," and "empower LGBTI Jamaicans" solidify the narrative of queer modernity. Canadian-based Jamaican activist Maurice Tomlinson's self-recorded reflection on his experience of 2017 Mobay Pride was featured by Daily Xtra and provided footage of various activities like painting the Freeport Police Station, a small protest with participants waving placards and rainbow flags, and a beach party. In this video, an on-screen message reminded viewers that "sex between men is illegal in Jamaica and **many LGBT Jamaicans face persecution and violence**" (Daily Xtra 2017; emphasis in original). As a remedy to this reality, Tomlinson (2017) reflects on the importance of visibility:

> It is very important that we show members of the LGBT community that we are here, the community in general that we are here. Because you don't know who is passing in the car and don't know that they are not the only gay in Mobay. A lot of kids don't know that they are not the only gay in Mobay . . . somebody is watching out there and saying "bwoy we here, I am not the only one in Mobay" . . . I hope that we will eventually get to the point where we can do a proper march (laughs with applause in the background) or some kind of public demonstration, with the police protection.

Even in his imagination, there is still a need for police protection; he envisions a perpetual threat. The reiteration of violence reaffirms the positionality of the white savior who will liberate the queers from the homophobic state. The contrasting images of "queer freedom" and death to Jamaica's working-class gully queens drive home the revelation that these Black queer bodies are used as capital for investing in queer modernizing projects by the Global North—in this instance, Canada. Or to borrow from Vanessa Agard-Jones (2013, 187), these queer Caribbean bodies move from innards of embodiment to the space of global capital.

In addition to publicizing these celebrations in Jamaica, international queer media has simultaneously relied on queer people's stories of extreme destitution, positioning working-class trans women, trans sex workers, and other queer people as poster children for their work. A Vice News documentary titled *Young and Gay: Jamaica's Gully Queens* does just this, by focusing on the volatile situations faced by homeless youth who do sex work in Kingston, Jamaica. Narrating how gully queens are forced to seek refuge in the capital city's storm drains away from homophobic attacks, a white British reporter descends into the community to get a tour of the gully and to see "what life is like living under the streets of Jamaica" (2014). Although the documentary initially gives a sense that the trans women can find community there, the story quickly turns into a depressing conversation about illegality, death, and illegibility. At the other end of the narrative, a community gatekeeper accompanying the reporter leads him through the paces of seeking a pretrial hearing, being rejected, and having "to leave Jamaica once again for fear of his safety" (ibid.). Here the interlocutor's safety abroad stands in stark contrast against the immobility that characterizes the gully queens' lives that they are shedding light on in this production. At the end of the documentary, the queens are filmed dancing in the street for a birthday celebration, under the bright lights and cameras from the film crew. However, the narrator sends a strong and emotive message: "With homophobic violence still such a prevalent part of Jamaican culture, and the buggery law looking to likely remain a long-standing fixture of Jamaican law, things aren't looking great for its LGBT community. Though the party down in Kingston's gully is a loud and proud show of defiance, the reality of what the gully queens and other gay, lesbian, bisexual and transgender Jamaicans will wake up to the morning after remains as bleak as ever" (ibid.). It authenticates the sentiment of at-risk queer Caribbean people to sustain continuous sympathy from the outsiders who are investing millions of foreign dollars in the region with projects that authenticate disease and mortality. These complicated relationships function on numerous levels that keep all stakeholders in place since human rights funders are less concerned with confronting the "complex relationships between eroticism, colonialism, militarism, resistance, revolution, poverty, despair, fullness, and hope" (Tinsley 2010, 204). In presenting unsettling stories like the one about Kingston's gully queens above, activists in the Global North provide ample justification for the exportation of neoliberal pride celebrations to the island. It is important to underscore, however, that queer people are negotiating their sexualities, identities, and positionalities in complex ways as they actively navigate and resist prevailing homophobia, transphobia, and discrimination while envisioning other ways of existing and thriving in the region.

These examples of conditional queerness illuminate the unwillingness of organizations outside the region to work more closely with the communities they attempt to assist and limits their abilities to do more meaningful work. Caribbean people remain the property of queer homoimperial outsiders who, because of their financial and political clout, continue to dominate the region's queer politics. Their voices and stories are silenced by this domination, which also reminds us that our Caribbean bodies continue to be unfortunately tied to long histories of Canadian imperialism that continue to satisfy the desires of the sympathetic white savior to modernize Others. In this situation, the Caribbean is produced as anachronistic: "prehistoric, atavistic and irrational, inherently out of place in the historical time of modernity" (McClintock 1995, 41). This kind of arrangement places regional activists in a conflicted position where they too sometimes further complicate these relations when international funding is added to this dynamic.

THE IMPACTS OF CONDITIONAL QUEERNESS ON QUEER COMMUNITIES ON THE GROUND

The distribution of funds is closely tied to assumptions of the victimhood and (un)productivity of trans bodies. In my discussions with trans women and other smaller community organizers, it became clear that a lot of aid and outreach was focused on urban, middle-class populations, and typically on issues faced by gay men and trans women. The deeply complicated needs of those who resided in nonurban areas and survived in socially and economically precarious situations were often ignored. Even when the larger and more popular civil service organizations provided support to queer people, their focus on specific interventions like HIV/AIDS meant that some lesbian and trans communities were bypassed. I met with a UNAIDS representative in Guyana who echoed these sentiments, stating that the organization has decided to strengthen its focus on "key populations," which he explains as persons engaging in "high risk activities, particularly among men who have sex with men." He further emphasized that UNAIDS has been "very instrumental in ensuring that the LGBTI, particularly the MSM, are given special regard as far as HIV/AIDS programs are concerned. In the process we have been successful in ensuring that funding for programs geared towards what we call *key populations* are developed" (Interview with UNAIDS Rep., December 2016).

UNAIDS's goal at that time was ensuring the provision of "the services we think they need to receive," such as "testing, talking about the use of condoms and lubricants, we make sure that those are provided [to the organizations]." While acknowledging that other communities would sometimes voice their concerns of being left out, the representative reiterated the organization's agenda to target "key populations" based on data. He explained to me: "What we are saying is that the approach that looks at where the disease, the condition is in populations, it looks at location, and then also we apply interventions which we know are of good effect" (Interview with UNAIDS Rep., December 2016). In this discourse, "key populations" are positioned as vectors of disease that need to be contained. This idea of who needs help is critical, as it facilitates an obvious erasure of how queer and trans people are deemed productive or not. Or as Alexander (1994, 6) theorizes in her analysis of the legislating of heterosexual citizenship in the Caribbean, particular segments of queer communities are seen as "pos[ing] a profound threat to the very survival of the nation" because of the toxicity of their sexual desires in infecting "proper" citizens. When pushed to comment further on the responsiveness of civil society groups in Guyana that do HIV/AIDS work, to whom UNAIDS provided funds, the representative noted that some "are very good at it, they are very organised and very strong" while others have challenges, hinting that the competition would be dominated by the organizations with more capabilities and those who demonstrate a willingness to allocate the funds as UNAIDS saw fit. Smaller entities "assume that it is their money, you know that kind of thing. The wrong kind of thinking, instead of asking how the money can be used properly, you know" (Interview with UNAIDS Rep., December 2016), with UNAIDS being able to determine what "properly" means.

A lesbian activist from the civil service organization Quality of Citizenship Jamaica (QCJ) explained in our interview that she was unfortunately on the neglected end of this relationship between international funding agencies and activist organizations in the country. QCJ was barely functioning in 2016 because of dwindling funds and eventually shut its doors permanently in 2018 (QCJ 2018). We spoke at length about how the funding climate affected her organization and the struggles she experienced in tailoring initiatives to suit the little money that was made available. She explained that their main source of funding came from Canadian-based AIDS-Free World, which allowed them to attend the Inter-American Commission on Human Rights summit and to purchase office equipment. Or as she mentioned to me: "The laptop that I'm on right now, that kind of thing . . . they gave us the freedom. You know certain things we had to do, one of them was to present at the OAS—we made sure that that happened. There were a couple other things, which we did, and the rest of the money was up to us." Another potential funder was FRIDA: The Young Feminist Fund, but applications for support were unsuccessful. She lamented, "You have to come up with something exceptional that they will feel is better than somebody else's own." The main bulk of funding was also being allocated to HIV, and while they provided HIV education to lesbian and bisexual women, infection rates were lowest among this group than any others, so the organization could not justify their need for funding. Further, she believed that the prevalence of white gay men as funders determined their focus on HIV and "at-risk" communities:

Global Fund specifically targets most "at-risk" populations—MSM, transgender community, sex workers, the disabled—those are some of the groups they target. In there, the only women that they are talking about is sex workers. Yes, there are lesbian or bisexual sex workers, but they are small in comparison to anybody else, but that is the only way we can get funding for that, and you will have to have a program for that who will be affecting a larger group of people than this small group. There was pressure to provide what the funders say we need to . . . without acknowledgement for how the disease actually impacted people in the region. We need to include women because women have been the support for gay men for many years. They are the ones that when dem sick and died [when they get sick and die], it was the women who were there to support them. What about the issues that women deal with? The stigma and discrimination that they face because they are helping you? You don't look at any of that . . .

In Trinidad and Tobago, I met with two founding members of Friends for Life (FFL), the oldest activist civil service organization in the country that works "mainly with working-class and poor persons and all the things that come with that" (Interview with FFL, February 2017). FFL has experienced numerous changes in the funding climate, and as Lyndon Gill (2012) notes in his ethnographic study on the organization, it has had to confront many issues associated with maintaining funding arrangements, including dealing with the consequences of poor financial decisions and mismanagement (2012). Or as they emphasized in my interview with them:

We were young, I will be very clear about this. We were a very young organization at the time. All of us in fact were working class people who I don't think had university education and it was simple things . . . you know when you do things not according to your MOU (Memorandum of Understanding), funders come down on you for it. But there were ways that they were very blaming, and just stupid. The other thing they did was blacklisted us, so they told organizations around the world who were doing LGBT work with that this organization was f-cking up money, and then to realize that this was happening in not just Trinidad but in the Caribbean and other countries. So, they did not pay attention to what organizations were doing, and then all of sudden when there was a problem, as opposed to "let's fix this," it was "y'all are horrible and bad, pack up your shop, we not giving you no more one, and we will tell everybody not to give you anymore." But those things come from, not international funders; it came from local people, local Trinidadians and Jamaicans who were running the Caribbean office. And what happens all the time in these situations, is that when somebody from a third world country or a developing country has to answer to somebody from an international country, they whip their own people and blame "no no no, I don't know why they doing it like that." We had a lot of that. (Interview with FFL, February 2017)

At the time of our interview, the organization's resources were on the decline, in part because it had decided to change its focus from only working with vulnerable gay men and trans women to more of a social work capacity-building agenda. One member exclaimed, "We send in a proposal and get a no because it doesn't have enough HIV in there . . . I'm done; I'm not doing any 4-day HIV workshop again, that's stupidness." Such a stance is poignant, especially when there are many other issues that foster vulnerability and need to be addressed. Or as they put it,

Things like homelessness, substance use, I think just the general f-cking trauma of homophobia. The way that family members or communities are homophobic, how that puts you at the risk of developing relationships that are abusive. You put yourself in vulnerable places over and over. I can tell you about HIV from now until the cows come home, but you may not get HIV but a Black eye or something. Youth being beaten by family members for claiming a gay identity, and being put out of the house, leaving them out on the street and at risk for HIV because you have to survive. Survival may mean a blowjob or selling unprotected sex and all the other things that might go with it. (Interview with FFL, February 2017)

Family support services and public education can thus be critical resources for reducing the flow of queer youth into homelessness and sex work. FFL and other civil service organizations are therefore pressured to tailor their work to meet the needs of the community while still meeting the outcomes desired by funders, which threatens to "change[s] what you do as an organization. It changes you; you end up doing things that is not your forte" (Interview with FFL, February 2017).

What FFL has been experiencing reminds me of Jamaican scholar Honor Ford-Smith's (1989, 15) reflection on some of these tensions in her work as cofounder and artistic director of the Sistren Theatre Collective, an independent women's organization that has been described as "a unique way of organizing, as an example of popular theatre in action, of the empowerment of working-class women, and of effective working-class self-management." Reflecting on the hardships experienced by the Collective, Ford-Smith reflects that the national poverty situation along with the poverty of members of the group made managing the collective a complex matter (56). With dwindling opportunities for local financial support, it sought funding from agencies in the "so-called advanced capitalist world" (58). However, these funding agencies and their policies, as she reminds us, "are often tied to the politics of their governments or of powerful special interest groups in their countries. Aid, to put it somewhat crudely, is related to both a search for markets and the search for international political support" (ibid.).

One of the biggest struggles the Collective had to come to terms with once international funding had been received was the issue of accountability. Or as Ford-Smith (1989, 64) questioned: "The main interest of many agencies was to fund short-term projects which produced quick and measurable results" on their terms and based on their standards. These grassroots communities were not always able to engage in such measurable projects. This pressure therefore produced unwanted unequal hierarchies of power among the women, with those who had particular skill sets being placed in positions of power, despite the Collective's desire to be nonhierarchical and self-managing. Ford-Smith explained further: "On the one hand then, agencies claimed that they were setting up self-reliant grassroots structures, but on the other, those organizations required processes of accounting and reporting which could only be done by people who had either university-level qualifications or many years of experience" (66). She acknowledged further that although the international agencies providing funding helped the Collective "to survive a very difficult period" (68), "the demands of the agencies withdrew energy from the group that could have been used in directly addressing the question of accountability both within Sistren and the women it served" (69).

I draw reference to this experience because I see strong connections with what was being expressed about funding relationships and how they impacted the work being done across the research sites. From these experiences, it is easy to understand the limits of technical funding for queer activism in the region. Funding sources at the time of my fieldwork[11] were not only severely limited but were also quite limiting in the room being provided for activists to do the work that is needed. As a result, queer people, especially those who are poor and in need of immediate intervention beyond HIV/AIDS support such as access to safe housing, state protection, and sustainable food supplies, are insufficiently accommodated. This ongoing scenario is detrimental to queer people's ability to live in the region and further complicates the ways they are allowed to exist conditionally.

FUNDING PRODUCTIVE SEXUALITIES: THE IMPACTS OF CONDITIONAL FUNDING ON TRANS ACTIVISM

Trans bodies are plagued by medicalized discourse. In the Global North, emphasis is placed on gender-affirming procedures and trans identities as psychological conditions, while the trans bodies of the Global South are marked by disease. All the trans activists I interacted with across the region longed for more inclusive interventions to be invested in the multiple issues affecting them, like those that Friends for Life highlighted above. Some of the funding agencies activists mentioned and continued pushing their human rights agendas on issues of HIV/AIDS and decriminalization of sodomy laws, and this has largely dictated the investments they are interested in making. Once allocations are made, there is little room to address the complicated needs of the silenced gender-nonconforming communities—like access to housing, food, medication, and employment. In instances where trans organizations receive funds from international or local ones, it is either delivered in a backhanded fashion or on the condition that moneys and resources be used for disease prevention interventions that continue to push a homonormative agenda and cannot truly account for working-class trans people's realities.

Guyana Trans United (GTU), located in Region 4 and in the capital city Georgetown, expanded its operation since it was established in 2009, directly because of the cross-dressing laws and the clear absence of activism on trans issues at the time. GTU's director mentioned the focus on lowering infection rates meant that trans clients would only be provided with condoms and lubricant but nothing else to help with other issues they face as trans people. Despite being able to rent a space and provide capacity-building training (sewing, pastry making, floral arrangement classes) to mostly Afro-Guyanese trans women from the surrounding areas, the organization has also had to streamline much of its services due to funding regulations. Thus, although it initially attempted to address the marginalization that trans women experienced in larger organizations like SASOD, it has suffered a similar fate of having to abide by limiting guidelines for its activism. GTU's director explained the gap between "the service that they desire, to what the community require" [sic]:

> They require for a fact in drawing your blood. Drawing your blood and to find you positive and to link you to a clinic. The community don't have a problem giving blood. They don't have a problem if you find them positive, and they don't have a problem to link you . . . but they have a concern: Okay I am now doing a test for you. When I finish this test that you want me to do, and if I found out I'm positive, my life now change. I might fall into a state of depression. I might fall into a state of not wanting to be among normal society, but I going to be [sticking] around this organization cause they test my blood and they know what going on with me. I want to be there, but then I can't come to the office because they does not provide a hot meal . . . the service don't provide that because of the funder. So, we will have to do this thing on we own . . . When we advocate for it, they say we don't support these things. So, there is this big gap within the service and what you want. (Interview with GTU, December 2016)

Many activists gave examples pertaining to food and housing insecurity, including an Amerindian trans activist[12] residing in Region 3, West Demerara, in Guyana. She ran a small community-based organization, Candle in the Wind, for mostly Amerindian and Indo-Guyanese trans women and gay men in that region. With a membership of about twenty-five persons, Candle in the Wind received limited funding from larger organizations like SASOD and GTU to conduct small group activities. The group was started in 2007 when its leader, a social worker and activist, decided that there was a need to bring members of the LGBT community together to "socialize and have fun" (December 2016). She has, however, recognized that the critical needs of working-class trans women located outside the city were being ignored due to funding arrangements and regulations:

> What I have noticed for a fact is that most persons, like 50% of the members, who make up the entire population of LGBT in Guyana fall below that economical poverty line . . . the funders have their own agenda and some of their agenda is about LGBT advocacy and running administration which I don't see is the real need. The people on the ground, the persons in the street, they need places to sleep, food to eat, clothes to wear, and maybe help them to build capacity, and to go out there and to do their work as a very positive person. So, for now, for me, it's too much of laws and getting and fixing and by the time we fixing, our members are starving and dying. (Interview with Candle in the Wind, December 2016)

In Barbados, a trans activist helped me to understand the inability of human rights work to address the specific needs of trans women in the region. The civil service organization, which she runs out of her rumshop, is in an inner-city working-class community in Bridgetown. Unlike some of the bigger and more well-known organizations, she was adamant that she needed to pay less attention to providing "services" to the working-class trans women and sex workers and more energy on understanding their needs, since using formal outreach channels can sometimes be off-putting for potential clients. She acknowledged the displacement of people in the community, noting how the marginalization of certain physical spaces triggered stereotypical judgments and inhibited their opportunities. "Sometimes, it's hard for people when you go for a job and you say Reed Street and people have their own preconceived notions of what your intent is, rather than employ you to do the work. It's hard for some people, so the street comes with its type and the treatment comes with it also." These urban spaces may have low income or education levels, but the attached stigma means denial of employment opportunities and having to turn to sex work. "When I go on the streets to work, male sex workers, transgender, sometimes people living with HIV, bisexual men . . . is a big group that I work with," she said, noting some of the strategies needed to engage that demographic, like her bar:

LIBERATING THE QUEER CARIBBEAN

So sometimes I will be here, and the guys will come in and check me. They will say thing: "you look nice . . ." You engage them in conversation, you start the convo. I also do this, "I hope you are protecting yourself. I hope you not engaging in this kind of behavior . . ." Sometimes you even get them saying "I have a problem in X area, where could you refer me, where could I get help?" They may need condoms, etc. But directly going and approaching the people, even the same people, when I do voluntary testing in collaboration with the ministry of health, and I meet them, there is questions you ask like "[you] having sex with men?" Some of dem don't be honest, but I guess one on one they can be honest with you because I know you, you know me, so I can be honest. But in big crowds and where it is official, they are not too prone to give that. (Interview with trans activist, September 2016)

She too was constrained by the overemphasis on HIV testing but recognized it could be useful. "For me, one of the things you will look to see is just like how the trans community has access. There are some things that you'd need but it might have to turn to HIV for you to access [the funds]. Sometimes it could be a bit challenging" (Interview with author, September 2016).

A lesbian activist working with Kingston's gully queens also recalled her experience of applying for funding in Jamaica and how such arrangements pigeonholed her organization's objectives:

So, you apply to tell them that, okay this is the work you want to do; most times when you apply you're not gonna get it because if you're not like a JFLAG and a Jamaica Youth Support for Life (JASL), they're not gonna look on you. And then what happens is when these bigger organizations apply for these funding and they use the word "all" then they have a $2,000 US left and they didn't meet their target, then they throw it to Colour Pink Group and say, "Here do some work, send me a report" and that's it . . . We want the work to be done so yeah, most times we're left with no options, but to just take it and do it. (Interview with lesbian activist, August 2016)

Another trans activist in Trinidad and Tobago shared a similar experience being sidelined because of this sole focus on disease reduction across the region. She was adamant that organizations like hers needed to change the narrative, despite funders' unwillingness to address such concerns:

Linkages, a few US-based groups—PEPFAR, USAID, FHI360—and all of these US-based NGOs come together to form one NGO to work on testing. Their goal generally is to see if they could get more testing done—they trying to find more positive. Their issue is really testing, and in the Caribbean here HIV is just a drop in the bucket. HIV is not our whole life, because we have a lot of issues. In terms of food, the trans women, I ask them if when they realize that they HIV positive, why they not starting medication. One of the reasons is where do I stay? If I access this medication and living on the street, how do I store my medication? What do I eat when I want to take this medication? Would I have something to eat? These are some of the issues, and Linkages only came here to find positive and they not really searching or researching the other issues that the community is actually facing. . . . I ask them what coping mechanism that they had in place for drug users, 'cause drug use is one of the issues along with mental health and depression. Now that we have discovered what you want, are you willing to hear what these persons want, what their needs are now? And no questions could be answered. (The funders were unable to answer these questions.). (Interview with trans activist, March 2017)

International funding agencies failed to address the needs of the communities they serve. In fact, the UNAIDS representative I interviewed made it clear that UNAIDS is not an implementing agency, and its aim is to influence policy, strategy, and national programs on what it believes are the "bigger problems." Further, he reiterated that the organization avoids "direct engagement with the small communities" (Interview, December 2016). This reminds me of CAISO: Sex and Gender Justice late founding director Colin Robinson's explanation that much of the organization's earlier work had occurred on policy levels, with less direct engagement with communities on the ground. However, it is important to note that much of CAISO's focus has expanded to complement this kind of work in recognition that while laws may change, there is still extensive work to be done to change the minds and hearts of Caribbean people, especially when there is little immediate and tangible downward impact on queer and trans communities from this kind of policy advocacy. I reflect on my conversations with Colin and explore these tensions further in the next chapter.

Despite international agencies' domination of the queer human rights aid industry in the region, the more complex work of community mobilization extends beyond their mandate. Organizations like UNAIDS use international United Nations political conventions as a platform to share discourses of tolerance and rights yet monopolize the conversation to pathologize queer and trans bodies of color as disease ridden. Despite such grand aspirations, backed by very decided interventions, pressuring local organizations to focus extensively on disease prevention or discovery, as activists in Guyana and Trinidad and Tobago put it, limits the ways in which sexuality and identity in the fullness of their complexities can be conceived. On the one hand, it constructs Caribbean people as inept and unable to identify their needs to determine valid courses of action. On the other, by finding more "sick" people, funders justify their helping imperative to manage the disease-ravaged bodies of poor, Black and brown, "underdeveloped" trans women and gay men based on limited and conditional ideas of queerness.

LIBERATING THE QUEER CARIBBEAN

The experiences of displacement presented in these narratives speak to the larger issue of how working-class populations are treated in the Caribbean, especially when they reside and work in communities and engage in activities regarded as unproductive. They also emphasize a reality of unbelonging within mainstream queer communities that reifies the existing race, class, and gender tensions of the day. In focusing extensively on litigation, institutional advocacy, and disease prevention among "key populations," well-established activists and funders encourage the creation of homonormative activism that fails to address and disrupt the systems of oppression that keep queer and trans people subjugated.[13] As such, Black working-class queer people, especially working-class trans women, remain outside the reach of queer human rights activism, with little choice to mobilize community from the periphery. Plus, as these trans women gesture, their complex situations are exacerbated by the current conditions of activism. Despite this, some activists like those I mention here continue to play an integral role in informing the dialogue, creating community, and more importantly, resisting even though they have less and often complicated access to the grand narrative about their needs. I take up these ways of community making in the following chapters as I think about how queer people, operating outside the confines of activism, interpret and navigate the region's cultural mores to develop creative and radical ways of living and thriving in the region as queer and transgressive subjects.

CHAPTER 2

On the Ground

CHALLENGING SEXUAL POLITICS IN THE REGION

Heterorespectability and the Production of Caribbean Queerness

The postcolonial nation is built on heteronormative conventions of personhood and desire which assume that identity, sexuality, and gender are fueled by a "natural" affinity to opposite-sex desire and attraction. Nationalism is premised on these conventions, and Caribbean nation-states maintain hold of these gendered ideas of citizenship to survive, even as they reconcile the long and lingering legacies of colonization that continue to impact the region.[1] These sentiments are laid in concrete terms through the regional laws that replicate colonial ideas about the proper kind of citizen and translate into beliefs about aberrant non-heterosexual practices in ways that promote limited ideas of citizenship and belonging.

Legal feminist scholars Tracy Robinson and Yasmin Tambiah have offered that Caribbean states have morally coded and discursively constructed themselves as prosperous through their oppositional construction of homosexuality as criminal and unacceptable. Robinson (2009, 4) argues that regional laws, through drafting and revision, have worked to "continuously define boundaries of authorized sex and sharpened the notion of danger of the homosexual other." She posits further, "In the early twentieth century the sex you *did* and its contribution to reproducing the nation helped to define your worth as a citizen. By the 1990s *whom* you had sex with was being increasingly affirmed as a yardstick for belonging in criminal family laws" (12; italics in original). Therefore, some bodies are policed and even silenced, while being coerced into modes of acceptability. Through these regional laws, there comes a reassertion of heteronormative gender norms that are in turn "performed" in order to address acts of deviance and punish "gender traitors" (Alturi 2001, 9). Hence, the state and society continue to punish homosexual men and women for deviating from heteronormative standards, reinforcing belonging and citizenship that are linked to conformity to the nation.

Additionally, Christianity has strongly influenced the region's sexual politics, throughout its colonial history and even today. In speaking of Jamaica, Latoya Lazarus (2013, 336) acknowledges that the Christian church is popularly portrayed "as tending to perpetuate somewhat the fire-and-brimstone caricature that has impeded much meaningful engagement" on sexual and reproductive rights, yet she noted "some more conciliatory scenarios in which the endeavors of Jamaican churches and church folk have converged with those of progressive rights defenders." Lazarus observes, "These 'other' Christians, who also belong to various denominations, call for a more critical reading of Biblical texts so as to avoid reproducing and legitimizing the oppressive relationships such as patriarchy and heterosexism that underlie heteropatriarchal cultures and heteronationalist states like Jamaica" (343). Despite this effort by less conservative segments of the Christian population to nuance approaches to human rights, many secular advocates remain suspicious about churches' involvement in contributing to local human rights movements. In this context, these advocates question: "How much of a guiding framework can churches be in furthering a local understanding and respect of human rights? Which churches will provide such a framework? And how do you work with the contradictions that exist even within churches?" (Lazarus 2016, 45). Religious outrage against homosexuality has led many Trinidadians and Tobagonians to "regard homosexuality as not only repugnant and deviant but also sinful from a Christian context" (Tambiah 2009 9), an opinion that continues to prevail when discussing legal issues affecting the queer people. Their sinfulness and immorality are used to justify their persecution, criminalization, and social unacceptability. While spirituality and religion can provide space for the inclusion and acceptance of same-sex desire, mainstream religious bodies continue the rhetoric of damnation, "love the sinner, hate the sin," and other narratives of unbelonging.[2]

Many examples of state-sanctioned homophobia also abound in the region, where queer people, especially Black working-class gay men, trans women, lesbians, bisexual men and women, intersex people, and other gender-nonconforming people are victims. An important example in Trinidad and Tobago is that of Kenty Mitchell, a Black working-class, openly gay Trinidadian man who was incarcerated and de-robed—literally and figuratively—through a homophobic strip search procedure by local police officers after being arrested for a nonexistent warrant that was the result of a computer error at that police station. More importantly, Mitchell successfully sued the state for this wrongful incarceration and demeaning and emasculating experience at the hands of the police officers; it was probably one of the few instances in the Anglophone Caribbean where a Black, working-class person has won against the state despite their sexuality and gender identity.[3] Mitchell's openly gay Black body made him "hypervisible as a transgressive subject" (Wahab 2012, 493). As a Black man, he was ridiculed for his effeminacy and his incapability to "demonstrate moral rectitude" (Alexander 1994, 13), which contravenes the nationalist construction of Black heteropatriarchal masculinity. As Amar Wahab highlights, Mitchell's "small" penis, revealed in the strip search, "symbolically poses a threat to the normative codices of a virile heteronationalist Black patriarchy" (493). It was solidified, as he argues, in the especially public staging of the strip search in the outer area of the cells ... in full view of anyone who desired to pass along the corridor, spectacularizing "that small cookoo you have" (494). This ceremonial shaming "effectively stabilizes the state's discursive authority through constituting Mitchell as a nonviable, feminized, and failed masculinity" (ibid.). Recalling Alissa Trotz's examination of the incident in which Colwyn Harding, a twenty-three-year-old African Guyanese man was hospitalized after being sodomized by the police, and Sandy's experience of being force-fed the baton by police officers in Trinidad that I reflect on at the beginning of this book, it is clear how such an assault serves to emasculate sex and gender transgressors and reinforce violent heteronormative norms of masculinity.[4] In these incidents, the state has placed sexual inscriptions on some bodies, thereby outlawing their very existence, yet "unproductive sexuality" can be used to destabilize dominant heteropatriarchy (Alexander 1994, 2005).

In this chapter, I explore the legal context determining queer people's relationship to the nation and how activists located within the region are carving out space as they engage with and disrupt dominant sexual politics in their countries. Feminist scholars have extensively theorized the implications of restrictive legal structures in the Anglophone Caribbean and their purpose of determining who can and cannot claim citizenship and belonging to it. The current historic moment also exposes these limits of belonging and is characterized by the strident efforts of queer activists who are continuously challenging discriminatory laws, beliefs, and practices to claim citizenship. I explore how Caribbean queers are envisioning home despite being forced to reside on the borders of citizenship and belonging. I also examine the rootedness of contemporary values and beliefs about sexuality and the colonial referents that influence powerful discourses of state and church to marginalize queer people, thus inspiring the gender and sexual rights work of queer activists in Trinidad and Tobago. In detailing these legal cases and their outcomes, I trace the narrative of queer citizenship as it is being written and articulated in these momentous adjustments to the region's laws. Despite legal efforts having slow but significant impact, they have laid a necessary foundation for new and exciting forms of activism to thrive over the last decade, ensuring that the issues that queer people face are continuously being engaged on national, regional, and international levels.

Religious Nationalism and Neoliberal Queer Resistance: *Jones v. The Attorney General of Trinidad and Tobago*

On February 23, 2017, activist Jason Jones filed his historic constitutional case against the State of Trinidad and Tobago; Chief Justice Devindra Rampersad ruled in April 2018 that Sections 13 and 16 of the country's Sexual Offences Act (1986), which criminalized anal sex between consenting adults, are "unconstitutional, illegal, null, void and invalid and are of no effect to the extent that these laws criminalize any acts constituting consensual sexual conduct between adults." This ruling promoted Trinidad and Tobago to the rank of countries in the Caribbean, South America, and Central America (the Bahamas, Belize, Bermuda, and Suriname) that recognize a need to address homophobic legislation; it has also initiated the tenuous process of having sodomy legislation removed from the books.[5] Despite the significance of Jones's successful case, the ways it has been positioned and taken up internationally has controversially silenced the contentions lingering in the ruling's wake. Below, I explore some of the complicated dynamics arising between activists and moral gatekeepers from Trinidad and Tobago and other Caribbean islands following the ruling.

When Jones filed his case in February 2017, it moved quickly through the various phases of the judicial process in just over one year. While the proceedings initially held low public interest, on April 6, 2018, a Christian nongovernmental organization, *T&T Cause*, whipped the country into a state of pandemonium after holding a mass protest through the streets of Port of Spain. Evangelical and non-Christian religious leaders spewed a familiar homophobic rhetoric of the destruction of Sodom and Gomorrah, about the laws of God being the laws of the land, and of impending disaster when the gates of hell fly open. These sentiments incited intense anxiety among some members of society who utilized deeply limiting understandings of gender identity and sexuality to determine the limits of morality. Evident in this stance is an idea previously echoed by the evangelicals in Jamaica in 2011 about the impossibilities of removing that country's sodomy laws, where militaristic action situates these dominant, conservative organizations as the last frontier of citizenship, whereby Caribbean people are commissioned to protect the nation. Shirley Richards (2011), past president of the Lawyers' Christian Fellowship in Kingston, Jamaica, exclaimed, then, "The battle has only just begun. Now as never before in our history, churches are going to have to unite to fight a common battle. Weapons will have to be carefully chosen. This battle is not one to be fought with weapons of war as in the Middle East. Instead, we will have to fight back cultural imperialism with a moral revolution!" While these arguments define the parameters of acceptable sexuality, implicit were also concerns of threats to heterosexuality, the sacred and well-being of the nation, exposing the conservatism embedded in these ideas about the productive citizen.

Following the judgment in Jones's favor, T&T Cause invited religious clergy from other Caribbean islands, including Jamaica, where Bishop Dr. Wayne West of the Jamaican Coalition for a Healthier Society blamed the judiciary and media for increasing acceptance of queer lifestyles. He called on participants of their rally to "make your politicians defend your values against judicial activism. Fake science and fake news also has [*sic*] a role to play in this continued push for the gay agenda. This is no longer about what goes into the bedroom, it is about what we decide to base our society upon" (Superville 2018). This rhetoric incited further anxiety about queerness, seeing a group of religious leaders in Trinidad and Tobago forming a deeply concerning alliance with local NGO RebuildTT in June 2018 to speak against the threat of what they consider to be an LGBT agenda that threatens the nuclear family (De Souza 2018). In this meeting, the group of men made several erroneous claims about the current state of queer issues in the country and used misinformation to fuel fear of an imposing queer agenda. However, members of the local community immediately sought to remind the society about some of the issues that queer people face, fervently pushing back against those dangerous messages. In a statement, the Alliance for Justice and Diversity (AJD), a social justice coalition comprising seven civil service organizations responded to this meeting and the members' claims:

> The six men united despite their well-known theological divisions over the age of marriage and the decriminalization of homosexuality to call, in their own words, for "no amendment to the Equal Opportunity Act to accommodate any LGBTQIA issue." Their position responds to recent public calls to strengthen legal protection for LGBTI persons against discrimination. Several young LGBTI persons were evicted by landlords after they appeared in the media celebrating an April court ruling decriminalizing sodomy. LGBTI persons who have filed past cases with the Equal Opportunity Commission (EOC) have received determinations that the cases were not within the EOC's jurisdiction. The EOC Chair has affirmed this in a media statement following reports of the evictions and of firings of other young people for similar reasons. The Commission has been on record since 2014 asking for the authority to receive complaints of sexual orientation discrimination. (AJD 2018)

This statement goes on to list numerous inaccurate claims made by these men, including an unfounded relationship between expanded human rights protections in the law and increased HIV rates, ideas about nurtured genders and sexualities, and a statement that the small queer population was not representative of the national community (AJD 2018). One member of the RebuildTT team even claimed that the queer community's fight for rights included "the right to be married, and to change the education syllabus" (De Souza 2018). He also acknowledged that "[an] international agenda was being pushed on people so RebuildTT felt the need to push back" (ibid.). Some local activists continued to emphasize, however, that this was not the focus of the current struggle.

While the mainstream discourse by Fundamentalist Christian groups received extensive attention, it was not entirely representative of the larger religious discourse circulating during these moments. In fact, prominent leaders from different religious faiths took completely different stances on the matter. In response to the situation, Hindu pundit Satyanand Maharaj condemned the religious groups who supported sodomy laws, arguing:

> Buggery, these religious right zealots fail to recognize, is not the providence of only the gay, but consenting straight couples also engage in this sexual exercise. The buggery laws on the statute books for over a hundred years have witnessed the rise of the gay lifestyle . . . To those who are fighting to prevent these people from their inalienable human rights, how will you react if your only child comes out to you? Will you abandon and disown them? This is an issue where our humanity is being tested. A person's humanity is not related to their sexuality. (LoopTT 2018)

Likewise, Father Jason Gordon, archbishop of the Archdiocese of Port of Spain, sought to intervene in the discussion arguing that "the [Catholic] church made a very clear statement that buggery should not be criminalized and that any country that has buggery as a criminal offence, that the church should find ways to remove it from the statute books" (Sant 2018).[6] What these scenarios reveal is that reminiscent of Lazarus's findings about religious perspectives on Jamaican sexuality, despite the more popular homophobic religious rhetoric, there is indeed much more nuanced discussion and consideration being given as people continue to reconcile the sacred with queer sexuality and gender identity.

Consequently, fundamentalist groups have resorted to fear tactics, exploiting the anxieties they have seeded within the public. Their misinformation, emphasized that an international agenda threatened to implant itself in the region and would destabilize the moral and religious fabric of the land. They were fearful that the globalized image of "gay identity" was going to be transplanted and become the norm there. For them, activists like Jason Jones are the embodiment of that fear—a depiction of queerness they have created as the enemy of their moral and respectable culture and nation.

Queer activists central to the case, and the international media's coverage of it, have pushed a neoliberal queer agenda that threatened to undo much of the headway made by activists on the ground. Indeed, Jones, the defendant, was himself a controversial figure before, during, and after the ruling where he made several statements that mobilized a queer identity politics familiar to places like Europe, the United States, and Canada. His visibility in international media coverage of the case highlights the clashes that occur between how activists on the ground perceive their work and their role and how these things are viewed from a "Western" gaze. This includes the debate about what "rights" should be pursued, implications of international funding, and the depiction of "queerness" in the Caribbean as a position of death and denial rather than a more nuanced and balanced image.

Jason Jones and the late Colin Robinson (well-known human rights activist and founding director of CAISO in Trinidad and Tobago) had a public disagreement on the importance of legal activism. In an interview with the Institute for War and Peace Keeping, titled "Trinidad and Tobago: A Nation in the Closet," Robinson expressed the view that legal challenges like these "were not fundamental to improving the status of LGBTQI people on the islands . . . the law doesn't make people homophobic; culture and religion do . . . the sodomy law isn't necessarily what most affects LGTBQI people in their daily lives" (Vivero 2017). In response, Jones indicated that he was "working on ten asylum requests from LGBTQI Trinidadians" who were "expelled from their families," hinting that this reflected what Trinidadian society was like for queer people. Additionally, he lamented the lack of support from CAISO, saying, "I'm very disappointed with CAISO. They don't fight for same sex marriage. Robinson also said that my lawsuit was useless because it wouldn't change people's hearts and minds" (ibid.). Instead, Jones thanked "white cisgendered people doing it [providing legal support] for free" (Browne 2017), emphasizing the amount of financial, administrative, and legal support he had received from England for the case.

In a brief news interview shortly after filing the lawsuit at T&T's High Court of Justice, Jones pointed out that "if this country seriously desires to gain first world status, the law must be amended. . . . We've been independent for 53 years, so what's going on? These laws are originally British colonial laws so if Britain removed the laws so many years ago, what's going on here?" (Browne 2017). Here he positions Britain as teacher and uses the Gay International's white neoliberal rhetoric to emphasize some of the issues, like marriage, that he positions as markers of what Jamaican scholar Carla Moore calls queer modernity (2014).[7] The United Kingdom also took advantage of the opportunity to further cement its location as savior ushering in change, with (then) British prime minister Theresa May affirming that "nobody should face discrimination or persecution because of who they are or who they love and the U.K. stands ready to help any Commonwealth member wanting to reform outdated legislation that makes such discrimination possible" (Lang 2018).

After the ruling in 2018, queer international media missed the opportunity to highlight the actual issue: the removal of the country's sodomy laws that criminalize sexual activity between consenting adults and what that meant for the country and the region. Media coverage by Gay Star News, Pink News, and the other queer media instead focused on casting the UK as a savior with the power to "help" change circumstances and address its historical role in current homophobic legislation around the world. For example, Pink News was excited to announce the UK's decision to fund initiatives to encourage change. UK home secretary Amber Rudd exclaimed, "The anti-LGBT laws in some Commonwealth countries are a legacy of Britain's colonial past." She continued, "The UK Prime Minister made clear on Tuesday that we have some deep regrets about Britain's historical legacy of anti-gay laws across the Commonwealth. . . . I'm pleased to announce we will provide £5.6m for a program to support LGBT and gender equality, working with organizations including the Kaleidoscope Trust, the Royal Commonwealth Society, the Human Dignity Trust and Sisters for Change to support the reform of the laws" (Butterworth 2018).

Logo TV's NEWNOWNEXT used the moment to congratulate the region for its slow progress but also emphasized the ways that the criminalization of homosexuality variously affects queer people across the world, reminding the activists to remain committed to ending criminalization (Avery 2018). Gay Star News, on the other hand, ran a series of features highlighting what this ruling meant for gay Trinidadian men in the diaspora. One Trinidadian living in London provided a moving story of his forceful departure from a "country that doesn't accept you" (ibid.). He positioned London as a city in which he was able to come into the fullness of his queerness, with opportunities to immerse himself in activist work. This ruling, he continued, "reminds me that my home, the place I grew up, the place I loved more than anywhere else—does accept me. And also, that one day a young gay man can sing our national anthem with pride and truly believe the words, 'here every creed and race find an equal place'" (ibid.).

It is this rhetoric of an enlightened outside and hostile region that makes the conservative right anxious; they imagine gay people performing their sexual identity as they have seen depicted in queer media, with scanty dress in Pride events, public displays of affection, and raising families, all of which they consider contrary to their values. People like Jones are fighting for necessary change, but this is a fight deeply entrenched in an idea of queerness not readily available in the space(s) wherein they seek to intervene—hence, the reaction from religious organizations about an infiltrating "outside" agenda. This notion, however, is disrupted as I show throughout my discussion of queer place and trans space making in the Caribbean that are rooted in communities that exist outside the confines of formal activism in kinship formations, bars, and rumshops, and across several other geographies. In fact, while a decriminalization of consensual sexual intercourse between adults can be legislated, it remains necessary to consider how this could translate to the everyday needs of same-sex-desiring and gender-nonconforming people, especially those who are working class or home challenged, or those who engage in sex work. In the next section, I explore activism in Guyana around the cross-dressing laws that have impacted trans men and women.

Crossing Dressing and Crossing Boundaries of Respectability in Guyana: *McEwan, Clarke, Fraser, Persaud and SASOD v. The Attorney General of Guyana*

153. (1) Any person who does any of the following acts shall, in each case, be liable to a fine of not less than seven thousand nor more than fifteen thousand dollars...

...(xlvii) being a man, in any public way or public place, for any improper purpose, appears in female attire; or being a woman, in any public way or public place, for any improper purpose, appears in male attire...

Between February 6 and 10, 2009, seven transgender women were arrested in Georgetown, Guyana, and fined under the country's Summary Jurisdiction Offences Act of 1893, which criminalizes, among other things, cross-dressing by men and women for a vague charge of "improper purpose." This issue engaged numerous human rights organizations and legal experts, as various rescheduled court appearances resulting in a Guyana Court of Appeal decision in February 2017 that "upheld the decision of former Chief Justice, Ian Chang that cross dressing is allowed once not done for 'improper purposes'" (Guyana Chronicle 2017a). On November 13, 2018, however, the Caribbean Court of Justice overturned all previous rulings in favor of the appellants.

Through the years preceding this final decision, the litigants and interested parties had to navigate stringent social and cultural restrictions that impeded their movement through the justice system. In reflecting on SASOD's ten years of existence as an organization in Guyana, its director noted that these human rights infringements had engaged the organization's attention even before this arrest:

In May 2006, SASOD became aware of an arrest and prosecution for cross-dressing through a Stabroek News report. Through our community networks, we reached out and found Petronella who was arrested and fined several thousand dollars for this victim-less offence. Petronella joined SASOD representatives on a live program on state radio for International Day Against Homophobia and Transphobia on May 17, 2006. In February 2009, there was a more extensive, state-sanctioned crackdown as various sections of the media reported the arrests and prosecution of 7 persons within a 48-hour period for cross dressing. This police crackdown was particularly offensive as the 7 persons suffered a range of rights abuses beyond the arbitrary arrest and detention—including sexual harassment while in police custody and disparaging remarks about their gender identity and sexuality from the then Chief Magistrate Melissa Robertson, who took the opportunity when sentencing to share her gospel of Christ from the bench. In February 2010, 4 of the persons

ON THE GROUND   61

arrested and prosecuted, along with SASOD, filed suit against the state for
these unconstitutional violations. (Simpson 2013)

The case was initially adjourned until June 4, 2013, and then to September 13,
2013, where Chief Justice Ian Chang determined that "the police violated the
human rights of the four litigants in the case during their crackdown in February 2009 when they arrested them under section 153(1)(xlvii) of the Summary
Jurisdiction (Offences) Act." Each of the four trans women was awarded $40,000
GYD [approximately US$190] "for breach of their rights to be informed as soon
as reasonably practicable as to the reason(s) for their arrests under Article 139
(3) of the Guyana Constitution" (SASOD 2013). Despite establishing that cross-
dressing was no longer deemed to be illegal unless done for an "improper purpose," Chang failed to provide any clarification on what constitutes an "improper"
purpose" (Wills 2017a). With legal counsel from a team of attorneys from the
University Rights Action Project (U-RAP) comprising lawyers and professors
from the University of the West Indies, the litigants proceeded to appeal Justice
Chang's decision in Guyana's Court of Appeal on three major grounds: that trans
women remained unprotected by the chief justice's decision; that the "hopelessly
vague" cross-dressing law failed to provide a precise explanation of what is being
prohibited; and that it contravened Guyana's constitution in which "all persons
are equal before the law and entitled to the equal protection and benefit of the
law" (SASOD 2016). The implications of such vagueness materialized with Chief
Magistrate Robertson's declaration "that [the trans women] were 'confused' and
should 'go to church and give their lives to Christ'" (Trotz 2013), which revealed
how tethering the legislative to the religious defined what "improper purpose"
meant in that context. It was again evidenced in January and March 2016 when
Petronella, mentioned by Simpson above, was barred from entering the court to
appear before Magistrate Dylon Bess because she wore female clothes. "Bess
reportedly told [her] he only knows about two genders, which are male and
female" (Wills 2017b). Scholars have interrogated the dangers of problematic
ideas like these. Or as Alissa Trotz (2013) argues, "The imprecision attached to
'improper purpose' gives wide discretionary powers to the police and the justice system in a context where the cards are heavily stacked against LGBT
persons."

After several other postponements by the court of appeal, the appeal was
finally heard on November 18, 2016, with judgment being delivered on February 27, 2017, in the state's favor. The *Guyana Chronicle* (2017b) reported:
"Chancellor of the Judiciary, Carl Singh, Acting Chief Justice, Yvonne Cummings-
Edwards, and High Court Judge, Justice Brassington Reynolds, unanimously
upheld the decision made by Justice Chang in 2013. Singh reasoned that an
improper purpose would be a man dressing as a woman, and using this female

image to solicit services from a taxi driver, after which he robs the driver." The case was again heard at the Caribbean Court of Justice (CCJ), Guyana's highest appellate court, on June 28, 2018, with the court finally proclaiming victory for the appellants on November 13, 2018:

> The Court held that the law was also unconstitutionally vague, violated the appellants' right to protection of the law and was contrary to the rule of law. A majority of the judges, President Saunders and Justices Wit and Barrow also upheld the appeal on the basis that the law resulted in transgendered and gender nonconforming persons being treated unfavourably by criminalising their gender expression and gender identity. The Honourable Mr. Justice Anderson in his judgment commented that the law wrongly sought to criminalise a person's state of mind as there is no test to determine what is an "improper purpose." Mme. Justice Rajnauth-Lee's opinion focussed on the vagueness of the law in question.
>
> The CCJ also found that the remarks made by the Magistrate, immediately after sentencing the appellants and while the Magistrate was still sitting, were inappropriate. According to the Court, "judicial officers may not use the bench to proselytise, whether before, during or after the conclusion of court proceedings. Secularism is one of the cornerstones upon which the Republic of Guyana rests."
>
> The Court ordered that Section 153(1)(xlvii) be struck from the laws of Guyana and that costs are to be awarded to the appellants in the appeal before the CCJ and in the courts below. (CCJ 2018)

Like Jones's case, this was another important moment in the region's queer history. Not only does it emphasize the fact that trans women are constantly policed, but it also points to a larger issue of regulating the ways that poor Black and brown people can occupy space—especially when the private becomes public for many, like those who live on the street and do sex work. Such acts by agents of the state fulfill the precedent of colonial vagrancy laws where, in countries like Guyana, it remains illegal for persons deemed socially and politically illegitimate by the society to occupy public space and use it to survive.[8] Janeille Matthews and Tracy Robinson (2019, 143) argue that "the line between vagrancy offenses like loitering and wandering and the constitutional right to freedom of locomotion is a fine one" when the country's colonial laws are used to continuously criminalize particular segments of society, such as the "idle and disorderly persons, rogues and vagabonds, incorrigible rogues, or other vagrants" (Phillips 1995, 1371).

These working-class trans women must therefore be understood as multiply displaced in ways that move beyond just a discourse of queer rights, as much of the rights talk mobilized by these arrests obscures the other ways in which they become criminalized. What would it mean then to consider how these litigants were fighting against not only a system of gender and sexual oppression but also one rooted in longer histories of racial and class apartheid? This is especially apparent when we observe that those charged under colonial vagrancy laws were working-class Afro- and Indo-Guyanese people with limited access to private space, whose experiences of enslavement and indenture were also marked by displacement.

I place these trans women's experiences with the state squarely within the confines of this historical legislating of acceptable productivity and legitimacy, especially because how they have been occupying urban space both historically and contemporarily—as gender transgressors and sex workers—is deemed "improper." M. NourbeSe Philip's recollection of how the jamettes of Port of Spain in Trinidad used their sexual agency to disrupt the order of the day is a beautiful and precise explication of this power that these trans women hold. The jamettes, Philip (1999, 74) argues, utilized the power that "the space between" give Black women to reclaim the trauma of years of control as an active way to say, "We have a right to be here" (82). As both jamettes and these trans women in Guyana show, that right should be exercised to demand belonging to a space even when that occupation of the space is disruptive.

Evidence of the trans women's disruptive illegitimacy lies in the ways the cases were handled and the numerous charges stacked upon the initial one of cross-dressing. For example, charges also included damage to property, larceny, and loitering, as reported in the local news:

> It is alleged that on February 6, the seven men were all dressed in female's clothing. According to them, it was "unisex" clothing. It is also alleged that on the same day Bess, Fraser, Peters and Persaud damaged the trunk of Steve Donlop's bus, costing $12,000 and that on the same day Fraser stole a cell phone valued $90,000 from Donlop . . . Donlop stated that on the day in question several boys were interfering with Bess, Peter, Fraser and Persaud. He said that shortly after the boys started to pelt bottles towards the four men who fled the area. Fraser had ran inside Donlop's bus for cover and when Donlop had instructed the boys not to damage his bus with the glass bottles, Fraser snatched his cell phone as he was about to call the police. Donlop later made a report to the police station and the four men were arrested and later charged. (Stabroek News 2009)

Such claims frame their behavior as "improper" and tether their criminalized cross-dressing with the other offences of aggressive larceny and damage to property. Therefore, by arresting them, the state maximized, as a matter of historical precedent, an opportunity to cleanse urban public spaces of such activity through detainment. These trans women's perceived criminality provided the perfect opportunity to attach disruptive characteristics to further solidify their positionalities as unbecoming of productive citizens.

Conditional Lives: Belonging, Queerness, and Citizenship

This perceived criminality of trans women and working-class queer people also makes its way into queer activism through the seemingly deliberate exclusion of persons coming from these backgrounds. In the previous chapter, I noted how this near-invisibility, or what I define as conditional queerness, is necessary to keep in place the homonormative arrangements that currently structure regional organizing, especially that which is closely tied to funding from outside the region. Here, it is notable too that mainstream activism within the Anglophone Caribbean sometimes produces a culture of conditional queerness that privileges limited acceptable ways of being queer, while silencing people's deeply complicated realities. For example, an activist working closely with the poor inner-city trans women in Kingston, Jamaica, explained to me her frustration about a blacklisting of trans women by what she positioned as a prominent "uptown" organization there:

All these other organizations are for the rich, the rich members of the LGBT community. So, it sort of puts a strain, because then when these organizations are applying for funding and they're saying that they're inclusive and it's for all members of the community. Then you get the funding and you're only working with a certain section of the community. What happens to everybody else?

... There's a few of the organizations here that work with the LGBT community, [but] they're all afraid of working with the homeless population. And that's because none of them are not open to why the queens behave that way—the reasons behind their behavior, how hard it is for them to adapt to certain situations ... what they've all been saying is that there is nobody else that they can call and say, "this is what's happening to me" and they'd come out there and sit with them. It's sort of like they're exiled, they're hidden away, nobody business about them. Unless some [foreign] organization comes to Jamaica and wants to do a documentary and brings some money, that's the only time [local activists] come around ...

These [local] organizations are very against the homeless population; they don't want them there. But these are my babies, they are my kids, I love them. When they're having training, they don't want them there; when they're having events, they don't want them there. So, when it is that you're going to be having celebrations and you're going to be feeding the five thousand and you're not even feeding your own homeless LGBT community that says a lot. And when it is that you're going to be having events and you're putting members of the homeless community blacklisted, that they're not allowed to attend, that causes issues.... It's like they really just for themselves and it's the top of the LGBT community here in Jamaica. (Interview with author, August 2016)

Evident here is a similar criminalization of Jamaica's working-class trans women where particular unproductive and unrespectable stereotypes are attached to them. Their communal blacklisting calls attention to some of the respectability politics that circulated within the communities in that moment. Like the instances of working-class trans women being arrested in Guyana for cross-dressing for "improper use," this interaction tells an important story of how particular queer bodies are made to occupy space in the region; sometimes in ways that perpetuate and collide with long-standing ideas of the respectable, productive Caribbean person.

A long-standing condition of our colonized existence is our perpetual quest for normalcy, productivity and ultimately legitimacy, which does a disservice to "the unmanageable" (Philip 1999, 295), who need to be managed in order to produce the "respectable queer," predicated on claims to citizenship. However, these discourses further position working-class trans women on the periphery of these claims, as their aesthetic, gender, and erotic practices are "dangerous," "unruly," and disruptive. In the previous chapter, I argue that global funding structures produce certain bodies as worthy of intervention through patholo-gizing discourse—those diseased bodies that remain outside legality and legi-bility in the state narrative. In contending with the ways that queer and trans people are rendered unintelligible systemically and culturally, and unlike the prescriptive tones of international human rights activism, regional activists have actively been seeking to create more inclusive images of the queer citizen. It is important, then, that I turn to the work of CAISO: Sex and Gender Justice (CAISO) in Trinidad and Tobago, officially formed in 2009. The organization was inspired by the country's national calypso tradition, Kaiso music, which uses the art form to engage social and political issues in song. CAISO's work, there-fore, functions as an act of political intervention in sexual politics. In Trinidad and Tobago, CAISO has been one of the most prominent queer activist organ-izations fighting against homophobia and discrimination across state, religious, and cultural boundaries. Among other critical work, CAISO has long called for protection against discrimination on the basis of sexual orientation and gender identity, particularly for expanded protections in the country's Equal Opportu-nity Act through its Add All Three campaign.[9]

At the time of my research, CAISO catered to a largely urban, Afro-Trinidadian middle-class population, and its founding director, Colin Robinson, was inter-ested in a nationalist politics of inclusion. To this end, much of its work had been in the areas of advocacy for legal and policy change with numerous appearances in the media (newspaper articles, advertisements, editorials, and talk shows), community mobilization, protests, and faith-based organizing. Since its incep-tion, it has remained invested in coalition and alliance-building work and has been pivotal in several collaborative social justice projects in the country.

66   DEFIANT BODIES

Angelique Nixon, CAISO's current director, explained the importance of this focus:

> Since 2020, CAISO has expanded its work to reach more community members especially working-class people and trans and gender non-conforming people. They do this through a programme called Wholeness and Justice which provides legal and psycho-social support services for LGBTQI+ people living in Trinidad & Tobago who experience human rights violations. The programme is committed to responding to violations of LGBTQI+ community members, with an emphasis on trans, non-binary, gender-non-conforming and intersex people. The goals of the programme are to deliver clinically competent, trauma-informed interventions that enable healing and resilience. We have been able to do this through strategic politics and engagement with funders where we insist on operations support. This has taken years and years to develop and build through partnerships, alliances, and an insistence on listening to and meeting the needs of local and regional communities as the priority—particularly those who are most vulnerable and marginalised. Other important projects we have initiated in the last two years include "Sign Together"—training LGBTQI+ people and service providers in Sign Language, offering support for Deaf LGBTQI+ leaders, and providing LGBTQI+ sensitivity and deaf culture training for sign interpreters and service providers; and "Finding an Equal Place at Work," which builds upon the workplace policy through education and training for organisations. In June 2021, CAISO launched a Caribbean Responsive Grant Mechanism for Caribbean LGBTQI+ organisations (in partnership with Astraea Lesbian Foundation for Justice), which funded 13 organisations across 8 countries in Cycle One and 14 organisations across 7 countries in Cycle Two. The decolonial methodology and regional review process for the Responsive Grant Mechanism was co-created by CAISO, Astraea, and a regional committee.

CAISO's Homosexual Agenda

I am particularly interested in CAISO's "Homosexual Agenda" project as I reflect on how its locally rooted approach to organizing influences its activism and mobilizing. In 2010, a self-professed ex-gay American evangelical pastor, Phillip Lee, made his first of many trips to Trinidad and Tobago to speak against same-sex sexuality. In partnership with the Hospital Christian Fellowship, Lawyers for Jesus, and the Emmanuel Community, he made a series of appearances at local media houses, secondary schools, and the University of the West Indies and "declared war on the issue of same sex attractions" (Daily Express 2010). While Lee's campaign to "straighten" Trinidadians may have received significant traction in local and regional religious circuits, intervention by activists overshadowed his venture. Led by the newly formed CAISO, a team of students from the University of the West Indies, and other supporters staged a series of protests to highlight the dangers of such attempts to regulate sexuality and primarily "target poor women and GLBT people's rights by whipping up fears about abortion, same-sex marriage and 'same-sex parenting' as threats to the 'traditional' family, even in places like Trinidad & Tobago where same-sex marriage is not even being debated" (CAISO 2010a). CAISO attempted to shift the discourse surrounding the event, insisting that it will not be remembered for Lee's role as

> a "reformed" American gay man who came to combat growing acceptance of homosexuality here . . . to deliver a message that homosexuality is acquired . . . reinforce the Lordship of Christ and the authority of scripture, which says homosexuality is a sin . . . and spread the news that no one has been delivered from homosexuality except through Christ. It will instead be about three other stories:
>
> 1. That the GLBT community in T&T is ready to organize and advocate visibly for equality;
> 2. That public opinion in T&T is that gay people should be able to live their lives; and
> 3. That young people care about something other than themselves, and that they hold a vision for citizenship that is about taking care of each other and standing up for what they believe in. (CAISO 2010b)

CAISO developed its "Homosexual Agenda" T-shirt campaign to counteract Lee's imported homophobia, by claiming the occasion "for those of us committed to building a local culture of inclusion and progress in Trinidad & Tobago to stand together and stand up for our values around sexuality and citizenship, and to contrast them with destructive messages being exported by the United States Christian Right in the name of Jesus" (Robinson quoted in Gosine 2015, 869). These T-shirts displayed the three main "agendas" of local homosexuals: (1) To buy Crix, (2) To spend time with family, and (3) To work for equality (CAISO 2010c). Like many other organizations, CAISO engages a vision of inclusivity and legitimacy based on ideas of fully integrating into the heteronormative nation. This witty attempt to normalize and legitimize queerness works to remind people that queer people want and should have a right to access these mundane things. This homosexual agenda campaign is instructive for thinking about the complex ways that the organization negotiates prevailing ideas about sexuality and queer legitimacy, yet another framing of the queer Caribbean subject emerges. As Andil Gosine argues, "The T-shirt speaks to both the banality of sexual rights on the one hand and the 'normalcy' of queer people on the other; all homosexuals want to do is what other Trinbagonians want as well: 'Buy Crix' (a reference to the popular local biscuit and, simultaneously, shared economic struggle)." An additional play on words would be the allusion to their signature slogan "Crix goes with everything." While the reference to spending time with family may have been normative, Gosine (2015, 867) reminds us that in Trinidad, "family" connotes broader and looser networks of attachment than the nuclear Euro-American notion of kinship.

This campaign, though, seemed to be emphasizing normative gay identities, with less attention to the experiences of those queers who do not easily fit into prescriptive race, gender, and class categories; who work and live in marginal spaces; and who are unable to participate in the kind of normalcy being emphasized because they exist in heightened illegality, darkness, and secrecy. The bullet points on the T-shirt, then, may not necessarily align neatly with the more deeply complex issues affecting queer people. The Homosexual Agenda campaign was revamped in 2015, through a series of advertisements in the Trinidad Express Newspaper that further mobilized a normalizing rhetoric. Each ad called on different segments of the Trinidadian society to be accountable for a local politics of inclusion. Two ads from this series reflected on this idea of national belonging, calling on people to "better follow the two highest Christian commandments" (CAISO 2015a); and to "let friends, family, coworkers and caregivers whom you trust know and love the real you" (CAISO 2015b). This nationalist desire for respectability and inclusion sought to produce and portray well-mannered and productive Caribbean queers who are able to satisfy or mimic dominant tenets of heterorespectability. In fact, I see that CAISO was aiming to achieve the opposite of what the discourse coming out of the cross-dressing case in Guyana did as a deliberate strategy: the cross-dressing case challenged people to reconsider the ways that dominant ideas of respectability, belonging, and nationhood continue to work as forms of social control and exclusion to the detriment of those, like working-class trans women, who fail to live up to these kinds of standards. On the other hand, CAISO's homosexual agenda invited queers to participate in and benefit from dominant and normative ways of existing in Trinidad and Tobago. This desire may have been influenced by the organization's nationalist investment and initial focus on activism at a policy level rather than through sustained engagement with people in their communities on the ground, as expressed by members of the organization in their interviews with me. The founding director explained to me in 2016 that:

> The mission has been providing voice and policy change. The initial groups that we developed natural affiliations were the feminists who were advocating for sexual citizenship issues before gay men came along. So, folks like FPATT (Family Planning Association), IGDS (Institute for Gender and Development Studies), to a lesser extent Network of NGOs (Non-Governmental Organizations) were some of the early relationships that developed. WINAD (Women's Institute for Alternative Development), ASPIRE and in part by

ON THE GROUND 69

working on some of the broader issues, Gender Policy, some children's issues but also by, you know, kind of working together on some stuff and people began to include us in. Like FPATT had us when they did their sexual rights; when they did a Caribbean launch of this sexual rights declaration that they had done, they asked us to speak and that was sort of a defining moment in terms of our public visibility, so stuff like that . . . We wanted to be this nation-building group, so we are trying to do nation-building things. One of the domestic alliances that we have developed . . . I mean one of the things we did was, we thought initially that we wanted, we saw a clear link between our work and other bodily rights groups work. (Robinson, September 2016)

In sitting with Robinson's vision, I must reflect again on issues of access as I consider the kinds of influence these policies and relationships with technocrats and civil society have for members of Trinidad and Tobago's queer communities. As Robinson himself lamented in his response to Jones's constitutional challenge, such top-down approaches may not be as effective as more sustained on-the-ground strategies. I remain curious, then, about the tangible outcomes of this type of advocacy.

By normalizing queerness and including queers in imaginations of citizenship, CAISO and other civil service organizations in the region have been inadvertently seeking to produce a homorespectable queer who is legitimatized as a subject that embodies all that heterorespectability commands. In seeking to normalize queerness, the group disciplines queer bodies through their relationship with and longing for legitimacy within the nation. Or as Jasbir Puar (2007, 50) explains in her theorization of homonationalism, they reiterate heterosexuality as the norm and foster nationalist homosexual positionalities indebted to liberalism. This inherent indebtedness diminishes the organization's desire to transgress normative gender and sexuality as it revolves around normalizing tropes of queerness. In doing so, these kinds of projects prevent a more fulsome acknowledgment of the complicated ways that queer and trans people really exist.

An important distinction must be made here that this focus does not necessarily mean that the organization is not working with communities. Queer activism is indeed dynamic, intersectional, complex, and always evolving. In fact, CAISO's activist repertoire has expanded significantly over the years to include other projects and provision of services—namely, its "Wholeness and Justice" program, which seeks to increase access to psychosocial and health services to queer people, and especially trans, nonbinary, gender-nonconforming, and intersex people. Another important project is its responsive grant mechanism in collaboration with the Astraea Lesbian Foundation for Lesbian Justice. With two successful cycles in 2022, the organization has been able to provide financial support to community groups across the region to guide "LGBTQI organizational sustainability and capacity needs, community building, strategic advocacy actions and policy-shaping opportunities, unexpected networking and alliance building opportunities, and COVID-19-based responses and needs" (CAISO 2022).[10] By engaging this analysis, I intend not to disregard the organization's accomplishments; I aim instead to emphasize the complicated negotiations of resistance that exist as activists continuously navigate and maneuver the messy terrain of queer politics as they continue to formulate and reformulate objectives that seek to move away from and incorporate dominant ideas of belonging and citizenship in the region.

CAISO's Ongoing Negotiation of Trinidad and Tobago's Queer Sexual Politics

While conducting fieldwork and as a research intern at CAISO, I was able to experience firsthand how the organization's work was constantly evolving. In 2015, it spearheaded the formation of the Alliance for Justice and Diversity (AJD), a social justice coalition of organizations and allies comprising a group of Trinidad and Tobago's LGBTQI-focused NGOs: CAISO: Sex and Gender Justice, Friends for Life, I Am One, the Silver Lining Foundation, Transgender Coalition of T&T, Women's Caucus of T&T, and Womantra.[11] The coalition aimed to establish a common policy agenda and present lawmakers with a prioritized list of policies and practices that would improve the lives of LGBTQI+ persons living in Trinidad and Tobago. Together, they also continued to work on CAISO's ongoing Add All Three campaign, renewing calls on the government to include three statuses of protection to the Equal Opportunity Act—age, health conditions, and LGBTI status—in response to community engagement on policy actions most needed to fight against discrimination.

In 2016, the AJD partnered with the Institute for Gender and Development Studies at the University of the West Indies and received a grant of 166,000 euros for a collaborative project: "A Sexual Culture of Justice: Strengthening LGBTQI & GBV Partnerships, Capacity & Efficacy to Promote & Protect Rights in Trinidad & Tobago" (European Union External Action 2017). Each member of the AJD was given the opportunity to contribute to a joint, multi-organization, three-year venture that allowed them to work on their individual projects within the confines of the grant.[12] As organizations were shaping their individual and collective projects, the year 2017 began with an upset. Three gay men—two immigrants and one Trinidadian—were murdered in suburban neighborhoods close to the country's capital city, Port of Spain. By this time, Jason Jones had also submitted his constitutional case against the State of Trinidad and Tobago, and this presented an opportunity to build momentum for his case internationally, by using the murders to emphasize the violent realities that gays experienced in T&T. The British *Guardian* newspaper even highlighted this in a feature about the case: "Jones, who lives in London and is a dual-nationality British citizen, claims that a serial killer targeting homosexuals murdered five gay men in Trinidad in 2017" (Surtees 2018). Recognizing the damaging potential of these unfounded claims, members of the AJD convened an emergency meeting to devise an immediate strategy to counteract this sensationalism in the media and to steer attention toward some of the other issues facing queer people in the country, like access to equitable employment and health care and addressing issues of discrimination. At that meeting, a decision was made to design a series of quick messages to acknowledge this threat of violence and murder in the community, but also reminding queer communities to be accountable for their safety in a moment when there was an apparent resurgence of homophobic attacks.

I designed five posters, which were distributed by the AJD at various queer events during the 2017 Carnival season. Each poster, as I discuss further below, sent a specific message: (1) "Watch Yuh Friend Back And Save Dey Life," (2) "How Do We Stop The Threat Of Violence And Death," (3) "Send Your Location," (4) "Speak Out," and (5) "When Meeting Someone." Soon after the first round of distribution, CAISO received a small grant from the Canadian High Commission in Trinidad and Tobago to print and distribute more of this material across the country in a project titled "Watch Stop Send" (more popularly called the "Keep Safe" campaign), which aimed to "offer simple messages: Be aware. Watch out for each other. Help find solutions" (AJD 2017). A CAISO representative explained in a media release, "Our LGBTQI communities here are resilient and have a long history of collaboration and of solution-seeking. Instead of panic, fear, and victimhood, we are calling for people to increase our responsibility and vigilance, to take more loving care of each other, and to ensure each other's protection" (ibid.). It is from this experience that I began to better appreciate the complicated negotiations that activists must make in their envisioning of queer liberation. I noticed how this project both complemented and contradicted CAISO's nationalist politics in its "Homosexual Agenda" campaign, as it sought to have a conversation, via the posters, with community members rather than with the state. In this instance, the organization shifted focus from seeking belonging in the mainstream society to carving communal space that was safe and welcoming for various queer people. This decision to shift focus and to also accept funding from Canada is significant in the context of my discussion in this work and in CAISO's typical stance about the nature of the work being supported by international groups. It is important to note here the context in which this funding was received—not only was it unlinked to any other projects being done by Toronto-based organizations but CAISO was given free rein on the type of messaging that it desired to produce for the community. This is reflected in the local dialect used and references to specific realities at that time. One unavoidable condition of this campaign was the inclusion of a small Canadian flag to signal the High Commission's involvement. By doing so, Canada has been able to place its mark on this campaign to remind people of its ability to intervene in sometimes-subtle ways.

As I participated in this campaign by designing the posters, it became more important for me to locate myself as a researcher critiquing Canadian homoimperialism, but simultaneously contributing toward a vision of queer Caribbean freedom through my conceptualization of these designs. I constantly wondered if my involvement contradicted what I was attempting to investigate and analyze. However, following transnational feminist Chandra Mohanty's call, I saw this as an opportunity to extend my feminist praxis and pedagogy beyond academic scholarship and to also participate in activism and struggle outside the academy (2003, 523). I appreciated this campaign because it diverted from the more popular rhetoric of danger in a moment of threat to queer life, instead encouraging persons to be vigilant and in control, characteristics barely afforded to the vulnerable queer subject in the region. Below are the posters with a short description of their objectives.

On January 25, 2017, forty-four-year-old Guyanese national Kwesi Mona and an unnamed friend were found at Mona's home in Curepe, Trinidad (see figure 1). Mona was dead, while his friend was unconscious. The police and members of the community suspected that Kwesi was attacked by this friend, and autopsy reports concluded that he was "beaten on the head and strangled with a belt. The cause of death was ligature strangulation, but the several blows to his head resulted in no head trauma" (Stabroek News 2017). This poster played on the imagery of the violent death that gay men were experiencing and sought to call on the community to literally watch each other's backs so they can help save people from being attacked and killed.

Figure 2 draws attention to the reality that each person has a duty of accountability in minimizing the risk of violence and death among members of the community. The rhetorical statement aims to get people thinking and hopes to encourage conversations among groups of people or at least bring more awareness about the reality of homophobic and transphobic violence in Trinidad and Tobago.

Figure 3 reminds persons that they should always let someone know their whereabouts, especially when meeting people with whom they are unfamiliar. This was an ongoing conversation among community members who were constantly reliving encounters of violence when they or their friends fell prey to attacks from perpetrators under the guise of meeting up to socialize or for sexual encounters. The committee felt it necessary to encourage this practice so that friends and family can lend assistance if necessary.

Figure 4 was designed to encourage a more inclusive queer atmosphere. There was a general sentiment by gender-nonconforming persons that queer spaces catered to gay men and that these spaces were sometimes intimidating or

Figure 1. "Watch yuh friend back." CAISO: Sex and Gender Justice.

Figure 2. "Stop the Threat of Violence." CAISO: Sex and Gender Justice.

Figure 3. "Send Your Location." CAISO: Sex and Gender Justice.

Figure 4. "Speak Out." CAISO: Sex and Gender Justice.

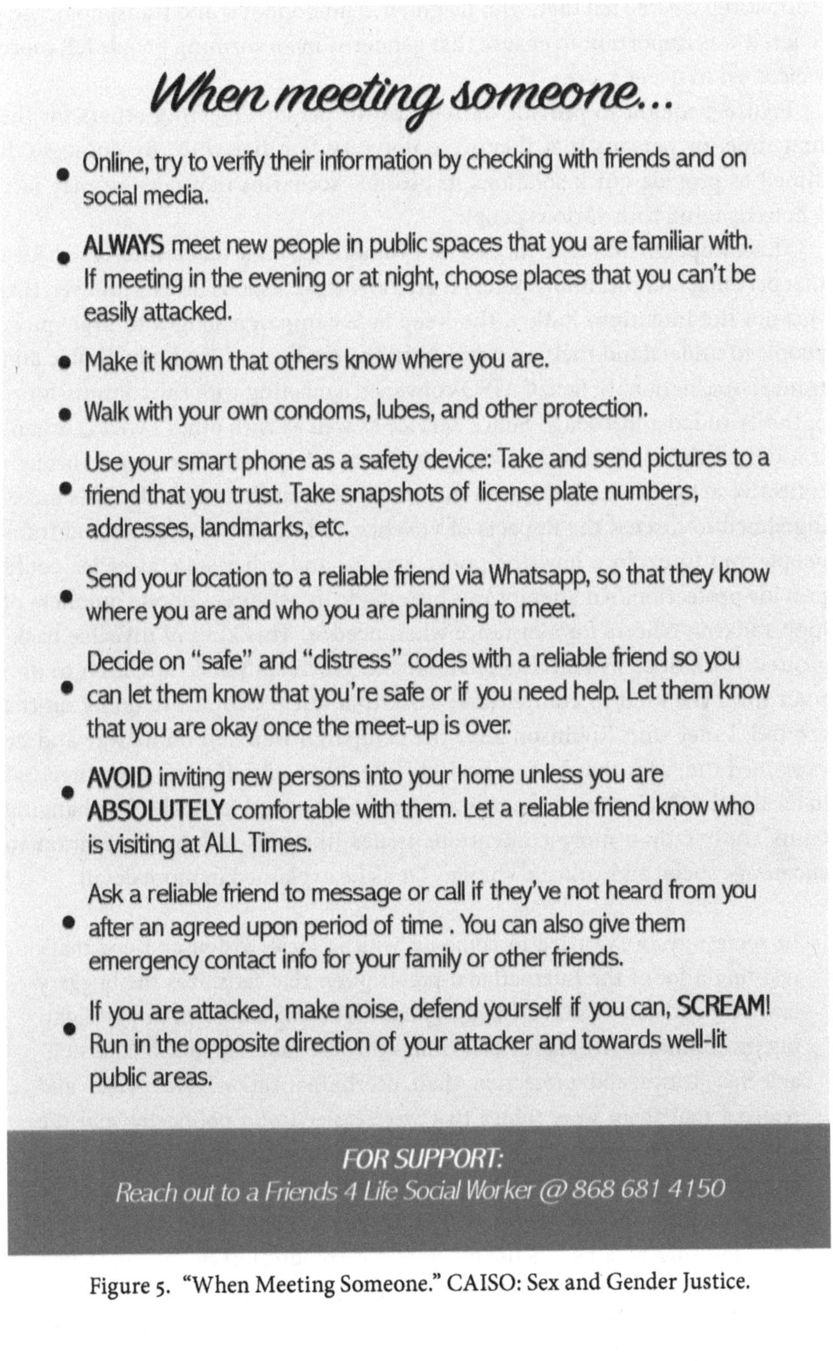

When meeting someone...

- Online, try to verify their information by checking with friends and on social media.

- **ALWAYS** meet new people in public spaces that you are familiar with. If meeting in the evening or at night, choose places that you can't be easily attacked.

- Make it known that others know where you are.

- Walk with your own condoms, lubes, and other protection.

- Use your smart phone as a safety device: Take and send pictures to a friend that you trust. Take snapshots of license plate numbers, addresses, landmarks, etc.

- Send your location to a reliable friend via Whatsapp, so that they know where you are and who you are planning to meet.

- Decide on "safe" and "distress" codes with a reliable friend so you can let them know that you're safe or if you need help. Let them know that you are okay once the meet-up is over.

- **AVOID** inviting new persons into your home unless you are **ABSOLUTELY** comfortable with them. Let a reliable friend know who is visiting at ALL Times.

- Ask a reliable friend to message or call if they've not heard from you after an agreed upon period of time . You can also give them emergency contact info for your family or other friends.

- If you are attacked, make noise, defend yourself if you can, **SCREAM!** Run in the opposite direction of your attacker and towards well-lit public areas.

FOR SUPPORT:
Reach out to a Friends 4 Life Social Worker @ 868 681 4150

Figure 5. "When Meeting Someone." CAISO: Sex and Gender Justice.

uninviting. CAISO felt that, with heightened homophobic and transphobic violence, it was important to ensure that gender-nonconforming people felt more welcomed in queer spaces.

Figure 5 sought to provide dating tips for persons meeting others for the first time, or persons that they were not very familiar with. By doing so, it aimed to provide quick solutions to possible scenarios that persons may face when engaging with various people.

This campaign may be critiqued for promoting a logic that reinforces an idea that personal and communal safety is an individual responsibility. However, this was not the intention. Rather, the Keep Safe campaign sought to urge queer people to understand their agency within the confines of the homophobic and transphobic nation. In fact, CAISO convened a meeting with the commissioner of the Trinidad and Tobago Police Service as well as with other LGBTQ organizations, at that time, in acknowledgment that safety must be ensured through collective action and allyship—even with the discriminatory state. This meeting aimed to discuss the impacts of violence and murders on queer and trans people and to explore how the police service and other state agencies could provide protection. An attempt was also made to get direct phone numbers of high-ranking officers for assistance when needed. This kind of invisible background work done by activists often fails to get much public attention to distract from the kind of complicated work that queer people are doing on the ground. I met with Robinson after the campaign was well on its way and he explained the work that he saw projects like this doing. Having been involved in local activism since 2007, he now appreciated the need to tackle "low-hanging fruits" rather than more contentious issues like anti-sodomy legislation to encourage social and cultural change. Or as he explained in more detail:

In some ways we've tried to come up with [a local] vision and one that's resisting a lot of the international prescription that fetishizes the buggery law. Very early on we said the buggery law isn't being enforced, why we fighting up around it? Are there other things that are more important and valuable for justice and protection than decriminalization? We polled and realized that there were things that were easier to do politically, and the political capital required to destabilize is high. So why would we get rid of a law that is not being enforced? What could change the next day? Should we focus on other things? We needed to develop a community ethos where, when someone became a victim other people wouldn't just steups[13] and laugh or gossip; that we were engaging with some kind of healing with people who experienced trauma and violation; that we were developing a communal sense of taking care of each other and of communal justice-seeking. (Robinson, October 2016)

These sentiments are captured in CAISO's Keep Safe campaign, where the messages remind persons about their responsibility in ensuring community safety rather than resting it in the hands of the state, the gay international, and their agents. They recognize the everyday interactions that queer people have, as they exist in the society, not as outcasts but as persons with the agency to navigate their sometimes-hostile surroundings. One important project that came after this in 2018 and 2019 was the Safer Together initiative, which offered three series of community-based workshops across the country with different members of the community and focusing on trans and gender-nonconforming people and community members who are hearing-impaired. This Keep Safe campaign therefore grew into community-based action and training.

As these examples show, Caribbean people are actively navigating and disrupting prevailing homophobia, transphobia, and discrimination on the ground. This is despite a dominant rhetoric emanating from North America and Europe, and even within the region, that the Caribbean is in dire need of saving from "degenerate, barbaric, savage, or inhuman" others (Kempadoo 2004, 30). More importantly, though, they also bring to the fore the messy and deeply complicated negotiations that queer activists engage, some of which sacrifice a more radical approach to queer liberation. Despite this, these rich engagements with heterosexist, homophobic, transphobic regional structures reveal that queer people are envisioning various ways of being despite legal, political, and cultural hostility that cast long discriminatory shadows on the Caribbean. It is therefore necessary to deepen the conversation about these issues even further in acknowledgment that queer and trans people, especially those sidelined in the narratives, are actively carving out space in truly radical ways.

At the time of my research, trans women and gender-nonconforming people were not being extensively engaged by many civil society organizations; however, many trans-led groups have since been established, and with more recent responsive funding opportunities, they have been able to prioritize trans, intersex, and gender-nonconforming people and sex workers. While in Trinidad and Tobago (and elsewhere) sodomy laws are being decriminalized, there are still other legal frameworks that criminalize these queer and trans people's economic activities, like a lack of protection from hostile employment environments and access to health care and housing, and sex work, to which they must turn when all other doors are closed to them. Activists must therefore assess the realities of the communities they intend to assist to effectively respond to their needs.[14] This means listening attentively to truly hear what these complicated needs are. Saying that the voices of the marginalized are silenced does not mean that they are being silent; they are speaking out if we listen, or if we look. The next chapter peers into such typically ignored derelict spaces to recover silenced (not silent) queer voices.

CHAPTER 3

Between the Walls

RUINATION AND NEW SEXUAL WORLDS IN BARBADOS

On an academic trip on the eve of the 2018 tourist season, I stayed at a small, locally run hotel, on Barbados's southwest coast. This villa, as I quickly learned, was situated next to the abandoned Four Seasons Hotel that continues to be haunted by a fascinating story. My first hint at the deep ambivalence over this site, even before seeing it myself, came from the nervous responses by Barbadians who gasped every time I mentioned where I would be staying. As if in concert, every person exclaimed "you have to be careful 'cause dem does do bad tings dong dere.'" Each time, I prodded further to understand what people meant. Was it in reference to violent criminal activity? Was it a warning about some mystical happenings fit for a blockbuster science fiction movie? Or, as I eventually realized, was it a hint about the unmentionable activities that occur in the dark, unlit abandoned crevices surrounding the villa? The occurrences at the hotel were un secreto abierto (King 2014), an open secret, that "[bring] into focus aspects of everyday physical life, the disavowed, and abject (low class life, low brow, low down) that are usually excluded from the 'high' political realm" (Sheller 2012, 24). Such transgression is often relegated to sites of abjection such as the inner-city rumshops, the dimly lit roads and alleys, and even abandoned buildings.[1]

The Anglophone Caribbean is characterized by a long, tenuous, and indeed complicated queer history that is often sustained by narratives of extreme violence, disease, and death for queer people who are deemed to be unproductive by their heteronormative societies and who are simultaneously exoticized and pathologized in the transnational gaze. Barbados, like the other locations addressed in this book, has been greatly influenced by colonial legacies of control, but it stands out, as David Murray (2010, 4) notes in his study of the sexual politics on the island, as a country of interesting contradiction. Historically, it has gained the reputation of being very proper in relation to its Caribbean neighbors—more English than the English themselves. Whether this stereotype is true or not, it makes sense to question what it might mean to examine sexual transgression as a form of "slackness" that butts up against dominant social norms and mores in a space understood to be one of the most respectable in the Anglophone Caribbean. In this chapter, I present a series of images of the abandoned Four Seasons Hotel to examine the fascinating stories of colonial ruination, normativity, and transgression being told there.

The discourses examined in the two previous chapters situate the Anglophone Caribbean states as homophobic and suffocating for queer praxis, but with activists and organizations working to empower and create space for queer Caribbean subjects. The same can be said of the abandoned hotels, now occupied under cover of the dark for queer pleasure seeking; they facilitate the actualization of queer sexual desire. The site provides possibilities for queer people with "relative rather than absolute citizenship, or rather none at all" to actively confront dominant sexual politics on the island (Alexander 1994, 52). While this may be true, I engage a deeper critique of these spaces as sites of colonial ruin, symbolic of the processes of ruination that empire has set in motion, including the dominant discourses of legitimate and respectable sexual practices that continue to impact the region's sexual politics. In *Imperial Ruin*, Ann Laura Stoler (2013, 7–9) distinguishes between "ruins as sites that condense alternative senses of history," and ruination "as an active, ongoing process that allocates imperial debris differentially . . . an ongoing corrosive process that weighs on the future." In other words, they provide an aperture, an opening or a lens, for viewing multiple temporalities (Anderson 2015). These abandoned hotels are sites of ruin, telling of their loss of financial utility for Global North investors, while also having meaning for *others* who occupy them as spaces of local pleasure. They are also sites of ruination, emphasizing how imperial power occupies the present through their continued role in exploitative industries, driven by colonial and neocolonial ideologies and capital, which have lasting impact on the region's political, cultural, economic, and sexual health.

The "Caribbean" and "queerness" emerge as almost synonymous with ruin and ruination, as symbols of degeneration and collapse (Anderson 2015), of decay, disease, and disorder, disparate from the civility of the norm. A popular Global North discourse about the Caribbean is that it is a place that exists in anachronistic time (McClintock 1995), out of sync with the rest of the world, where queer people are incapacitated in their attempts to attend to their deeply complicated needs. Such a narrative erases the role of colonial institutions and practices in orchestrating this region's sexual politics. Thus, I examine the ruins and relics of the abandoned hotel as an anachronism, telling a story of colonialism and its lasting imprints on Caribbean soil, even after the (neo)colonizer has retreated. In her provocative study of queer sex in Martinique, Vanessa Agard-Jones (2012, 340) offers that "while the sand's referents are far from concrete, they provide a model for one way to understand the memory of same-sex desire and gender transgression on the island—as diffuse yet somehow omnipresent." Thinking closely with her, I too argue that this soil—the dirt, mess, and litter, relics of homosexual encounters—is symbolic of the defaming of the region for sexual practices that are glorified in the Global North. Stoler (2013, 19) also urges an examination of colonial ruin not through the relics within the "center," the spaces from which the colonizer came, but through scrutiny of "situations and sites that appear in formerly colonized regions." She warns, "The 'interior' and 'exterior' spaces of imperial formations may not correspond to the common geographical designations that imperial architects scripted themselves," meaning that while the colonized regions were deemed "peripheral," they are in fact the "core" sites to examine the true work of imperialism in its mutability, its various forms and iterations. She details many sites for examination, including "the breadth of corridors in which people can move, the virtual barriers by which they are cordoned off, the kinds of infrastructure to which they have access, the selective dumping of waste, the preemptive racialized exclusions and exemptions in which they live" (ibid.). This chapter engages in such an examination, although not looking at the estate houses and destitute sugar mills of the old colonial era sprinkled throughout the interior but rather at the abandoned hotels that dot the coast, their foundations almost washed by the ocean waves and tides, their walls exfoliated by the blast of sand and salt. I interrogate what spaces like these tell us about the truly transgressive nature of queer sex in Barbados and the Caribbean, and what it might mean for us to reposition these activities as a yearning for another way of being in the world.

Tourist Hotels: An Architecture of Neglect

At night, there is little evidence beyond the shadow cast by my body, basking in the full moon, of what lies in the distance. Darkness fills the atmosphere and dances with the creatures that sing a festive melody in the dense bushes at the corner of my eyes. As morning breaks, images of desolation emerge as quickly as the sun shoots higher and higher into the sky. I cannot help but notice the abandoned resort buildings, shingled roofs caving in under the weight of over a decade of rain, sun, wind, animal excrement, dead flora and fauna, and sea blast. These buildings immediately remind me of the region's deep-rooted histories of colonization and the violent ways that outsiders continue to occupy space until it is no longer of value to them. They remind me that the Caribbean is an "invented landscape" that has been the causality of romanticism, since the eighteenth century, for the uses and pleasures of inhabitants of the Northern Atlantic (Sheller 2003, 46). This invented landscape has led to a taste for places that appear untouched, unspoiled, wild, and primitive (ibid., 53–54). This site alone, like many others across the island, has fallen victim to these dynamics

BETWEEN THE WALLS 83

Figure 6. The abandoned Four Seasons Hotel viewed from the sea. Photo by author.

where the capitalist outsider rapes the land and leaves their mark for generations to remember.

In 2005, British hotel industry and real estate magnates Michael Pemberton and Robin Paterson created quite a stir among foreign celebrities and Barbadians with the announcement of a grand plan to construct a multimillion-dollar villa resort at Paradise Beach. They envisioned the project in competition with Sandy Lane resort, which "for a few weeks each year, around Christmas and New Year, this spot appears to be the epicenter of a showbusiness earth tremor" (Dovkants 2012). International celebrities immediately purchased villas, won over by the thought of escaping to the exclusive, high-end resort with prime access to the white sand beach and picturesque ocean. Icons like UK-based singing competition *The X Factor* mogul Simon Cowell; British composer and musician Andrew Lloyd Webber; and CEO of Universal Music Group, Lucien Grange, invested millions of dollars for their dream properties on the island (Winner 2010). Despite the initial hype, the fantasy resort was soon entangled in controversy and began receiving extensive media coverage locally and internationally for delayed construction and dwindling funds. British news monitored closely, speculating what was at stake for these foreign celebrities who were on the brink of losing their money. Filmmaker and media personality Michael Winner wrote for the *UK Telegraph* in 2010 that "angry villa participants

Figure 7. View of ocean from "yard" of abandoned Four Seasons Hotel. Photo by author.

who'd put down massive cash to be embroiled in this mess wondered what fees Michael Pemberton and Robin Paterson had taken and if they were to be put back into the diminished pot." He questioned Pemberton, who wrote, "I have passed your communications to my lawyers." Local media, such as Barbados Underground, highlighted the labor issues and noted that Barbadians viewed the project as unsustainable. The project failed to secure banking investments and labor contracts, for which they controversially brought on Chinese workers. In an ill-conceived attempt to save this monstrosity of a project, and much

Figure 8. The beach of the abandoned Four Seasons Hotel. Photo by author.

to the dismay of Barbadians, the Barbados government sought to intervene by way of investing 60 million U.S. dollars to revive the project, with a plan of maintaining 20 percent equity in shares (K. Hudson 2010). This is despite the reality of a rapidly declining economy at the time and the mounting battles among investors who continue to seek legal and financial redress for their failed investments. Despite vocalizing their commitment to a 2011 completion date, the project was eventually abandoned; the company formed to manage it, Paradise Beach LLP, was formally dissolved in 2016.

Sites like these remain contentious across the Caribbean, and in Barbados alone numerous unfinished and abandoned projects dot the island's coastline with little sign of completion. Such projects of notable mention include a seventy-acre Merricks Resort in Saint Phillips and the Harlequin Hotel complex on the south coast in Hastings, both amounting to approximately $600 million in debt owed by British investors (Cumberbatch 2017). In Barbados, a country largely dependent on tourism, larger issues such as job security remain within the tourism industry and continue to affect locals. Barbados Tourism Investment Incorporated (n.d.) estimated, for example, that in 2014 tourism remained central to the country's economy and employed 14,000 persons directly with 12 percent of GDP attributed to the tourism industry. Locals also own and manage small hostels and apartments that provide low-cost accommodation to tourists, hoping to capture the market of visitors who do not stay at the island's many expensive resorts and all-inclusive hotels. However, small hoteliers and those employed in tourism-related services are constantly threatened by the expansion of the all-inclusive hotel model on the island, which results in exclusive, predetermined packages for guests and little benefit to Caribbean economies.

This is a problem that affects all tourism economies across the Caribbean. Matthew Bishop (2010, 107) reveals in his investigation of Saint Lucia's tourism development strategy that "the all-inclusive model accounts for between 65 per cent and 80 per cent of the island's rooms (Government of Saint Lucia 2005) and this means that, aside from unskilled work as bartenders or maids and the 8 per cent government room tax, St. Lucian society is excluded from many of the economic benefits of an industry where the bulk of the financial transactions between producer and consumer take place in the metropolis and rarely touch the Caribbean shore." This model excludes locals from access to income from tourists who no longer have need for goods and services outside the resort, so much so that even Caribbean governments do not have adequate share in the industry that dominates their economies. Angelique Nixon reminds us of this in her interrogation of how Caribbean people across the region and its diasporas negotiate production and consumption. An overdependence on tourism by regional governments, she theorizes, remains a major problem and "reflects the extent to which decolonization in both economic and cultural terms has not been realized across the region" (2015, 13). Despite this inaccess, local restaurants, artisans, and retailers continue to depend on tourist visitors to purchase their items and continue to suffer from diminished patronage due to corralling of visitors within the resort's walls.

It is important to acknowledge, however, that the formal tourism sector alone is insufficient for providing sustenance for locals. In fact, tourism scholars have theorized extensively the ways that the informal tourist economies in the Caribbean involve not only what is popularly dubbed as "sun sand and sea" tourism but also an integral, but illegal, underground aspect of sex tourism. Since the 1980s Caribbean governments have invested extensively in the tourism industry, with rigorous attention to privatized all-inclusive schemes to market the island's top holiday destinations. As these niche tourism services were being promoted internationally, "another less welcomed niche service, sex tourism, began to expand" (Mullings 1999, 55). Not only are tourists disembarking on the unspoiled white sand beaches of the island but they are also accessing a particular brand of pleasure-related services from men and women made available to visitors. This dynamic is maintained, as Kamala Kempadoo (2004) notes in her study of Caribbean sex tourism, because of the continuous decline of regional economies that decreases people's access to particular standards of living. Sex work thus provides for many Caribbean people "an opportunity for meals, cash, accommodation, access to exclusively tourist spaces, [and] access to travelling abroad" (118).

Of the situation in Barbados, David Murray (2012) has begun a vital discussion on the ways that gay Caribbean people engage in nuanced relationships of pleasure with visitors to their countries. In his work on gay Barbadian queens, he explores a popular tourist idea of a society of Black gay men that prey on white gay tourists for money and stability. His main informant, Edward, a white Canadian living in Barbados, depicts a northern imagination of a gay life filled with exoticized gay Caribbean men, and the disappointing reality that he could not fulfil their desires. On the other hand, he alludes to a Barbadian version of this tourist/local relationship that "emphasizes the predatory sex tourists who came to Barbados to lure young men with money and other material goods, and any Bajan man who did pursue this kind of relationship was deemed not respectable" (61). To this end, Murray concludes that the Barbadian tourist landscape perpetuates a colonial narrative of consumption, economic exchanges, and negotiation of respectability politics that have characterized the relationship between the North American metropolis and Caribbean periphery (63).

These studies provide rich context for my analysis of gay male eroticism in Barbados, and from which I explore the ways that men desiring same-sex intimacy can navigate the prevailing political, cultural, and social circumstances influencing or even inhibiting these desires. They help to contextualize what this abandoned landscape and architecture tells us about sexual practices and desire. Reflecting on Nixon's (2015, 196) call on us to rethink sites of Caribbean rebellion and freedom, I consider this site of abandonment and ruin as one of resistance that allows us to explore "complex sexual relationships and understandings of sex and sexuality in [and outside] families, that work against a politics of respectability." I therefore focus on the potentialities that male eroticism within these spaces offer as a commentary of not only sex but also the state of other economies of intimacy and desire. This materialist visual analysis is innovative and charts new territory for an understanding of sexual economies in the Anglophone Caribbean. Or, in acknowledging Krista Thompson's (2007) notion of "tropicalizing images" and their effects on an imaginary of the Caribbean as a carefully crafted and manicured space for tourist consumption, I present a sexual politics of eroticism that resides outside a picturesque Caribbean, and instead, within spaces of ruin.

Sites of Ruination

After standing on the white sand, cooled by the gentle waves and crushed between my toes, I am compelled to look back at the barrenness that pierces through me. No longer focused on this pristine aquamarine fantasy, I pivot 180 degrees, allowing myself to confront the imagery of abandoned dreams, colonizing investments, and bad financial decisions. This image is unsettling, and it reminds me of the fearful comments made by those who warned me about the area—"dem does do bad tings dong dere." Homophobic messages are plastered on the dilapidated walls, and I know them all too well. They are the ones that people in North America and Europe have grown accustomed to hearing about the backward, hostile Caribbean. They remind me of what many people endure in the region.

Figure 9. "Sickly 'Skunk' Gay Men Beware." Photo by author.

But as Stoler (2013, 5) explains, and has accomplished in the edited collection *Imperial Ruin*, we must "identify new ways to discern and define what constitutes the tangibilities of colonial pasts and imperial presence." When I stare at the abandoned hotel, I see the tangible remains of neocolonialism and ruination. Stoler believes it is a key matter of perspective to rethink and expand how we approach the "tangible" effects of ruination, not only as that which can be touched, but as that which is substantial and capable of being perceived (ibid.). Thus, I gaze upon these ruins with a new perspective, not as empty or abandoned but inhabited and full of meaning. In describing Manhattan's West Side, Fiona Anderson (2015, 138) offers that "the structural decay that made the warehouses so dangerous rendered them more appealing cruising spaces: long corridors facilitated wandering; empty door frames provided peepholes; and cracked windows and broken floorboards created accidental glory holes." Stripped of their original purpose, the hotels "encouraged the projection of phantasy, distinct from the ordinary urban time–space of work, public transport and apartment buildings" (ibid., 140). The decaying architecture at Four Seasons creates an erotic opening. Among the windowless graffitied walls, blasted by ocean breezes, in the debris of their nighttime escapades, I see the absented presence of queer desire. In the absence of bodies, their presence can still be witnessed. Or as Jose Muñoz (2009, 42) has instructed, "To see these ghosts we must certainly read the 'specific dealings, specific rhythms' that bring to life a lost experience, a tem-

Figure 10. "Bullerman Car." Photo by author.

porally situated picture of social experience, that needs to be read in photo images, gaps, auras, residues, and negations." He offers, "If the eye is sensitized in a certain way, if it can catch other visual frequencies that render specific distillations of lived experience and ground-level history accessible, it can potentially see the ghostly presence of a certain structure of feeling" (ibid.). Below, I sit with what my eyes see, sensitized to perceive the evidence of queerness in this abandoned space, the debris, and ephemera.

Consuming Pleasure

While the issue of people's homosexuality exists as an open secret in the Caribbean, queer people often face the threat of being "outed" because of their sexual behavior, as shown in Figures 9 and 14 (later on). Additionally, there is a further stigma about HIV/AIDS that it is still considered to be a "gay man's disease." As this, and the following pictures show, there remains a high level of policing on the issue of sexually transmitted infections (STIs). Here the "Sickly Skunk" is exposed as a warning to gay men who may encounter them. These markers are important, with the word "sickly" conveying the popular impression of HIV/AIDS as an illness infecting Caribbean people, and gay men in particular. Furthermore, "skunk" as a derogatory term classifies the perpetrator as a vile creature and vector of disease that must be avoided. This type of negative naming is rooted in long histories of extreme surveillance of nonheterosexual sex among Black men across the world. Marlon Bailey (2016, 240), in his study of raw sex among Black male communities in the United States, argues that such discourses "scrutinize and penalize black gay men, placing blame on us by constructing us as vectors of disease who should not have sex at all, let alone risky sex." A similar rhetoric, as I explain in earlier chapters, has been adopted extensively in the Caribbean through initiatives by large international funders and civil society organizations doing work with communities that they consider "key populations," like men who have sex with men and sex workers, to be at risk of contracting and spreading HIV/AIDS and other STIs. The Caribbean region has been continuously haunted by alarmingly high statistics around HIV infection rates. For example, UNAIDS reported in its 2018 review on the status of the epidemic that as of 2017, there were 310,000 reported cases of adults and children living with HIV, and 15,000 and 10,000 newly reported cases and AIDS related deaths respectively reported in the Caribbean (UNAIDS 2018). "HIV prevalence among gay men and other men who have sex with men is particularly high in Trinidad and Tobago (32%), Bahamas (25%) and Haiti (13%). Among transgender people, it is highest in Cuba (20%); and among prisoners, it is highest in Dominica (29%)" (ibid., 6). Interestingly, the report showed higher condom usage among young men than young women. Sixty-seven percent (Belize) to 79 percent (Jamaica) of young men (aged fifteen to twenty-four years) reported using condoms at last sex with a nonregular partner; however, young women (aged fifteen to twenty-four years) had lower condom usage, at 49 percent (Dominican Republic) to 57 percent (Jamaica). This is troubling when we consider that oftentimes, men who have sex with men also have sex with women, forming a bridge between "key populations" and other groups of people. While in the Caribbean, gay men and other men who have sex with men accounted for nearly a quarter of new infections in 2017, "key populations and their sexual partners" represented two-thirds of new infections (UNAIDS 2021).

While the graffiti throughout the space, such as that in Figure 9, label these queer bodies as the bearers of disease and command visitors to "Beware," I wonder if these statements serve as a reminder of disease, an urging to be cautious and careful, or if it is it a threat of outing. The presence of the condom packet in Figure 11 indicates that the imminent threat of sexually transmitted infection may be understood by those who occupy this space, whether as a result of national, regional, and international emphasis on safe(er) sex practices or because of an acute awareness of the tangible effects of such infections on queer communities. While the discourses highlighted above invade this site through the messages of HIV/AIDS plastered on the walls throughout the building, I see the condom packet serving a dual function of reminding us about the agency that those occupying this space enact while actively seeking out opportunities for pleasure. I understand pleasure in this context, as H. Shariff Williams (2012,

BETWEEN THE WALLS

235) theorizes, as "a means through which men could feel and be felt by each other . . . [receiving] pleasure through physical connection and intimacy, release of and freedom from pressure and stress, and facilitation of another man's pleasure." While these communities are pathologized in wider national discourse, it is evident here that they confront these realities by being actively in control of their sexual activities, which may involve condom use as integral to their seeking pleasure while simultaneously protecting themselves from contracting STIs.

The condom wrappers are the debris, the remnants of an encounter, almost mockingly lying before a spray-painted threat of exposure. We do not see people's bodies here, but the wrapper is indicative of their presence, their bodies engaged in pleasure seeking directly in front of these words, as if to bring the equally anonymous writer to bear witness to their act. Also discarded, the empty rum bottle, like others left lying across the site, informs us of another item being consumed here: alcohol. Like sex, alcohol is surrounded by stigmatizing and pathologizing discourses in wider national and regional contexts. Alcohol consumption statistics across the region are also startling, with strong and easy connections made between excessive alcohol abuse and societal issues like high mortality rates, alcohol-related health issues, and intimate partner violence. For example, a 2015 national survey on Barbados conducted by the Ministry of Health in partnership with the University of the West Indies, the Pan American Health Organization, and the World Health Organization found that one in ten men engaged in excessive alcohol consumption over a thirty-day period, with "one in three men aged 25–44 years reported binge drinking in the past 30 days" (Rose AMC Unwin et al. 2015, 7). These statistics are linked to "biological risk factors" such as hypertension, diabetes, obesity, and heart attack affecting citizens (ibid., 25–37). Another study, commissioned by the European Union on gender-based violence (GBV) in Barbados and Grenada, also found a strong correlation between physical excessive alcohol use and psychological domestic violence by men against women and children (Boduszek et al. 2017).

Alcohol and substance abuse continue to impact Caribbean people in deeply complicated ways. However, in reality, alcohol and other recreational substances possess a world-making ability to encourage particular interactions between people who may not necessarily encounter each other. The strewn alcohol bottles beg the question of what possibilities might be afforded by alcohol consumption within the walls of this decrepit site, as a mechanism for easing tensions and fears among occupants who seek out transgressive interactions with each other. The debris does not tell the whole story of the interactions that occurred in the space. While I might like to focus on alcohol's role in facilitating transgressive interactions, I cannot be sure that the connotations of abuse are not also present. Was the interaction entirely consensual? Was coercion, drunkenness, and violence used to access sex? I continue to look, as Stoler (2013) urged, with

Figure 11. Alcohol and condoms. Photo by author.

new lenses at what can potentially simultaneously be evidence of violence and of queerness; same-sex intimacy is not devoid of violence (Kumar 2018). Preity Kumar (2018) notes that violence within same-sex intimate relationships is inextricably linked to heterosexism, heteronormative and homophobic contexts that render invisible the violence itself and the ways in which selfhood gets configured through the enactment of violence. In other words, same-sex-desiring persons see violence at work in their environment and in turn utilize it to maintain intended power dynamics. Other studies have also found that stigma

BETWEEN THE WALLS 93

related to HIV and MSM exacerbated experiences of intimate partner violence among men, which in turn, results in higher levels of potentially risky sexual behaviors, substance abuse, and sexually transmitted infection (Wang et al. 2020). As described in the previous chapter, risk of violence is a reality for pleasure-seeking same-sex-loving and gender-nonconforming people. The debris left behind in these abandoned hotels exemplify the juxtaposition of potential pleasure and pain for queer subjects seeking self-actualization in these spaces of ruin, ruination, and unbelonging.

THE LOVE ROOM: NATIONALISM, CITIZENSHIP, AND QUEER UNBELONGING

Taking a few steps back, I capture another image, a bigger picture, shown in Figure 12 below. Beyond the wall where "sickly skunk" is painted, there is a room, not fully enclosed, residing amid homophobic graffiti, which another author dubbed "The Love Room." The inscribers focus on Jesus's love, while in another part of the hotel, an evangelical booklet tells those who visit the space about "salvation and its benefits." Both the inscription and the booklet recall the rhetoric of neocolonial evangelical missions in the Caribbean whose religious clergy and supporters preach a homophobic Christian doctrine that seeks to "save" the nation from queer people; they encourage loving the sinner and not the sin. This message is used to bring deviants back to Christianity with the promise that if they resist their sinful urges and practice a life of celibacy in service to God, they can still be saved. Moreover, it allows "Christian" practitioners to hold on to their prejudices and hatred while purporting to do something righteous (Ghisyawan 2022). The previous chapter detailed how religious homophobia becomes part of the state's rhetoric and practice, and in Barbados, it is no different. In fact, in 2019, a group called Family-Faith-Freedom Barbados informed the government of Barbados that it was mandated "from God of an overwhelming majority . . . that it should use its power for good" (ibid.). Their vision of "good" meant the continued exclusion and vulnerability of queer persons, to protect "traditional home" and family structures, which they felt would be threatened if same-sex couples were allowed to marry and adopt and raise children. They were fearful of the social, religious, and political implications posed by the legal challenges to the country's buggery laws, which if successful, would decriminalize sex between consenting adults of the same sex (K. Smith 2019). The inscriptions on the walls of the abandoned hotel, along with the booklet promising salvation, similarly insert religious homophobic rhetoric into so-called un-Christian spaces (as Evangelical Christians would see it), under the guise of love and compassion.

According to the 2010 census, 75.6 percent of the population of Barbados considered themselves to be Christian, 2.6 percent have a non-Christian religion, and 20.6 percent have no religion. Of those considered Christian, the largest

Figure 12. The Love Room. Photo by author.

group (23.9%) follow Anglicanism, represented by the Church in the Province of the West Indies, within which the island belongs to the Diocese of Barbados. Pentecostals are the second largest group (19.5%), followed by other smaller sects, like Seventh-day Adventists (5.9%), Methodists (4.2%), Roman Catholics (3.8%), and other Christian sects. Of the non-Christian worshippers, 0.7 percent are Muslims and 0.5 percent are Hindu, most of whom are immigrants or descendants of Indian immigrants; Rastafari (1.0% of the population), which was introduced to Barbados in 1975; Jews (0.05%); the Baha (0.04%); and Buddhists. Although these groups are smaller, their differences in race, in dress and aesthetic, like Rastafari dreadlocks, mark them as different, making them hypervisible in the space.

Confronting Morality and Guarding the Nation

Rastafari combines Protestant Christianity, mysticism, and a pan-African political consciousness; its principles of anti-Babylon livity[2] insists on purity and disassociating oneself from the evils of the capitalist nation. Roderick Hewitt (2016, 17) explains that Rastafari's selective use of the Hebrew Scriptures to oppose homosexuality constitutes a potent subcultural force within that promotes negative influences of homophobia and stigma against people living with HIV. This has compounded other forms of public opposition in Jamaica, and elsewhere,

Figure 13. Salvation. Photo by author.

that prevents governments from being brave enough to address discriminatory colonial laws against sodomy. It follows then that the Rastafari brand of Black nationalism is also patriarchal, including defined gender roles and moralistic understandings of sexuality (Bedasse 2017). Terms such as "Rastaman's woman" and "daughta" are used to emphasize the belief that women are not the spiritual, moral, or intellectual equal of men. Monique Bedasse (2017, 37) posits in her groundbreaking book *Jah Kingdom: Rastafarians, Tanzania and Pan-Africanism in the Age of Decolonialism* that, "The men of the URIA [Universal Rastafari Improvement Association] worried about the impact of sexual deviance on the construction of the morally sound African nation they sought to build, and the lion's share of this burden to uphold the moral rectitude of the African nation fell on Rastafarian women themselves. As men saw it, sexual deviance pertained to the 'choice' to use contraceptives, to abort babies, or to engage in sexual activity solely for pleasure." Sex was for procreation, and was policed mainly through the behaviors of women, who were cast in colonial rhetoric as hypersexual and "available for rape" (ibid.). Preserving the race meant "affirming motherhood as the primary role of women, policing sexual conduct, and establishing a link between gender norms and morality (ibid., 21). This means that non-procreative sex, including same-sex interactions, were deemed immoral and impure.

The graffiti shown next in Figure 14 aligns the sexually deviant Rasta with disease and impurity, but at the same time, it disrupts the notion of wanton homophobia in Rastafari communities.[3] It is written as a statement of fact, portraying a different type of Rasta—one that moves beyond the stereotype, and who engages in sexual relations beyond the procreative norm for legible citizens and Rastas. By also exposing the reality of AIDS infecting and affecting them, this imagery asks us to rethink the ways that Rastafari is positioned as only anti-Babylon, to instead appreciate Rasta communities as consisting of people with tangible sexualities, identities, and desires that move beyond heterosexuality. Yet, like queer people in other homophobic religious communities, they are bound by the religious rhetoric and policing. Simply put, this imagery asks us to contemplate the idea that Rastas too can have queer gender and sexual desires, and praxes. Sexual praxis is "sedimented social practice rather than social identity," thus I recognize "the existence of persons whose social identities, sexual practices or physical bodies do not adhere or conform to [dominant sex and gender] categories" (Kempadoo 2009, 2). By centering this understanding, the Rastas being referenced here emerge as people whose identities, desires, and practices are not limited by heteronormativity, despite their beliefs being instrumental in creating normative gender and sexual ideals in the Caribbean, where Fundamentalist Christianity has taken hold and influences all aspects of life.

In another part of the hotel, there is a pointedly political inscription, shown in Figure 15. There is "evidence coming soon" to expose the prime minister and calling on others to vote her out in 2018 by selecting the Democratic Labor Party (DLP) and not Mottley's Barbados Labor Party. Another person crossed out the DLP and added the United Progressive Party, launched in February 2017, but which failed to secure votes in the 2018 election.[4] This image captures M. Jacqui Alexander's (1994) sentiments about the outlawing of inappropriate sexuality,

Figure 14. "Rasta Mean Have AIDS N Bull." Photo by author. While in many Eastern and Southern Caribbean islands the term (v.) "bull" often refers to sex between men and women, it has also been used to refer specifically to sex between men. Variations of the term include (adj) "bulling" and (n.) "Buller."

and provides tangible evidence of how state-sanctioned homophobia is mobilized in ideas about legible sexuality in the Caribbean. This picture reminds us that:

> Although policing the sexual (stigmatizing and outlawing several kinds of non-procreative sex, particularly lesbian and gay sex and prostitution) has something to do with sex, it is also more than sex. Embedded here are powerful signifiers about appropriate sexuality, about the kind of sexuality that presumably imperils the nation and about the kind of sexuality that promotes citizenship. Not just (any) body can be a citizen anymore, for some bodies have been marked by the state as non-procreative, in pursuit of sex only for pleasure, a sex that is non-productive of babies and of no economic gain. Having refused the heterosexual imperative of citizenship, these bodies, according to the state, pose a profound threat to the very survival of the nation. Thus, I argue that as the state moves to reconfigure the nation, it simultaneously resuscitates the nation as heterosexual. (6)

This stance was made abundantly clear during Barbados's general election campaign season in May 2018, when a scathing attack was launched by former

Figure 15. Heteronormative nation. Photo by author.

Speaker of the House and member of the dethroned Democratic Labor Party, Michael Carrington, who felt it necessary that Mia Mottley "declare publicly if she is gay or not, insisting Barbadians had a right to know what kind of leader they could be getting" (Barbados Today 2018). Mottley's name and reputation was sullied in this attack out of desperation in this repulsive attempt to retain power, and clear lines were drawn to demarcate the relationship between the state and its citizens on the premise that the ability to govern the country was reserved for persons who (must) profess their heterosexuality.

Even the political and religious discourse circulating in the region in light of recent constitutional developments around the issue of queer human rights is provocative in revealing the legislation of the region's sexual politics. In this historic moment political and cultural tensions continue to remind queer people about the boundaries of acceptability that prevent them from honing the fullness of their genders and sexualities, and there remains a clear tethering of the state to the church, and the state and church to the social and cultural. Recall here my discussion of how Jason Jones's successful constitutional challenge against Trinidad and Tobago's anti-sodomy laws in April 2018, for instance, resulted in a series of discriminatory events by religious and secular groups that sought to prevent the disruption of a homophobic status quo. While these arguments made by political and religious leaders define the parameters of accept-

Figure 16. "To [sic] Much Hate." Photo by author.

able sexuality, implicit here are also concerns of threats to heterosexuality and the sacred well-being of the nation. They also work to expose the heteronormative conservatism embedded in ideas about the productive citizen. These incidents continue to exclude groups of people from claims to citizenship and belonging, where queer people continue to be denied access to legitimate identities because of state inscriptions, infused with religious and cultural mores, that mark their bodies as illegitimate.

The Love Room is emblematic of this juxtaposition of love and hate, acceptance and exclusion. The messages on the walls urge love (Figure 12), lamenting that "There is to [sic] much hate in this world." Another message says, "World and Island respect IT," appearing to urge that same-sex desire be respected and insinuating that the "hate" they are referring to is the intolerance for queer people. But the Fundamentalist Christian rhetoric of "love the sinner, hate the sin," along with other contrasting messages that vow exposure and pathologize queer bodies, demonstrate that tolerance and acceptance is conditional. On the one hand, queer sexual and gender praxes are relegated to the private, hence needing to be "exposed" or made public. Yet on the other hand, sexual and gender praxes are limited through the strictly defined parameters of acceptability. So, while the impulse to lessen hostility toward queer people may bear some truth in particular instances, in others there still needs to be significant change.

Something for Everybody

These inscriptions around the hotel offer an obvious juxtaposition of Barbados's regulated queer sexuality against a more liberated story of sexual pleasure among men on the island. Scattered throughout the abandoned hotel, they raise questions of purpose: Why are they here? For whom are they intended? By whom were they written? How do the readers respond to the messages? The message in Figure 10 threatens to expose the "bullerman" and includes the license plate of one person's car. These messages may be understood as warnings and threats, but they could also be seen as invitations, attempts at making connections. Various other messages possess these valances, capable of being read in any of these ways. It is certainly possible that the words were not written by "outsiders" but rather by those who themselves use the space. While several warnings to the transgressive occupants are plastered throughout the site, others are scribbled as advertorials of the pleasures available within. These messages provide an explicit guide to men seeking out particular fantasies of anal and oral sex with other men. Thus, I extend an invitation to view this ruined hotel as a site of community inscription, a safe space in which those who occupy it can communicate with each other about the issues affecting them. I offer a provocative notion that the information being provided by and to persons in this site can be appreciated as a tool to make connections with people who are not visible as queer in the larger Barbadian society but engage in sexual activities with other men.

I avoid reading this message, then, as an attempt to bring shame to them via "outing." For example, while the car registration plate in Figure 10 may be identifiable by some, and a limited analysis would position this message as detrimental to their safety, I argue that it is also important to consider the audience receiving these messages. Who are the people accessing this site? How do they engage with it? The words act as an introduction, telling the readers, the persons who occupy this space of abandonment, that the driver of that car is similarly transgressive. Figures 17, 18, and 19, seemingly written by the same hand, each invite the pleasure-seeking reader, decidedly male, requiring a penis to consummate the encounter, to be present in the space at certain times to have their desires fulfilled. While cruising the space, they encounter the phantasmic, or spectral bodies of these other men, who they are prepared to consume.

Sara Ahmed's (2006) theorization of "bodily orientations" is important here for understanding how queer men reorient themselves within the space in opposition to the prevailing heteronormativity outside it. In her theorization, she argues that political, cultural, and social structures leave their impressions and influence what is considered to be natural, reachable, and having integrity. These boundaries, or what she terms "bodily horizons," are heteronormative in nature and determine "the 'line' that bodies can reach toward, what is reachable, [and marks] what they cannot reach" (541). Therefore, "straightness" is marked by het-

Figure 17. "Sweet Man Ass." Photo by author.

erosexual culture as attainable, resulting in a risk of mal-alignment for queer people through their departure from the straight and narrow, and involving their "going astray, getting lost, or even becoming queer" (452). Ahmed theorizes further that one's bodily orientation within a space is determined by their temporal and spatial relationship to it (543). The queer subject disrupts the established order when his relationship to that space "tends toward" a different orientation that is not heteronormative. The men occupying this site, then, are able to undo restrictive ideas about heterosexuality and heteromasculinity by orienting their desires toward each other away from the gaze of the homophobic, heterosexist society.

When men visit this site, they are also able to negotiate their queerness in relation to their heteropatriarchal social and cultural responsibilities in the mainstream Barbadian society. Notice that they are invited to the space at particular times—at 6:00 A.M. to be f-cked, at 11 P.M. and midnight to be sucked. These times are certainly contradictory to normative time beyond the confines of the abandoned hotel. These inscriptions represent what Muñoz (2009, 32) refers to as "ecstatic time," signaling moments wherein one feels ecstasy, "announced perhaps in a scream or grunt of pleasure, and more importantly during moments of contemplation when one looks back at a scene from one's past, present, or future." Queerness is manifesting in these ecstatic moments, that resist "straight time," time's linearity and predeterminism. Instead, the inscription

Figure 18. "B Here." Photo by author.

Figure 19. "11:00 P.M. Each Night." Photo by author.

speaks of a time past where these pleasures were already enjoyed, a time present in a specific moment of enjoyment, but also a time in the future where queerness can be actualized.

These scenarios are quite telling when considered in relation to the region's political economy where Caribbean societies remain largely structured by a gendered division of labor where men continue to make up a large part of the manual and formal workforce, and women perform domesticated work within the household and in the service industry. A 2014 gender assessment of Barbados conducted by the Caribbean Development Bank indicates that a majority of Barbadian men were employed in "construction, mining and quarrying; wholesale and retail; transportation and storage, and public administration and defence" (Allen and Maughan 2016), revealing that they continue to replicate this pattern where they work outside the home for long hours during the day. Presumably, these men are able to negotiate and access same-sex sexual encounters by structuring pleasure time before and after they begin and end their workday. These men's identities are arguably formed in response to the cultural logics of heteronormativity and work to undergird state power (Muñoz 1999, 5). They are positioned between two worlds and must adopt survival strategies that "empower [their] minority identities and identifications," using the codes of majoritarian stipulations "as raw material for representing a disempowered politics or positionality that has been rendered unthinkable by the dominant culture." In locations like this, they "constantly find [themselves] thriving on sites where meaning does not properly 'line up'" (ibid.) This grimy building—its dusty, moldy staircases and its breathtaking views of the ocean—allows men to explore their desires while forgetting, even if just for a moment, the burden of compulsory heterosexuality on their innate sexual desires.

Leaving Paradise

The average (un)suspecting visitor to this beach may quickly negotiate this eerie abandoned site by avoiding its dark, mysterious crevices. They may only interact minimally with the imposing graffiti on the hotel's outer walls when they bathe in the pristine waters of the Caribbean Sea because these walls demand attention. People may be quick to dismiss the markings as mere idle notes about the island's sexual culture, but as I show, this site presents an opportunity to understand how Barbadian men are interacting with each other beyond legible rules of heteronormativity set by the nation. In this analysis, I gender the space as masculine, in my understanding that the graffiti illuminates the interactions between men who desire other men's bodies, asses, dicks, and bodily fluids. I also position the "bad tings" happening within the hotel's walls as pleasurable, unable to account for the possibility of transactional exchanges that may occur between transgressive inhabitants. I acknowledge, though, that this site is certainly

Figure 20. Leaving paradise. Photo by author.

not exclusive to men, and I am mindful of the ways that other queer people may utilize it for pleasure, to make money and to explore their desires, sexualities, and gender identities. Inspired by queer-of-color scholar Jose Muñoz (1999, 97), I believe that the "bad tings" happening "down dere" provide "a blueprint of a world not quite here, a horizon of possibility, not a fixed schema." By offering this analysis I draw attention to the fact that queer people, despite the horrors of compulsory heterosexuality in the Caribbean, are indeed actively envisioning opportunities to live in a moment that critiques the present, to disrupt dominant ideas of (hetero)sexual legitimacy and experience desire and pleasure (among other things) through disruptive and transgressive activities. Spaces like these are important for reminding us about our deep desires that we are continuously conditioned to ignore. Even in the absence of queer bodies, these spaces point to their practices of making and claiming space, of pleasure seeking and self-actualization.

The inscription of the graffiti in Figures 17, 18, and 19 demonstrate that this space is not static but alive. The persons there are interacting not just with others they might encounter in the space but with the messages that are being left there. They form part of the debris left behind in the abandoned Four Seasons Hotel, which tell a story, a narrative of the space, despite not being able to see the bodies within it, or what, if any, material or tangible thing is being taken out. According to Stoler (2013, 11), by definition, "ruination is a process that brings about 'severe impairment, as of one's health, fortune, honor, or hopes.' Conceptually, ruination may condense those impairments or sunder them apart. To speak of colonial ruination is to trace the fragile and durable substance of signs, the visible and visceral senses in which the effects of empire are reactivated and remain. But ruination is more than a process that sloughs off debris as a by-product. It is also a political project that lays waste to certain peoples, relations, and things that accumulate in specific places." By focusing on the space as "ruination," the hotel is witnessed as more than just a site of ruin, telling a story of the past; I recognize how this site engages with an ongoing neocolonial process that includes transnational capital and rhetoric, religious nationalisms, and homophobias which influence the physical and psychological environment, dislocate queer bodies, and necessitate creative space-making. Within normative spaces, queer bodies are already coded as "ruined," decrepit, diseased, disorderly, decaying, vulgar, and exposed, and are thus absented and pushed out of view. Thus, the site of ruin becomes the context wherein queer people have presence, even in their absence; like ghosts or spirits, they leave behind an echo of themselves that disrupts time and space, telling stories of trauma and resilience. The following chapters reconstitute these disembodied spectral beings, making them tangible through an examination of the self-making, space-making, and community-making practices of trans people.

CHAPTER 4

Queens, Kings, and Kinship Networks

QUEER CULTURE AND TRANS(GRESSIVE) COMMUNITY MAKING

Without community, there is no liberation... but community must not mean a shedding of our differences, nor the pathetic pretense that these differences do not exist. —Audre Lorde (1984, 112)

The dominant narratives of the Caribbean mark queer people as criminal, outlaw, and as "other," not aligning them with the projected image of the belonging and citizenship (Alexander 2004). Thus, the queer person falls into the space of exile, of banishment enforced through migration or through marginalization within Caribbean societies, a position called "internal exile." Internal exile may entail social, cultural, and institutional isolation, being cut off from support networks and social relations, separated from the "mainstream" by some boundary or barrier, whether material or ideological. It is a punishment for not belonging and has been used to discipline the "other." For example, gay people in fascist Italy (Garofalo, Leake, and Renga 2013); Dalit women in Andra Pradesh, India (Franca 2020); political opponents of Pinochet's military regime in Chile, against whom relegación or internal exile was used to suppress opposition by isolating community organizers (Barbera 2008); indigenous peoples, like the Maori in New Zealand (Oppenheim 1983); and other colonized peoples in numerous countries facing civil unrest and postcolonial anxiety (McCormack 2008). When there are people whose will appears incompatible with the dominant norms and unwritten rules of the society, power structures attempt to control them by disconnecting them from local communities, the country, and the resources and services they need to make a livable life.

In this chapter, I turn to ethnographic accounts and queer people's creative writing on their experiences in the Caribbean to explore the deeply complex, but truly radical nature of this process of internal exile, a praxis of space-making mobilized by queer people in the forming of community, kinship networks, and opportunities to thrive across the region. These stories, inspired by the region's social, cultural, and political characteristics, help to paint a picture of the possibilities that exist in queer embodiments that go against the grain and disregard prevailing mores and norms of Caribbean societies. I explore some of the ways in which trans men and women create safe spaces, bonds of kinship, friendship and community that resist the death narrative and demonstrate that queer people can in fact survive and thrive in Caribbean spaces. These strategies include drag pageantry; the use of social media and the creation of virtual communities; "down-low" encounters with men who desire other men; and the co-opting of mainstream bars, clubs, and urban night space. I frame these practices of transgression and subversion as acts of defiant survival, challenging norms through embodied practices that resist invisibility, isolation, negation, and death. I borrow from queer-of-color theorist Jose Muñoz (1999, 6) to document how queer people "work with and resist the conditions of (im)possibility that the dominant culture generates."

EXCLUSION WITHIN "QUEER" SPACES

Since queer communities are not always welcomed within normative spaces, queer geographies develop to cater to the needs of community members. As Krystal Ghisyawan (2016; 2022) documents, however, these spaces can still be exclusionary. Over the course of the eight-month fieldwork period, I spent many Friday and Saturday nights at various queer club spaces around Port of Spain in Trinidad, as well as events open to the queer community at public and private venues. On most visits, I noted the predominance of gay men, and I would document the ways that trans women interacted in the spaces, with other patrons and each other, whenever they were present. For instance, there was a popular Saturday night party catering to a largely middle-class, young professional group of Black men. Between July and December 2016, I attended some of their events, usually hosted at upscale venues farther from downtown Port of Spain. Popular entertainment included Afro-Trinidadian male strippers and speedo-wearing bartenders with well-defined bodies, playing into the sexual tropes of Black Trinbagonian men's hypermasculinity. These events were marketed to gay men. A Facebook advertisement for one of the more exclusive parties stated: "BOYS WILL BE BOYS. We have a Mansion to ourselves boys, so you know what that means right! Lets [sic] call all the other boys over. It's A freaking Party! House Party Style. It's summer so new experiences are necessary with [name omitted]. We promised you this summer that less clothes is better and you know from experience there's no dresscode @ [name omitted] and less is always more" (FB Post, August 9, 2016). The ad went on to list the pricing for the event, $100 with invitations, $150 if you were on the list, and $200 for those not on the list.

Ghisyawan (2016) has observed in her work that there are other "community" party spaces, open to all genders, and even all-women parties, where same-sex-loving women and gender-nonconforming women would be present, but these cis-male-centered events were exclusive, with women, trans women, and trans men being noticeably absent. She has also noted similar gender bias in queer clubbing spaces, particularly in a popular club, in one of the upper-class urban communities off Port of Spain's central business district, that attracted mostly Afro- and Indo-Trinidadian men who dominated the dance floor by about 1:00 A.M., when the venue became cramped. Female attendees, mostly Afro-Trinidadian, were usually in the minority and would typically lime on the periphery or outside on the balcony overlooking a steelpan tent to the left and a popular cricket stadium across the street (2016; 2022). These dynamics were much the same when I visited this club on June 24, 2016, as I noted in my journal:

> It is interesting to see how people occupy space in the club. The women were liming at the back left-hand corner close to the deejay in a group of about six. They were Afro-Trinidadian, probably in their 30s and 40s and wore clothes that some might consider to be butch/masculine (Baggy jeans, t-shirts, sneakers, low haircuts/locs/no makeup). The rest of the club was occupied by gay men who generally stood in groups of about 3–5, with the few couples in between. They [the gay men] were dancing with each other, or just drinking alcohol and watching the other people in the club.
>
> Two Afro-Trinidadian trans women danced in the center of the club just next to the four local whites. They seemed to be a bit out of place. Not physically out of place because of their queerness, but their cross-dressing stood out in stark contrast to the [men's] normative gender performances around them. Occasionally, they sauntered across to the center of the dance floor when the popular dancehall songs played. Even these performances didn't really elicit much reaction from the crowd, and people seemed to ignore them completely. I wonder if it was their out-of-place performance that made them invisible/unimportant to the space, or if their drag was just a "normal" and expected part of the club dynamics. Another young Black man also occupied the space with the trans women, and he too was out-of-place. He was obviously very young—maybe 17/18 years old, he was very effeminate, and danced fluidly to the music (especially the dancehall and soca) in ways that mimicked how Trini women would wine.[1] (Diary entry, June 24, 2016)

Although they appeared quite unremarkable in the space, with other patrons paying them little mind, these trans women were still able to access it, and enjoy themselves. At night, the nearby streets and dark savannah became the offices of numerous trans women who rely on sex work for a living. Perhaps knowing the terrain and the social vibe of the club rendered it "safe enough" (Ghisyawan 2016) for trans women to socialize there, whether or not they engaged in sex work. Most other queer club spaces that I investigated appeared to be inaccessible to trans people, either because of location or the discomfort aroused by other patrons present there.

The absence of trans people at the cis male centered party and trans women's awkward claiming of space at the club allude to the larger problem of conditional queerness in the region, whereby trans performances are not widely accepted or seen as respectable. The prevailing race and gender politics that inform queer organizing in the region means that Black, urban, gay, and cis-gendered men dominate it, at the expense of *other* queer and trans subjectivities that are accommodated "only insofar as they can be forced to hew to hegemonic modalities" (Gossett et al. 2017, xxiii) and are prevented from entering particular narratives of queerness from positions of agency. However, as I capture in the stories above, and through drag pageantry below, transgressive identities and practices are finding other more productive ways of engaging in the critical work of community building (Mohanty 2003, 231). They do this through the creation of space that is more transitory, moving around various subculture venues in the queer community, including normative spaces co-opted for a certain time or event, like the cis male centered parties (Ghisyawan 2016). As an integral aspect of internal exile, trans people therefore co-opt their own spaces and develop alternative activities catering specifically to their communities. The remainder of this book explores these spaces, the transgressions occurring within them, and the tensions and the politics that arise.

CREATING SPACE: DRAG, PAGEANTRY, AND PRIDE
Sariah

I extend an invitation to each of you, to not just visit, but live.
Live and experience the cultural diversity of my nation.
Our presence is unquestionable.
You doubt? Take note:
Skin never dried; hair never frizzed.
Our beauty reflects the love of life like diamonds.
I come to you with the poise and prestige of our forefathers.
I am educated. I am determined. I am accomplished. I am a woman!
Have you seen me? Have you really seen me?
I represent my country proudly.
I move the world with the rhythm of the kodjo drums,

And intrigue you with the stories of my ancestors.
All the while bombarding your taste buds with the delicacy of my land,
Influenced by the French and Arabic.
With the colours yellow and blue held high.
I come to you representing the third largest country of the largest
    continent—Africa!
And oh, before I go take note—tear it, wear and never bareback it.
Stop the spread of HIV and use a condom.
Bonsoir mes amis. Je m'appelle Sariah Dubla, 19, Miss Chad!
(October 2016)

Sariah, an Afro-Trinidadian trans woman, was just shy of nineteen years old when she won the prestigious Miss Queen of Queens drag pageant in October 2016. It was only her first time entering the pageant, but with detailed instruction and mentorship from past contestants, drag mothers, and pageant officials, she was able to snatch the crown from the other more seasoned queens who came from the various Caribbean islands. I met Sariah one night for our interview after being connected by a prominent queer community leader who thought that she had an interesting story to share. Once she completed high school and turned eighteen, she left her family home in Port of Spain and moved to a small suburban town in the east of the country. Sariah is petite and introverted but was not fazed by the fact that we sat in the food court at the local airport, chatting over a meal of bread and fried chicken, with other customers and their families dining at tables close by and possibly hearing our conversation. Initially she said that she would dress as a "woman" for the interview but came instead with "boy clothes" as she "wasn't able with all the stress of dressing up" (October 2016), these terms being used by her to signal how she presented herself at times. Her long French-tipped polished nails and green contacts were the only things that may have signaled to the others around that she might be queer or gender-nonconforming.

Sariah was shy and her answers to some of my questions were a bit short and seemed rehearsed. But our conversation about her recent pageant win ignited her excitement to tell me more about herself, which gave me some valuable insight about her experience as a young trans woman in the queer community. The Queen of Queens pageant is held every year in October, and trans women and drag queens from around the region compete for the coveted crown, a cash prize and a year's reign comprising several community appearances and performances, and free entry into various parties over the course of the year. Drag pageantry has always been an integral part of Trinidad and Tobago and the region's queer culture and remains one of the few avenues for trans women, especially Afro-Trinidadian working-class trans women who are excluded from activism and

QUEENS, KINGS, AND KINSHIP NETWORKS   111

community events organized by mostly gay men, to actualize their gendered agency. However, even these trans spaces are contested, as Sariah's experiences will elucidate. Sariah explained that one of the biggest aspects of the Queen of Queens competition is the delegates' coronation night introduction; they take that opportunity to deliver a witty, entertaining monologue intended to show the judges their talent and awareness of the competition's annual theme. Without hesitation she reenacted hers for me. Quoted above at length, I use this introduction to read into the multiple layers at play, not only in Sariah's experience in the pageant and queer community but also in the discursive currents that structure gender-nonconforming people's experiences of (un)belonging.

Competitors adopt a country and represent it through each stage of the competition—introduction, swimsuit, talent, evening gown, and interview. Sariah, embodying the "poise and prestige of our forefathers," invites us to live in the culturally diverse nation, Chad. She is deliberately "bombarding your taste buds with the delicacy of my land, influenced by the French and Arabic." She is also proud of her national flag "yellow and blue held high," while advocating safe sex, reminding us to "tear it, wear and never bareback it" (October 2016). The Chadian experience that she identifies is closely connected to that which has colonized Caribbean bodies for decades in the forging of acceptable and respectable identities. It is reminiscent of aspirations to embody the colonizer's greatness, and the ways that generations of colonial subjects remain haunted by a violent history of oppression. It is a haunting "whose public genealogy is one of pain. And killing. And mayhem. And tribes. And genital mutilation. And AIDS. And cannibalism. And incompetence. And army corps. And Dictators. And killing. And Killing" (Philip 1999, 25). Sariah's focus on her yellow and blue flag enacts a similar logic of citizenship that reproduces and privileges dedication to country and sends a reminder that queer persons must pay certain allegiance in order to belong, like the images of acceptable queer embodiment as depicted in CAISO's (2010) homosexual agenda campaign that invite queers to participate fully in national citizenship. Finally, her advice to engage in safe sex reiterates the idea of queer bodies at risk of disease and dying that permeate organizing in the region. Even here in the pageant sphere, many investments continue to surveil queer bodies to promote a homonormative idea of queer belonging, including how to behave in public as a trans woman.

At her age, Sariah feels that she is expected to fulfill a trope of "dizziness," a concept used by queers, especially gay men and trans women, to refer to persons who are easily swayed by potential suitors. Dizzy queers are also seen as promiscuous by virtue of their penchant for pursuing multiple relationships simultaneously or even moving from partner to partner in short spaces of time. These dizzy practices go against moral codes of proper behavior in the larger society and within the queer community. Sariah then feels that she is expected to be unstable, loud, raucous, and visible for the wrong reasons in the community. She explains:

> I mean sometimes they can take it a little overboard with the things that they say, but we tend to put ourselves out there to be obnoxious. Especially the young people. When we walk the streets, we tend to be loud, and cussing and disrespectful and real. I not saying you can't be real . . . It have a group of young homosexual people, anytime people see them they would say dem ghetto and disgusting. I don't want that, because I recently had a meeting with people from Johnson and Johnson when they came to talk about HIV and AIDS and people in the community, and the things they were saying about the young people; it was very disturbing . . . everybody tends to think that we are loud and obnoxious and we are going to destroy the community in the future, and "all she good for is lying down on a bed," and all those kinds of foolishness. I want to prove them wrong. (October 2016)

Even though she herself urged condom use in her speech, she recognizes that the narrative of promiscuity and HIV infections is damaging to the image of the young trans community. The rowdy behavior of the young working-class trans people, theirs being "loud, and cussing and disrespectful and real," is perceived as "ghetto and disgusting." They do not adequately embody respectability, and so are associated with the unacceptable queer body, diseased, aberrant, and threatening the societal moral order that conditionally does not belong.

As a young trans woman, the expectation is that Sariah too would behave similarly. She tells me of this perception through her interactions with other contestants in the pageant where, "everybody thought, she just young, she eh going to win, she just you know, she doh know nothing about Queen of Queens. I didn't but the thing is, as I told everyone, I listened. I listened; I take the criticism very well. It was not easy" (October 2016). She was privileged to have a support system to teach her the techniques to win the coveted crown. In the wider community girls like her stand out, and with few resources or community figures available to provide mentorship, many of them, especially those who are teenagers from the lower classes who lack family support, end up on the streets or in the arms of men who purport to provide help. Sariah goes on:

> And the thing they don't know is that a lot of the more mature people in the community take advantage of us and we don't know—they should be helping us. Is not like nobody going and come and say "well, doh (*do not*) do that child, this is what to do and this is what not to do." Even come and say "this is a douching bottle, this is a condom, this is lube, this is what you use it for." Nobody going to do that in this time. A lot of them make the young hoes lie down in dey (*their*) bed and give them a lil (*little*) hundred dollars and say bye bye. I intend to change that . . . because especially the younger generation,

we have no community to turn to. You don't even see the people who say they helping us in the parties or nuttin (*nothing*). Who dem is? (*Who are they?*) (October 2016)

Sariah's experience is exceptional; she had mentorship, unlike many other trans youth, who face exploitation from the only people who can help them: older trans women and gay men. They are not taught about sexual hygiene, finances, earning an income, or how to keep themselves safe from emotional or sexual predators. From Sariah's perspective, there is no formal community to which young trans people can turn.

Princess

Princess is a twenty-four-year-old Dougla and gender-nonconforming person from a small predominantly Indo-Trinidadian community in central Trinidad. She won the now-defunct Diva World pageant in 2009 but gave up her crown halfway through her reign because she felt that organizers had breached their contractual agreement with her. I had interviewed her for my previous project on local trans community-making strategies in 2012, and we reconnected when I visited Trinidad for research in 2016. During her reign, Princess felt unsupported by the pageant organizers, barely attending community events and parties. She became increasingly disconnected since her reign, and at the time of our 2016 interview she had severed all ties with the organizers and persons in the pageant circuit, explaining, "I doh have any conversations with the pageant holders, right! If we meet up in parties, they would just nod at me . . . we never had a relationship to be honest. We never had a relationship although I was carrying the crown for six months" (November 2016). Late one night, over pizza at a plaza in Chaguanas, near where she lived, Princess eagerly told me about the disappointing state of the pageant circuit and used that as an opportunity to tell me why she decided to distance herself.

The Queen of Queens competition had just passed about two months prior, and she was disappointed about the types of girls who were now entering, since they were not "crown ready." Princess identified these contestants as "the street girls, the prostitutes basically, or the girls who now coming out in the whole lifestyle and they just feel that, okay I could be a woman" (November 2016). One contestant in particular, a young trans woman who flew in from Grenada to compete, made her really upset when she saw her one night "crossing the road in Port of Spain in a panty thing, a slippers and a top . . . yeah a panty panty . . . a leather panty" (November 2016). Princess considered this attire too risqué for wearing in public as it signals promiscuity and unrespectability. Here, she reproduces larger societal associations of promiscuity and prostitution with shame and being unworthy of respect. In our conversation, she goes on to distance herself from these public displays and explains that girls like "Miss Grenada" were being influenced by the circle of friends that they maintained in Trinidad, reinforcing some of the experiences that Sariah had with "obnoxious," "ghetto and disgusting" behavior among her peers, as discussed above.

Princess lamented, "Yuh walking the street and yuh was in a slippers. I coulda see the stocking because yuh was padding (adding foam and other material to their thighs and buttocks to give the illusion of a curvy body). Even the night of the show I saw her, she was leaving with [certain people], so yuh know, again, yuh company will influence you. For me, luckily, I would say that I influenced in a way" (November 2016). She acknowledges that she is no longer being influenced by members of the local trans community, but rather by American television, which has informed how she navigates the local conditions:

> I'm now becoming Americanized because I'm watching RuPaul's Drag Race and ting. That's how I know about the whole genderf-ck and the boy-girl . . . what you call it? Androgynous. So, if I would have to pick . . . how I see it now, gender shouldn't be determined by the clothes you wear. That's just my take on it. I think it should just be by your sexual organs . . . Evolution occurs and everyday some part of evolution occurs. Eventually we might just see that if today I wake up as a guy and I feel to put on a dress and sneakers, and I feel to grow my hair down to my back because we living in a society . . . it's already Americanized. In the American society people can do it and they get away with it. (November 2016)

While Princess makes some complicated references to an assumed freedom offered to gender-nonconforming persons in America, she also longs to see such cultural and gendered (r)evolution in Trinidad and Tobago. Even though she thinks that the Caribbean has a "long way to go for these things to happen" (November 2016), she played with her gender expression in order to rebel against the dominant gender expectations within Trinidadian society. Unlike in 2012, when she rarely presented herself as a "girl," Princess explained to me that she now preferred to do "genderf-ck" when she goes out in public to "have them men dem dizzy" (November 2016). I return to her experiences later in this chapter.

Internal Exile in Hostile Spaces

Caribbean literary scholar Michelle Cliff's portrayal of Harry/Harriet in *No Telephone to Heaven* (1987) resonates with Sariah's and Princess's descriptions of the internal exile trans women experience within generally hostile spaces. Harry/Harriet's evolution is traced throughout the book, clearly showing on the one hand how they were able to maximize on gendered expectations to hone their queerness, while being able, on the other, to actualize the fullness of their identity, when they eventually declare to their lover Clare, ""Harriet now girlfriend . . . finally . . . the choice is mine, man, is made. Harriet live and Harry be no more"

QUEENS, KINGS, AND KINSHIP NETWORKS 115

Figure 21. *Queen of Queens Pageant Magazine* cover 2007. Wesley Nicholls.

(168). Prior to this, Harry is gendered male in the book, referred to with male pronouns. Cliff describes, "Then Harry/Harriet, boy-girl, Buster's brother-sister, half-brother-sister actually, who was always strange, since childhood, they say, but everyone tolerates him, as if measuring their normalness against his strangeness." She writes, "He is only one, after all, one that nature did not claim," suggesting that his inclinations were not just strange, but unnatural. Still, his family

Figure 22. *Queen of Queens Pageant Magazine* cover 2008. Wesley Nicholls.

felt the need to protect him, to keep him from ending up "some back-o' wall alley in Raetown f-cked to death." Cliff (1987, 21) writes: "Harry/Harriet puts on a bikini—bra stretched across his hairy, delicately mounded chest, panties cradling his cock and balls—and starts to dance to 'Hey, Jude.' People laugh, but nobody takes Harry/Harriet to heart. 'You won't laugh so when I am appearing in London with the Royal Ballet and the Queen come fe see me.' Laughs and more laughs. 'I shall be at Cable Hut tomorrow, dancing with the sun behind me.' Pause. 'Come if you want some p-ssy.' 'Lord Harry, where you get p-ssy?' 'You would be surprised, massa.'" Harry/Harriet performs an exaggerated sexual and comical persona, and as Chantal Zabus (2013, 57–59) argues, he, as Cliff genders him, is allowed to occupy a space of liminality because his initial aim is not to pass but to come across as comical. Although this makes their presence somewhat palatable to those around them and seemed to simply position them as the accepted other among everyone, Harry/Harriet provides a poignant glimpse later on into this relationship to the normative when questioned by Clare, who asks, "Harry, how come you talk this way when at the party you were going on about dancing in England before the Queen?" Harry responded, "Oh, man, girlfriend, is nuh what dem expect from me? Nuh jus' give them what dem expect? Battyman trash. No harm. Our people kind of narrow, pour souls. Foolish sometimes. Cyaan understand for the likes of me." He says that their people can't understand him. They are narrow-minded and even foolish. He notes that his performance in that public arena is to satisfy their expectations of him. He views these encounters as shallow, saying, "No, man, jus' give dem what they want. No need to get deep. No need to tell them my asshole was split when I was a bwai by an officer up at Park Camp—no need a-tall" (ibid., 128). He does not feel the need to bare himself, his history, or even his experiences of sexual assault to these people, as they are not invested in knowing him in that way. Harry/Harriet is resilient, skillfully maneuvering of the social and cultural climate in which they existed, even when this agency meant silencing trauma and despair at the hands of others. We also learn that the queer subject can have at their disposal, particular tools that equip them with a sense of agency as they carve a space for existing within and alongside the dominant culture. In this case Cliff asks us to consider comedy as an effective mechanism to bridge divides.

Cliff's presentation of Harry/Harriet's position of nonbeing through their transgressing of normative gender performance in Jamaica provides a good example of the ways that queer people can possibly claim and co-opt space. Toward the end of the story, Harriet, no longer Harry, actualizes the fullness of herself as a nurse and caregiver to an ailing Clare. Although her passing as woman may be read as her accepting binary ideas of femininity, it is this process of yearning for a different way of being and achieving it that situates her transgressive potential. Sariah and Princess are, likewise, transgressive figures engaged in a constant crossing of boundaries and gendered expectations. Even within the pageant and social circles, they are constrained by societal expectations based on race, class, age, and gender performance. Jasbir Puar (2002) notes this in her study of transnational sexuality in Trinidad similarly that racial, political, social, and cultural dynamics collide at these drag events, influencing the expectations that drag performers and their audiences hold of how drag should be performed by participants based on their social identities. Sasha and

Vik, Puar's main interlocuters, were the only two Indo-Trinidadian drag performers at the Diva World pageant in 1998 and helped her to understand some of the deeply complex ways that their Indo-Trinidadianness intervenes in and unsettles the largely Afro-Trinidadian characteristics of the spaces. Puar (2002, 1046) found that "different regimes of gay and lesbian identities [are] attendant to concerns of race, class, ethnicity, gender, sexuality and national identity as they occur in Trinidad," and use their understanding to shape their performances. At the Diva pageant in 1998, she notes,

> The performances ranged from spectacularizing glamour, to comedic parodies, to tragic depictions of HIV/AIDS, poverty, and sex workers. . . . In several scenes, participants emphasized similar tropes of beauty and glamour, wearing heavily sequined ballgowns and cocktail dresses, such as in a James Bond Goldfinger skit and an Annie Lennox impersonation; Patti LaBelle was the figure most often impersonated. In contrast, the more dramatic performances dealing with social issues included a remake of Queen's "Bohemian Rhapsody," in which a "Diva" performer snatched his wig off and threw it to the audience while lip-syncing the words "sometimes wish [sic] I'd never been born at all . . . nothing really matters to me." The dramatic performances also included sombre depictions of a patient dying of AIDS in front of an AIDS quilt as well as scenes of domestic abuse and a sex-worker being kicked around by her pimp. (2002, 1047–1048)

Although productions like Diva, hosted by prominent Trinidadian actor Raymond Choo Kong between 1993 and 1998; Golden Girls started by "Super Grand" in 1997; or Diva World started by Sean Edwards in 2008 are no longer being staged, the Queen of Queens pageant, which was first hosted in 1998, continues to reach a wide audience comprising people in the queer community, the wider local mainstream, and tourists who visit for annual Carnival and Pride celebrations. Uncle Cyrus, a queer community leader who has been photographing and video recording events since the early 1990s, reminisced in our interview that the competition, first started by prominent gay men Bryan Lucas and Sean Edwards in a small gay bar called Metal House in Port of Spain, held a grand coronation ball at the Chaguaramas Convention Center in 2007. Since Lucas's death in 2013, however, the pageant has been downsized significantly and is now being organized by other younger gay men in the community. The gay man to whom Lucas had handed over the duties of pageant organizing sought asylum in Amsterdam in early 2017. So, at the time of this research, the pageant was in a transitory phase. It is interesting to note that gay men have historically organized these parties and pageants in Trinidad and Tobago, and despite such a long history of pageantry, trans women continue to assume peripheral roles like helping backstage, hosting the events, and providing entertainment on coronation night.

During the months preceding these pageants, contestants prepared their highly anticipated performances and appearances. Sandy, introduced in the beginning of this book, also shared her experience as a Queen of Queens contestant in 1999: "It was nice, it was real nice . . . My costume was with wings, and I was portraying this song, it starting with 'fly . . .' is a woman sing it. An old, Black ageable woman . . . I cyar remember the song but it have a part with costume and it have a part for who could sing or whatever . . . well that dance was my part and I get to show off my talent" (November 2016). The pageants create a space where the negative perceptions of trans attendees and competitors are temporarily suspended, "no matter whom they desire or how they identify" (King 2014, 10). Events are openly marketed on social media, so the wider society is invited to witness their spectacular performances. In the past, they were promoted and reviewed publicly in local newspapers, and in the magazines pictured above. However, within recent years, much of the promotion has been done on social media platforms like Facebook and Instagram. The pageant sphere, then, allows trans women to embody a defined notion of drag identity that reiterates the bounds of respectable femininity, which both Sariah and Princess extrapolate to apply to trans embodiments of femininity. They both deride the failure of other trans people to observe the respectability politics of the society, which, in itself, is a deliberate transgression. They also believe the title of "Queen" should uphold certain principles of respectability in appearance, dress, and decorum. Additionally, both women registered discontent with the lack of community support, even in pageant circles, and the abundance of abusive treatment from peers and elders. Yet, the pageant space offers a framework for making new bonds of friends and family, on which some trans people thrive. The following section addresses this utility of the pageant space for fostering alternative kin bonds.

HOMEMAKING AND KINSHIP PRACTICES
AMONG TRANS PEOPLE IN TRINIDAD

Queer people have developed solid support systems with friends and chosen family that provide additional opportunities for them to take ownership of their lives. Many of the people I interacted with were estranged from their biological families but believed that ties to brothers and sisters or mothers and fathers were not restricted to blood and were formed through the friendships and relationships that they developed with other queer and trans people. Marlon Bailey's (2013, 49) work demonstrates how Butch Queens in Detroit create a "minoritarian sphere for those who are excluded from or marginalized within majoritarian society" through their ballroom community.[2] Similarly, the pageant community in Trinidad develops "houses" to which trans participants can belong, gain shelter,[3] make kin and friendship bonds, but importantly, gain mentorship and guidance. Sariah had just created Prestige House, a small family for young gay men and trans women, at the time of our interview. She saw it as a place, "where young people who [are] willing to change the way people view them, and change their behaviour come together." Sariah lamented, "It ridiculous 'cause more mature people want to watch us and say you see how dem getting on? They say we make the pathway for all yuh and this is how all yuh getting on and embarrassing us?" Yet she noted that the lack of community played a crucial role in the actions of young trans women. "We have no unity as a community," she said, "especially the younger generation, we have no community" (October 2016). She felt the houses would allow for social support and mentorship and could help sanitize the appearance of trans women to the wider community, which arguably alters their conditions of being, the ways that they are expected to appear to the queer community and wider society.

Sariah idealizes the heteronormative nuclear family as she envisions her kinship network, and even expressed that while the house would not be formal, she wants her members to know their specific roles and explained, "I still sorting out roles, like mother and father, it will have rules, so just know you can't be loud and on shit" (October 2016). The father is intended to be the one "who will give little advice and tell us how to manage things like going to school, making money, learning the ropes of the community" and knowing who will "just want to say [that] she now come out, she fresh, let meh [me] drama she a lil bit. Leh me jango she (take advantage of her)." The mother on the other hand is expected to be the nurturing one who will give advice on "things like relationships, presenting yourself in positively when you go out there. Typically, mothers are the ones who help their daughters to prepare for the crown to carry on the family legacy" (October 2016). Traditionally, family has been a regulatory space, with family structure and practices informing things like mating practices, household composition, and domestic grouping (M. G. Smith 1962, 3). These pageant houses seem no different, in that the roles performed within the house are viewed as functional, intended to train the family's subordinates to regulate their behaviors. At the same time, while these adopted roles appear to be appropriating the dominant practices and experiences from which they are largely excluded, their actual gender and sexual praxes upend the assumptions of normative nuclear families, which, as Caribbean feminist literary scholar Merle Hodge (2002) argues, is not the norm in the Caribbean anyway.

In the Caribbean, family is indeed not nuclear, and Hodge believes that a collective illusion that it is reflects how far we are away from coming to terms with varying meanings of family in the region. In fact, Hodge (2002, 274) argues that North American and European understandings of family and kinship are nonsensical when applied to the Caribbean. These popular clichés about the family include the nonworking housewife and single-parent families with absent fathers; when these situations do occur, it is clear that families are never really taken care of by one parent alone. Instead, she asks us to understand that Caribbean families are more of a network of grandparents, aunts, cousins, brothers, sisters, and even neighbors who all form a system of support for each other. Thus, she rightly believes that if the Caribbean region wishes to protect the "family," it needs to accept and address all forms of kinship present in our milieu (2002, 476). For instance, among Grenadian and Jamaican families, sociologist M. G. Smith (1962, 36) found that most households were headed by women who maintain relationships with men, usually their husbands, who may or may not reside with them full-time; an interaction he called modified monogamy. The Cohabitational Relationship Bill was passed in Trinidad and Tobago in 1996 to formally recognize the existence of intimate, heterosexual nonlegal unions in the country, known as common-law relationships. Rhoda Reddock (2004) has found that married couples, living in a nuclear family setup, had more clearly defined roles based on gender such as pooling of financial resources (in instances where the wife works) and men's assumed leadership role as household head, compared to common-law relationships where roles were less gender-determined. For instance, men in common-law unions "perform[ed] more regular housework than their married counterparts" (83). The fact that such law was proclaimed to acknowledge the prevalence of nonmarried unions points to this fact that many households in Trinidad and Tobago fail to live up to the dominant ideals of the nuclear family unit. The findings of this study also point to the possibility that the idealized notions attached to the roles of husbands and wives are intricately connected to assumptions about the gendered division of labor in a household that is strictly defined by law and enshrined in marriage.

Feminist scholars like Gloria Wekker and Audre Lorde ask us, however, to think differently about what family and kinship looks like in nonheteronormative contexts. Wekker's (2006) work on Mati women in Suriname makes a much-needed contribution toward a theorization of the ways that Black working-class women create family and a sense of agency through queer friendships, love relationships, and kinship arrangements. Mati work, Wekker emphasizes, holds special significance for women when many working-class men leave Paramaribo to do migrant labor, forcing them to fend for themselves. These relationships are built around women who care for each other and their families "not through heterosexual ties, but through 'cowives'" (ibid., 35, 138). These relationships are indeed sexual in nature but move beyond physical pleasure and also encompass emotional, physical, financial, sacred, and other kinds of support; all elements of the erotic as Lorde puts it and captures in *Zami: A New Spelling of my Name* (1982, 13–14): "Here Aunt Annie lived among the other women who saw their men off on the sailing vessels, then tended the goats and groundnuts, planted grain and poured rum upon the earth to strengthen the corn's growing, built their women's houses and the rainwater catchments, harvested the limes, wove their lives and the lives of their children together. Women survived the absence of their sea-fearing men easily, because they came to love each other, past the men's returning. Madivine. Friending. Zami. How Carriacou women love each other is legend in Grenada, and so is their strength and their beauty." Taking these arguments into consideration, I return here to Hodge's consideration that the Caribbean family is really anything but nuclear, and at times, not heteronormative. Queer kinship, thus, may not be exceptional at all, but rather a normal, although less visible, aspect of Caribbean society.

Queer Studies anthropologist Kath Weston (1991, 207) theorizes fictive kinship formations (in the Global North) as "capable of integrating relationships that cross household lines, exchanges of material and emotional assistance, coparenting arrangements, and support for persons with AIDS," similar to Mati work described above, and the care practices of gay activist group Friends for Life in Trinidad and Tobago, described by Lyndon Gill (2018), in his book *Erotic Islands*. Gill notes how the organization's members' erotic practices and similar vulnerability brought them together to support each other and provided a way for them to find a voice and sense of belonging and called these dynamics of support "erotic intervention." The friendships created by the trans women and men I met with are reminiscent of "contagious erotic subjectivities" as Gill (2018, 184) calls it, attending to their political, communal, and spiritual needs in a context of marginalization. Trans people at the margins "build protective boundaries around marginalized community" (Bailey 2013, 69) to reconceptualize their identities and communities. In doing so, they envision alternative ways to thrive, especially when facing ostracism by wider mainstream and queer communities, exacerbated by the discourses of human rights interventions that focus explicitly on death and dying, when they do manage to see these liminal groups at all.

TRANS MASCULINE[4] KINSHIP AS PRAXIS

Trans men are even less visible and less attended to in activism and scholarship than trans women, who are represented in narratives of transphobia, sex work, and transactional sex in the Caribbean. I was able to observe the kinship praxis of Black, nonurban, working-class masculine women and trans men in Trinidad, and am privileged to be able to recount their experiences. At a bar in East Trinidad, some friends who I call "the group of six" met almost daily to drink beer, rum, and Guinness; play cards; and talk about their events and experiences. On weekends, they would also typically host an all-fours card tournament with other Black masculine women and trans-masculine people from around the island. The bar provided space for trans men, trans masculine people, and other members of the queer community to share similar emotional, financial, and other kinds of support for each other. On one occasion, when a prominent lesbian in the community, Stacey Charles, died suddenly after a short battle with cancer (in July 2016), the rumshop became a space for support, togetherness, and mourning for members of the lesbian and trans male community. Local lesbi-

QUEENS, KINGS, AND KINSHIP NETWORKS

ans and trans men filled a large Pentecostal church known for its homophobic teachings for the funeral, where the very cautious pastor invited members of the community, who clearly outnumbered the congregation, to speak words of encouragement. Without hesitation many of Stacey's friends took turns to offer words of comfort to each other. One male-presenting person changed the tone of these reflections as they expressed disgust and disappointment at how Stacey's trans partner was being treated:

> . . . Lisa was like her riding partner, her soul mate, her everything beside her darling [Stacy's daughter] Siobhan. Even though they [the family] are not including them [Lisa] in their arrangements (loud cheers and shouts of support), I have a message for them: Stop discriminating, we are all God's children. We are! We are! Your daughter that you did not know, for everyone who is here today and ignoring the person who has been a part of Stacy's life, and all the spiritual music that y'all are listening to, do not point fingers and judge (loud cheers and shouts of support). You all have to answer to God and he knows our hearts; and if any of you have eyes to see and watch that beautiful woman in the coffin, is only peace, tranquility as if she is sleeping. So, people who are saying that [they] are "of God," stop judging and show love. (Diary entry, June 2016)

In this instance, we see a community standing up against religious hatred and confronting some of the tensions that structure queer people's relationship to the normative. Drawing on Sheller's (2012, 18) theorization of citizenship from below, I posit that in this moment the lesbian and trans male community "use[d] their embodied performances to infiltrate public [and sacred] space, exposing and possibly transforming assumptions about who is a free person, a citizen, or even a human being."

Once we arrived at the bar after the funeral for an impromptu wake, though they could barely function themselves, the group of six and all Stacey's friends ensured that her partner was cradled by their love, support, and compassion. This repurposing of the rumshop space, typically occupied by the group of six for entertainment, into a family space in a time of need "brings into focus aspects of everyday physical life, the disavowed, and abject (low class life, low brow, low down) that are usually excluded from the 'high' political realm (high class, high politics, high minded, high and mighty)" (Sheller 2012, 24). That moment provided an invaluable opportunity to not only see internal exile at work, but to also rethink the importance of kinship as an integral part of it. Andil Gosine (2015) theorizes that queer Caribbean family connotes much broader and looser networks of attachment than the nuclear Euro-American notion of "family," that U.S. and European gay organizations have tended to mimic in their homonormative agendas. These trans groups discussed here move away from normative understandings of kinship and family, providing invaluable support for members who reside outside the boundaries of legitimate family, sexuality, and identity.

Wekker's (2006) theorization of Mati also truly provides valuable insight from which to read this kinship labor being performed in trans communities. Mati work has survived African enslavement "marking disruption to the violence of normative order and powerfully so: connecting in ways that commodified flesh was never supposed to, loving your own kind when your kind was supposed to cease to exist, forging interpersonal connections that counteract imperial desires for Africans' living deaths" (199). As Wekker theorizes, Mati work "presents a configuration where erotic and sexual relations between women are public, acknowledged, validated and often openly celebrated" (73). We see this in the lesbian women and trans men's interaction and solidarity at Stacey's funeral where these bonds fostered the creation of family, community, and spirituality among them (24). These trans men, trans women, lesbians, bisexual woman, and others embraced their queerness in productive ways to envision other ways of being in the world. Visible here is evidence of how sexual and gender praxes disrupt ideas of the illegitimate queer that has no claim to citizenship. It also provides a glimpse of how trans men and women claim space and belonging in the Caribbean.

Trans Masculine Organizing: A Glimpse

As previously mentioned, there has been little work done to elucidate the ways in which trans men create community in the Anglophone Caribbean. Even in discussions with regional activists, little mention was made of trans male or trans masculine communities. This silence arguably stems from perceptions that these identities and practices are either not as prevalent in the region, that they are integrated into lesbian communities, or that they are less of a threat to the heteromasculinist mainstream and "[have] cross-culturally across time been regarded as an invisible or non-threatening position" (Chancy quoted in King 2014, 98). These communities were less accessible than the spaces occupied by trans women and gay men, especially in the realms of activism. In this section, I highlight the experiences of TransMan,[5] a small community group dedicated to providing physical, virtual, and communal spaces for trans male and trans masculine people in Kingston, Jamaica, and I Am One TNT, a similar group in Trinidad. While I Am One TNT does outreach work, here, I focus on their community building achieved through their drag king show. At the time of the research, I was unaware of any other trans masculine communities like these in Barbados and Guyana.

Kleos, a twenty-eight-year-old trans man who volunteered with TransMan, mentions that, although the group was just a few months old, it was created out of a necessity to educate themselves, the wider queer community, and the Jamai-

QUEENS, KINGS, AND KINSHIP NETWORKS   125

can society about their realities. In explaining its mandate, he explained, "Some people don't even know what it is to be a trans man and that is not just the general population, it is also within the queer population. So, you will now find that a lot of persons didn't know that they were trans, didn't know that there was a term for what they were experiencing or anything like that. So, we really have made an impact in helping people understand trans identity, to help them understand themselves, to educate people and sensitize them" (July 2016). TransMan has attempted to tend to the specific needs of the trans male population, like securing proper health care and reducing abuse in public agencies, "because there is a lack of resources for trans people. Of course, lack of awareness, and the legal situation that trans people are not recognized under the law because there is nothing there for gender identity or sexual orientation. You will find that they do not have insurance so they wouldn't be able to afford private health care. Private health care is very expensive. So, what people tend to do is that they tend to go to public health care providers. It is mostly in those spaces in which they are abused and mistreated due to gender" (ibid.). Although Kleos mentions medical treatment for trans people, he is not referring specifically to gender-related procedures. He explained, "Being trans is not about doing surgery. You don't want to reduce trans people to the surgeries they had or haven't had." Instead, he wants to draw attention to a system that "isn't trans friendly at all. In a sense, because we experience discrimination when it comes to housing, job applications. I mean, people are homeless because of their identity and not even their parent realize that it's not their sexual orientation that is really the problem. It is really their gender identity and they don't know how to handle it" (ibid.).

At the same time, in Trinidad and Tobago, the presence and needs of trans men were not coming to the fore in the same way. Instead, there was a small, but growing drag king pageant scene that offered a space for trans men and trans masculine people to create community and interact with the wider urban queer population. In 2016, the group I Am One TNT produced its first installment of "The Drag King Show" at a small artistic space in Port of Spain. I attended this inaugural event and immediately noticed the stark difference between what was happening there and what would typically happen at drag queen pageants like Queen of Queens. Pageantry for trans women is often serious business, and competitors make huge financial, emotional, and artistic investments for the shows. The atmosphere at this drag king competition was completely inverted, as the loosely organized show featured mostly unrehearsed, playful banter among the contestants. I capture this sentiment in my field journal entry below:

> Six kings modeled various designs made from yellow, red and black plaid fabric in the very informal segment and the participants laughed as they strolled across the stage, thereby inviting the audience to join in. This was the only segment for the first half, which shocked us, but we laughed it off as Marcus

whispered: "Yuh could tell is not hoes [gay men] doing this, cause the quality good bad!" The second half of the program was also loosely organized and playful. It included lip sync performances of ballads, a spoken word piece, an acoustic performance and DJ Yoshi performed in drag as an Indian man.

In the end, the kings randomly selected pre-determined questions to which they replied on the spot. These questions and answers evoked fits of laughter from the participants and the audience of mostly middle-aged Black women and a handful of men. What is your take on pregnant studs? Why did you enter the King Show? Name five different types of lesbians. Your Fem girl wants to switch roles, would you or wouldn't you support her? Although these questions were straightforward and received simple answers, they tackled key concerns of the trans male and trans-masculine population in Trinidad. (June 17, 2016)

These questions related to relationship dynamics, gender performance, societal expectations (even those of queer society), and reproduction as a gender-queer person.

One spoken-word piece, however, made a somber departure from the jovial atmosphere at the venue. In this piece the artiste, Danny, reflected on the various shortcomings that he was sorry for, recalling a long list of expectations that he failed to live up to. I attempted to meet with him in the following weeks, but due to time constraints and clashing schedules, it did not happen. However, Danny agreed to have the parts of the poem included in this discussion:

"I Am Sorry" by Daniel Trey Jayson Farrell (2008)
Does my "gayness" offend you?
Well, I am sorry
I am sorry, but I AM gay
I choose to love another woman
Rather than a man
I self-identify as a man
Rather than a woman
I am sorry that my lifestyle offends you . . .
. . . I am so sorry that my gayness offends you
It is not my intention
No, I just want to live my life
Love who I choose to love
I just want to be happy being me
I am sorry that you can't accept me

Danny reminds us of the harsh reality of the micro-policing of gender and sexuality at the intimate level of family. In the piece, he goes on to address concerns of being made to feel "like an ugly troll that lives under a bridge," and of his real-

Figure 23. "I Am One TNT Presents The King Show," June 17, 2016. I AM One.

ization that "you would live in hell because of me," signaling how his trans-ness made him illegible to his family. In the next chapter, I discuss how these trans spaces offer us valuable opportunities to think about how internal exile assists in decentering traditional notions of kinship when the queer community creates alternative support systems.

Figure 24. I Am One TNT, The King Show invitation poster, 2017. I AM One.

Although public trans male spaces are fewer in number, groups like I Am One have been making steadfast attempts to establish trans men–specific activities in Trinidad and Tobago's annual Pride celebrations in June and July, including the second installment of the Drag King Show. In its second year (2017), the promoters advertised more widely on social media, inviting drag kings from across Trinidad and Tobago to compete for the coveted "King's Crown." Social media advertisements stated, "Anyone can compete who wishes to flaunt their masculinity, celebrate the beauty of trans-masculinity, and find a safe space to perform. Welcoming trans men, as well as lesbian and queer-identified women and nonbinary persons who love to explore their masculine side" (I Am One TNT, The King Show, June 10, 2017). Despite still being in its early stages of development, the trans-male pageant scene in Trinidad and Tobago and across the region promises to be an exciting arena to further understand praxes of resistance through gender nonconformity.

The Pervasive Voice of Pathologizing Sexual Desire

Discourses pertaining to HIV and AIDS were present in both of these pageant spaces, for trans men and women. Recalling Pageant winner Sariah's experience, it remains the duty of the pageant queens to promote HIV and AIDS awareness, as the pageants were conceived of in this way by Queen of Queens organizer Bryan Lucas. The fact remains that many queer people, especially working-class trans people, are still dying from the disease, and there needs to be more effective ways of acknowledging and speaking about how the epidemic affects queer people in their everyday lives. These pageants provide such a space to do that because the trans women who participate are actively interpreting issues of disease and death through their personal and communal understandings and experiences of the epidemic, rather than through complex institutionalized discourse happening at larger activist levels. Unfortunately, this focus reproduces the pathologizing narrative of the HIV organizations discussed earlier in this book.

In conjunction with the FPATT, I Am One's 2017 Pride celebrations included voluntary HIV testing at several of their events, such as their Pride Arts Cabaret on Friday, June 9. In a Facebook post about the event, they shared, "Destigmatising the testing process is one of our goals. We believe all persons should #KnowYourStatus and recognise that our community's access to healthcare, counselling, and sensitive health-related support is limited at best. Even if you are not willing to be tested in a public setting, you can speak with the FPATT representatives on the night to set up a more private screening or counselling session" (I Am One TNT FB Post, June 6, 2017). More HIV testing was conducted at the annual Pride Memorial on June 25 as part of a joint project with Friends for Life and Linkages (the major funder mentioned by Trinidadian trans activists in the previous chapter). These deliberate attempts to test patrons at Pride events are at the very least problematic, as they serve as a reminder of queer people's diseased bodies at a time when the community intends to celebrate its accomplishments over the years. And while groups like FPATT have opened their doors to the community, and especially trans people, their mandate to encourage safe sex practices and to know one's status is out of place in these environments. This arrangement therefore reminds us that there is an ongoing need for the community to foster better support systems that strive to move away from this HIV and disease rhetoric.

One possibility might be to shift to proactive approaches to safe sex through education. As Sariah mentioned, mentors and elders could convey sexual hygiene, because no one teaches this to young men and trans people. It is critical to assess the readiness of youth for sexuality education, which the Silver Lining Foundation has deemed critical and urgent. In a survey of secondary schools in Trinidad and Tobago, it found that most students wanted sex education (64.4%), noting that they would feel more empowered in sexual situations. Students turned to peers (46%), media (45%), and pornography (30.7%) to answer their questions about sex. All students are potentially accessing misleading and harmful information about sex. Consider how this transcends into adulthood, predisposes the uneducated to abuse and violence, and influences the transmittal of preventable diseases (Ghisyawan, Kissoon, and Khan 2019). It is necessary to confront the fact that sex, in its plethora of erotic entanglements, is occurring across groups within Caribbean society (recall my earlier discussion of sexual encounters in abandoned hotels in Barbados) and thus should be engaged with to encourage awareness of safety, consent, and pleasure.

Among the forms of sexual praxis pursued by the trans women I spoke with included sex work, nonmonogamy and serial monogamous relationships, and casual sex with strangers. One of the main benefits of such rebellious praxis is an opportunity to make exciting, but sometimes potentially dangerous sexual connections. Although Princess and I had initially agreed to talk about her experiences in Trinidad and her ideas about some of the shortcomings of queer organizing, much of our interview centered on how these sexual encounters allowed her to accomplish her gender fluidity. She realized while young that many men were secretly excited by the idea of having sexual interactions with a man in female clothing, and maximized on this to also fulfill her sexual and gendered desires:

> Remember, is a vice for most people. Is a vice. Chicks with dicks are more fun, at least that's what they say. So, you having, okay . . . let me take it back a little bit further . . . a lot of guys like anal sex. They like to, yuh know . . . most times a lot of girls not into it, or they afraid and it does hurt; and whatever the case might be, they not accommodating. Right? So, they look for people who they think—they are not attracted to males, but they look for persons who look the most feminine to give that illusion and still have fun. Yeah, you have a dick but they not sucking it. They not playing with it, they not doing nothing. They not even kissing yuh! Yuh understand, is just a f-ck . . .
>
> . . . But the majority of men, they like backshot. Just the illusion of that hair going down yuh back is enough for dem. They don't have to see a face, just the illusion of the long hair going down on your back and yuh in a back shot, that is all that they really need. And that is the vice for dem. Yuh having the anal sex, and yuh just not having it with a female . . . Well most of dem, they just like to do it like a one-night experience because of . . . well remember dey watching porn and stuff like that, so they becoming exposed. Just like how any person before they going to sex, they will have a lil insight by watching porn . . . so they might probably stumble upon a shemale porn or something like that and that's how they would become introduced to it . . . (November 2016)

QUEENS, KINGS, AND KINSHIP NETWORKS 131

As Princess embellishes, she knows that men seeking sex with her may be seeking a new and exciting experience with a woman and are enticed by the idea of the "shemale" or the hyperfeminine "chick with a dick." She therefore embodies their sexual fantasies.

Trans bodies are entrapped in a matrix of desire, economic and social capital, and a need for survival, of which Puerto Rican author Myra Santos-Febres (2000) provides a provocative example in her novel *Sirena Selena*. In this soap opera–esque drama, readers follow a fifteen-year-old street-hustler-turned-drag-queen who uses their beauty and singing to bring them fame and stability. Selena is "discovered" by their mentor, Martha Divine, after their grandmother's death, being abandoned by their mother, and while hustling and doing sex work on the back streets of San Juan. Martha is thrilled by their talent and exclaims: "You have a beautiful voice papichulo. You sing just like Sirena. If you were a girl that's what I'd call you, Sirena . . . you remind me of your mother. If she hadn't gone astray, she would be a first-rate singer today" (28). Martha seizes an opportunity and takes Selena to the Dominican Republic with her where Selena begins what becomes a fascinating life as an exotic diva in Santo Domingo. It is here that they discover that their life in drag entertainment would be the beginning of a journey toward self-determination and stability. Like Princess, Selena is also able to utilize their gender fluidity to access a sense of happiness and satisfaction.

Selena and Martha Divine form a kinship bond with each other, where Martha takes the care and compassion to ensure that her adopted daughter feels loved while learning how to benefit financially and emotionally from the work she did as a cross-dressing entertainer. This knowledge is then utilized in Selena's bonds with other characters like Leocadio, Migueles, and Hugo Graubel, who all desire things like economic self-sufficiency, family bonds, and establishing themselves. Selena enters a tense but fruitful relationship with Graubel who leaves his wife after falling in love with her. She can enjoy success through his access to the rich elite business community and finds a way to establish herself while maximizing on the love and admiration he has for her.

> In Hugo Graubel she awakened more than desire; there was the curiosity to know more about this muchachity who knew exactly how to convert himself into the living image of desire, into the woman of his dreams, into the impossible . . . Sirena Selena was a magic well in which he could see things in the future and the past. But the reflections were haze, confused. Graubel was going to need time, more afternoons of rehearsals, unexpected meetings in corridors, conversations beneath a palm tree. Wooing was needed, and subtle distraction of his wife and children; he needed to but time to be able to immerse himself in the well (glorious or ordinary) that was Selena. (Santos-Febres 2000, 83)

Likewise, Princess is a fantasy, an escape, an enigma that drew men to her. Without a rich benefactor, she turned to social media, particularly Facebook, where men would send messages to her "girl page" and ask to meet up after chatting with her and "telling me all what they does think about doing" (November 2016). She considers herself lucky to be relatively safe, not having had any potentially dangerous encounters with these men. However, her safety remains an integral aspect of her negotiations for sex with them, since, as she explains, "the people I go with it is normal everyday . . . not to say thug-thug people . . . but sometimes is people selling weed [marijuana], is hustlers . . . yuh understand what I saying? So you really doh know who is who" (November 2016). Princess's safety routine entailed staying close to where she lived, in an area she considered her safe zone:

> How it works, I don't let . . . what I do for safety is I have this one place . . . there is a guesthouse there. Now, once I tried it with somebody and I went in there . . . what I normally do is, I go to the hotel, I will pay for my room cause is my vice too not only yours. Cause yes you like sex, but I looking at it as a f-ck too . . . just a f-ck. So technically that is how I conditioned my mind so that is why I don't get hurt . . . yuh understand. But I would go to the hotel, I would pay my money whether is for ah hour, two hours, three hours, whatever the case might be. And ammm . . . I would watch through the window to see the character coming in or whatever the case might be. So, if I don't want the person come up to the room . . . I just tell dem well I can't make it again. (November 2016)

This well-conceptualized plan once backfired when a familiar sex partner stole from Princess after meeting her a few times at the hotel:

> A time though I wasn't expecting it, I really, really, really wasn't expecting what occurred and the gentleman stole my phone boy! Yeah, it was terrible . . . it was terrible, terrible, terrible. Actually, that was somebody . . . the thing about it eh, I don't know why I is such a imps [fool] cause I know everything bout de man, I know where he working . . . I still couldn't believe it. I swear the man gone for breakfast or some kind of ting . . . that was the first time and I learnt my lesson . . . I don't ever fall asleep in the arms of a man. That is my number one rule. You leave. Normally what we do after the fact, if yuh want to bathe you bathe, yuh put on yuh clothes and go; or yuh just put on yuh clothes and go, and if I see yuh in the road I passing yuh straight like if I don't even know you . . . We spoke and ting [a while after] and he was like boy. After, he felt bad and ting, he tell me he was going through a real hard time or whatever the case might be and "oh ammm . . . Yeah boy . . . ammm . . ." and couldn't say anything. (November 2016)

She still continued to use these opportunities to connect with men but remained cautious about future encounters that were facilitated by her online connections.

In her experiences, at least three important issues surface. Firstly, recalling her story earlier in this chapter, Princess has been able to draw on popular gender references from American media (like RuPaul's Drag Race, mentioned earlier) to make her gender transgression palatable to the hypermasculine men that she desires, and who desire her. In doing so, she alludes to her ability to satisfy their fantasies, some of which they may have also discovered through international media and pornography. Secondly, her narrative provides a sense of how such access to trans women's bodies becomes a means through which some men can continue to play out their fetishistic desires of women's bodies, which some of these men may not be able to access from cis-gendered women, including hyperfemininity. Princess's hyperfeminine performance allows them to fulfill their desire for that type of woman. It is also important to note how Princess positions herself not as a victim of these misogynistic practices but rather as an agential subject who is simultaneously fulfilling her sexual desire, since as she asserts, "is my vice too not only yours, but I looking at it as a f-ck too" (November 2016). Notably, Princess's sexual escapades does not conflict with her opinions of femininity or feminine respectability, as defined by her pageant persona. One's way of dressing and presenting oneself in public must be respectable; but what one does sexually, when seeking pleasure, is one's own private business. Thirdly, Princess highlights the importance of safety in these interactions, especially when she seeks out these encounters knowing that the threat of harm is almost always immanent. I think about this question in relation to CAISO's safety campaign that I discuss in the chapter 3, along with my discussion in the next, and final chapter, which acknowledges these complicated negotiations that queer people must navigate daily.

Internal exile is a space-making praxis mobilized by queer people in the forming of community, kinship networks, and opportunities to thrive across the region, despite conditions that seek to isolate and undermine them. In real, lived contexts across the Caribbean, queer people devise strategies and create communities to claim space, which the stories in this chapter elucidate. These stories, inspired by the region's social, cultural, and political characteristics, help to paint a picture of the possibilities that exist in queer embodiments that go against the grain and disregard prevailing mores and norms of Caribbean societies. They demonstrate the need for sex and sexuality education for everyone, to better understand the complexities of gender and sexual identities, sexual and reproductive health that affect everyone, not just queer communities. Kleos's mention of the conflation of gender transgression with sexual transgression highlights its illegibility in the space, among the wider society and among queer communities. This ignorance hinders inclusive practices whether in kinship, education, economic, or social spheres. Thus far, the stories also emphasize the need for the pluralization of narratives and identities regarding gender nonconformity. The trans women and men I met and interviewed have varied experiences and subjective understandings of themselves within the society. It is important to maintain this heterogeneity when we discuss trans issues so as not to minimize their differences and particular needs. In the following chapter, I continue this examination of queer sexual politics from the margin by exploring queer people's lived experiences of transgression.

CHAPTER 5

Rumshops, Nightlife, and the Radical Praxis of Internal Exile

Formal activism often fails to capture the everyday forms of resistance that become part of embodied practices, including how queer people claim space. In this chapter, I share glimpses of how queer people occupy space in northeast Trinidad and Georgetown, Guyana, and the queer subculture in which they exercise agency by negotiating race, class, gender, and economic geographies. While, like the rest of the Anglophone Caribbean, issues of nonhegemonic gender and sexuality continue to define legibility, bars, rumshops, and nightclubs are actively and radically occupied at night, to disrupt the very structures that maintain hegemonic heteronormativity and binary gender conformity. These spaces provide an opportunity for queer and trans people to embody their defiant transgressiveness in ways that both reinforce and disrupt the hegemonic notions of race, class, and gender. These sites help to facilitate transgression within the confines of the law and prevailing cultural mores that determine gender and sexual legitimacy. They are using their bodies to navigate these geographies in exciting and radical ways sometimes under the (literal) darkness of the night. These spaces are not permanently available to queer subjects, but are instead transitory, or as conceptualized by Krystal Ghisyawan (2016, 181), they are "co-opted by queer subjects whose performances traffic through dominant spaces creating a web of relations." By navigating and negotiating the dynamics of each of these transitory spaces, I was able to experience how queer people, with the limited agency available to them, engage in small acts of rebellion to secure small levels of autonomy in their lives. Furthermore, as Cathy Cohen acknowledges in her work *Deviance as Resistance*, "while these choices are not necessarily made with explicitly political motives in mind, they do demonstrate that people will challenge established norms and rules and face negative consequences in pursuit of goals important to them, often basic human goals such as pleasure, desire, recognition, and respect" (Cohen 2004, 30). These performances therefore offer new ways to reposition queerness in the region. Space-making praxes provide evidence of "an alternative Caribbean ideology of freedom, one grounded in the living sensual body as a more fully rounded, relationally connected, erotic, and spiritual potential" (Sheller 2012, 23).

The sections in this chapter travel across and return to various spaces as I provide examples of how community is created, how social and cultural ideas of legitimate gender and sexuality are contested, and the wealth of queer possibilities that exist outside the activist and human rights realms that I explored in the beginning of the book. I consider the world-making potential of alternative forms of kinship and the value of mainstream sites like rumshops, bars, and nightclubs for the honing of a radical praxis of internal exile. In doing so, I shift the narrative of the Caribbean from being a place of *only* extreme violence, mortality, homophobia, and transphobia from which queer people need to flee and shed light on the tangible nature of queerness within this region despite all these issues.

KAY'S RUMSHOP: A HAVEN FOR TRANS-MASCULINE PEOPLE

In July 2016, the "group of six" Black, nonurban, working-class masculine women and trans men in East Trinidad, mentioned in the previous chapter, hosted a much-anticipated *All Fours*[1] tournament with prizes of cash and alcohol. Because I was already familiar with their preferred rumshop and knew most of the potential attendees from liming with them there and elsewhere, they invited me to attend this event. Although I was prepared to indulge in a long night of the card game, I was very surprised to see Kay, the owner and bartender, stop the music around 2:00 A.M. for an impromptu "show." Much to my fascination, and that of the other women and trans men around, the group of six modeled and danced in the center of the bar with their pant crotches stuffed to mimic a hard penis. Kay immediately began to play the dancehall song Dagger Dagger by RDX (2008) to complement their pelvic-thrusting simulation of aggressive penetrative sex. After about forty-five minutes of impromptu dancing, the card tournament resumed until well into the morning.

I visited the group of six one week after this event to lime and was able to reflect with two of the group's members about their impromptu show. Marc, who identifies as a man, couldn't control his laughter as he recounted "how big Pat make his prick,"[2] teasing him and saying, "like yuh wanted to shift de woman spleen with that!" Shortly after, Pat left to go prepare some food in the small kitchen, and on a more serious note, Marc explained to me what it meant for him to present as a man and spend time in a space like the bar:

> For me it simple eh Nikoli, I done live my life and make children and feel like
> I had to do certain things to get through in this life. Dealing with men in gen-

eral is always pressure because dem feel dey in control and I was not having that. I was always rough and rugged, not no lil pretty gyul going in Pennywise[3] to buy makeup and perfume. I go f-ck dem yes but is stiff prick for dem so. I like to wear my baggy jeans and big jersey with sneakers and take a skin fade cause it does go better with my finish. Imagine big broad back me in a flowers dress walking down the road. Nah that is madness! [laughs] And then too the kind of work I does do, laying tiles and mixing concrete make for this kind of dressing . . . This club here is the best place for me, we run things in here. You feel anybody could come in here just so and tell we anything? Look [pointing at two men sitting by the bar] everybody could come in here, but once they come in they have to get with the program quick. When I come here is like I home. Sometimes we does pull two table and sleep and get up in the morning and go. I eh have to worry about nothing when I up in here. This space is ours and we could do we own ting in here. (June 2016)

For me it's simple, Nikoli, I have lived my life, had my children and I feel like I had to do certain things to get through in this life. Dealing with men is always hard because they fell as if they are in control and I was not having that. I was always rough and rugged, not the pretty girl shopping at Pennywise to purchase makeup and perfumes. I will go f-ck them yes, but it is stiff prick I have for them. I like to wear my baggy jeans and big jersey with sneakers and take a skin fade because it goes better with my finish. Imagine big broad back me in a flowered dress walking on the street. No, that is madness! [laughs]. And then too, the kind of work I do, laying tiles and mixing concrete is made for this kind of attire. This club here is the best place for me, we run things in here. You feel anyone could come in here and tell us anything? Look [pointing at two men sitting at the bar] everybody could come in here, but once they arrive, they need to get with the program quickly. When I come here, I feel at home. Sometimes we pull two tables together to sleep and go home in the morning when we awake. I do not have to worry about anything when I am here. This space is ours and we could do our own thing in here.

Ghisyawan (2016; 2022) has noted that spaces like these are given meaning through their physical and social attributes, including how people inhabit them and move through them. She notes that the rules of a space may be unwritten, possessing what Pascar, Hartal, and David (2018) term "subjective boundaries." Its norms and rules are interpreted and learned through exposure to the space, so when others who are unfamiliar with it enter, they need to "get with the program quick," as Marc says above. They must quickly learn the rules and adapt, to preserve the space as the masculine women and trans men intend it.

Kay, the bar's owner, was an Afro-Trinidadian butch lesbian cis-woman, who passed away a few years after I did this research. She was the principal figure to give meaning to the space, both literally and figuratively "running the show," making the rules for how patrons were to conduct themselves on her property, consequently making it safe for same-sex-loving women and trans men. As they dominated the space, their rules became the norm, so that patrons, like the men sitting at the bar, knew they needed to respect the women's sexual and gender transgressions if they wanted to also enjoy this space. Ghisyawan (2016; 2022) also notes that such safety is not a constant experience, as changes that occur over time can render a "safe space" unsafe for someone in it; this can occur while others continue to feel safe and in control of the space. She asserts, "Vulnerability and violence can exist within any space, making it more accurate to term sanctuary spaces as 'safer' or 'safe enough'" (Pascar, Hartal, and David 2015 quoted in Ghisyawan 2022, 56). In the above quote, Marc designates this "club" as his safest space, calling it "the best place for me" and "home," to the extent that he would even sleep there and not worry about his personal safety, as a female-bodied man.

Marc recounts fulfilling the expectations of being a woman in our society as the "certain things" he had to do "to get through" in life, including having children and being with men. He even acknowledges that sex with men was not entirely displeasing, and that he would have sex with them, but disliked their need for control.[4] Older now, and not needing to be dependent on any man, Marc was more fulfilled in taking on a male gender identity and gender performance. He believed that his body structure and his line of work, in construction, were better suited to male attire. His decision to present as a man, and his textured experiences of it, can be read against the reductive and pathologized image of cross-dressing found in Guyana's legal framing, discussed in chapter 3. He actively seeks to disrupt normative ideas of gender that are unable to contain his experience and identity. In our short conversation, he explains that dressing as a man allows him to claim the liminal space of the rumshop, a traditionally male space, to explore these tensions.

In Peter Wilson's 1973 ethnography of social relations in the Columbian island of Providencia, he notes that rumshops are spaces "where men gather to drink, talk, and play" (168). More importantly, he theorizes that they facilitate male fellowship: "In them, the men of a community gather: here male concerns, interests, and cares are discussed and worked through; here males earn recognition in an environment that is their own" (ibid.). Similarly, Frederick H. Smith (2005, 243) notes that rumshops, bars, clubs, or social taverns in the Caribbean become "arenas for male drinking," especially for Indo-Caribbean males. The rumshop, he theorizes, holds cultural significance in the Caribbean, particularly for Indian indentured migrants whose proximity to the sugarcane plantations, where rum was a by-product, meant that rum was a "cheap and readily available" part of their social environment (184). The rumshop therefore became an arena for the production of Indo-Caribbean male kinship networks, homosocial bonds, and storytelling (Sidnell 2000). The masculine women and trans men flip the script in their particular rumshop, where they hold dominance; their concerns, interests, and cares are discussed and worked through, and they earn recognition in this, their own environment. It is not their masculinity alone that conveys spatial dominance, but Kay's proprietorship of the space permitted the group's control of its climate.

This establishment was frequented mainly by working-class Afro-Trinidadian people from different parts of the country. Queer patrons—gay men, lesbian women, and trans-masculine persons—even came from South Trinidad, noting that it was safe for them to be themselves there. Some assumed straight men from the neighborhood and friend circles would also lime there and knew fully the codes of what was permissible and what was not in this space. With Kay no longer there, I wonder whether this bar is still a safe space for trans men, whose everyday embodiment of masculinity may be viewed as threatening to the patriarchal order. I think closely here with Ghisyawan (2022) who retells the experiences of two nonbinary persons and two other masculine-presenting women who had experienced homophobic slurs, rude commentary, and public shaming for their gender transgression. They noticed that they received more hostility if they were in the presence of a femme-presenting woman. Ghisyawan writes, "If the pair engaged in behavior that might indicate they were a couple, they experienced even more scrutiny, and possibly more confrontational encounters. There is a constant fear that an encounter can become violent, especially for those whose appearance and manner do not neatly fit the societal expectations of femininity" (85). This rumshop was a site where sexual and gender transgression was permissible and even celebrated.

While the group of six's everyday embodiment of masculinity may not be overstated and brazen, their impromptu performance in the rumshop on the night of the card tournament demonstrates that they also reproduce somewhat problematic aspects of hypermasculinity, like the phallic Black penis and the aggressive penetrative sexual conquest symbolized by their daggering. Queer Caribbean diaspora scholar Ryan Persadie (2020, 72) notes that it is commonplace for the rumshop to afford "opportunities for Indo-Caribbean men to dance with each other and enact homoerotic behaviours where men compete with each other to see who can wine better, who can wine lower, encouraged by alcohol, and, interestingly, female spectators." That night's show highlights a similar opening for these trans men, to engage in homoerotic behavior, dancing together, and displaying their virility to the audience with their stuffed pant crotches. The audience laughed along and jeered at the playful exchanges occurring among the performers. Patrons heckled Pat and others; "Look how big yuh wood is!" one person shouted. Another voice asked, "You could use that?" Intrigued, someone requested, "Let me touch it nah!" while another demanded, "Show me how you does use it." The group's playful eroticism drew on referents of masculinity that still center the penis, using it to symbolize their own sexual prowess and dominance, despite not having anatomical penises themselves. As transgressive subjects, they can "develop not only different kinds of eroticism but also different vehicles of resistance ... [that] can become something that both females and males can claim and celebrate as [male identified people] loving women" (Tinsley 2010, 180). Yet their performance repeats problematic, essentializing racialized gender stereotypes, possibly because of their legibility. The connotations of the big, Black penis are well known and easily understood by the audience and other performers.

The "unproductive" sexualities and gender identities of these queer and trans subjects are being used to destabilize dominant heteropatriarchy, embodying what M. Jacqui Alexander (1994) theorizes as "erotic autonomy." These communities are "destabiliz[ing] that which hegemony has rendered coherent or fixed; reassembl[ing] that which appears to be disparate, scattered, or otherwise idiosyncratic; foreground[ing] that which is latent and therefore powerful in its apparent absence" (2005, 192). At the time of her writing, Alexander imagined the possibilities and power that sexually and gender transgressive relations held in crafting "interstitial spaces beyond the hegemonic where feminism and popular mobilization can reside" (ibid., 65). This community's erotic autonomy calls attention to the various ways that they are creating spaces of belonging, indeed "construct[ing] home when home is not immediately understood nor distinctively accessible" (1994, 22). Additionally, they find strength and fulfillment in their erotic practices, as Audre Lorde (1984) theorizes in "The Erotic as Power." In the setting of this rumshop, queer and trans people are able to actualize a sense of belonging that helps them to "fully feel alive in [their] doing" (54). It is by holding each other close and protecting this community in times of need and celebration that the group of six, the trans men, trans masculine, lesbians, and other queer people, are able to experience a sense of wholeness and satisfaction, or what Lorde understands as a "depth of feeling" (ibid.).

Trans-Femininity, Respectability, and Accessibility

During my fieldwork in Trinidad, I also interacted with many queer and trans people who socialized and worked in urban and suburban neighborhoods in the northeast of island. In Trinidad, I accompanied Sandy and her friend Big Redz to numerous bars as they partied and did sex work in a small suburban town. I opened this book with discussions of Sandy's exclusion from activist interventions being done in the country because she was nonurban and working class, with little access to resources from local activist organizations. Firstly, she did not know they existed, and after being attacked by police officers one night in Arima, she failed to receive any support to seek recompense. Rumshops and bars feature as a safe space for Sandy as well, who is able to form community, find safety, and sometimes even make a living in the typically hypermasculine space

RADICAL PRAXIS OF INTERNAL EXILE   141

of the neighborhood rumshop. It is in such space that her practices of agency are tangible as she negotiates her surroundings as a working-class, gender-transgressing person.

There was a bar across from the Savannah in Arima. It was the "scene," the place to be, on the weekend as it attracted a wide array of lower- and middle-class men from the town, many of whom were "down low" and engaged in secret relations with queer people. Sandy explained:

> I does go with my drag clothes normal. I does walk by the junction, go by the bar and go by the next bar—by [name omitted]—and drink two beers and go my way. Ah tell yuh nobody does be on me. I will take a taxi, walk through Arima and go straight to where I does lime . . . I like to go down by Savannah Bar[5]—dey come like [name omitted] too inno—there is [name omitted] part two. It does have hoes from Town dey and all on a Friday and Saturday. Doh get tie up inno. Yuh see dey, most of the people you see moving normal normal, dey like that!
>
> *I would comfortably go in drag. I would walk by the intersection, go to the bar and then go to another—by [name omitted], drink two beers and go on my way. I told you, nobody interferes with me. I will take a taxi, walk through Arima and go straight to where I typically lime. By Savannah Bar*—there is like [name omitted]—there is [name omitted] Part two. Savannah Bar usually has a lot of gay men, just opposite the Savannah. There are also usually gay men from Port of Spain on a Friday and Saturday. Don't be fooled you know, you see there, most of the people you would see acting normal, they are gay.* (November 2016)

As mentioned in the introductory chapter, Sandy lived close to and did domestic work around Arima. Here she compares Savannah Bar to another in Port of Spain, which was not the most open and accepting space, being dominated by Afro-Trinidadian middle-class gay men with all others occupying more peripheral spaces. The large numbers of men at Savannah Bar reminded her of this club. She presents herself in this space, and others, not as a gay man, but as a hyperfeminine trans woman, which she feels makes her presence more palatable. Her dress, mannerisms, and interactions with people are legible as feminine (enough), allowing her to successfully "pass" as a woman, resulting in the men she interacts with being more accepting of her. She found this to be true even when she visited the popular party strip in Port of Spain:

NA: So, how often do you go out on the Avenue now?

SANDY: I doh go plenty again cause of how the place get now [referring to less gay spaces in the area], but I does go like every month end, once for the month or so I does go.

NA: So, when you roll up in Smokey and Bunty, you doh get jumbie?
So, when you visit Smokey and Bunty, are you harassed?

SANDY: No, nobody doh jumbie me so that's why I does go by myself. Cause when I go out there nobody does really know cause ah does do it good eh [LAUGHS]

Nobody harasses me. That's why I would visit alone. Because when I visit, nobody really knows that I am trans because I pass well.

NA: You does do makeup and ting?

So, you wear makeup and stuff?

SANDY: Yeah, I does do it real good [shows me her pictures on Facebook].

Yes, I do it very well too.

NA: So, men does track you in those bars?

Do men hit on you in those bars?

SANDY: Yeah.

NA: They know about you?

Do they know that you are trans?

SANDY: Well some does know, and who don't know, I does tell dem.

Well some men know and who don't I tell them.

NA: And when you tell dem, what dey does say?

What do they say when you tell them?

SANDY: Well some does be for or against it. Some does say: "well I like how you moving; it's very kind of you to talk and say." They does watch the scenes and does be cool with it.

Well, some people either support it or are against it. Some say: "Well I like how you are carrying about yourself, it's very kind of you to let me know." They would watch how I carry about myself and are cool with me being trans.

(November 2016)

Sandy emphasizes here that she has been able to co-opt these mainstream spaces because she performs in a way that is acceptable by the men around her. She also fulfills their gendered expectations through her performance of such hyperfemininity. Even at home she fulfills these gendered expectations and sees herself as a well-integrated member of the community. In the interview I asked about her experience as being openly trans among her neighbors:

NA: In terms of living around here, how is it?

SANDY: It good ... Cool ... it have the fellas around here. Everybody, from the littlest child ... all my neighbours know. I could go on the block and smoke. I does go on the block with them boys and bun a weed. All dem block ... any block. They know bout me and is a norms. I gain a respect in [name of neighborhood omitted].

It's good ... cool ... there are men living around here. Everybody, from the smallest child ... all my neighbors know. I could go on the block to smoke. I usually go on the block with the boys and smoke weed. All the blocks ... any

RADICAL PRAXIS OF INTERNAL EXILE   143

block. They know about me and they are normal about it. I gained respect in [name of neighborhood omitted].

NA: What did you have to do to gain that respect?

SANDY: I think is just being cool, ain't being disrespectful, eh being this kind of loud up, loud up, loud up and in everybody face kinda ting, yuh know? Yuh know what yuh is, yuh now what yuh for. Yuh eh disrespecting nobody. If somebody come to you, you will . . . but you eh disrespecting nobody. Yuh know how much children is big man, I grow them up from baby? Plenty of them.

I think it's just being cool, and not being disrespectful, not being loud and boisterous and in everyone's face. That kind of thing you know? I know what I am, and I know what I'm for. I'm not disrespecting anyone. If someone comes to me, I will . . . but I am not disrespecting anyone. Do you know how many children are big men now, I took care of them since they were babies. A lot of them.

NA: You see about children too?

SANDY: Yeah home here or by their house. Plenty of dem is big man now and nothing never happen then and it eh happen now. It have people will tell you Sandy, I trusting Sandy with my children any day! And I believe is the way how yuh carry about yourself. Is the way how yuh carry about yourself. Cause I will tell you something, you see dem gays in town right? I doh know, but they doh really like me because . . . the reason they do like me to tell you the truth, because of how I does move right. Like how dem go like fight and ting, I'm not that kind of person. Yuh understand? I does be more cool. I doh go nowhere to look for fight. If I see something, I gone from there. If somebody say something bout me I pretend I eh know what they saying.

Yes, either here or by their house. A lot of them are big men now and nothing ever happened then and it won't happen now. There are people who will tell you Sandy, I trust Sandy with my children any day! And I believe that it's the way that you carry about yourself. It's the way that you carry about yourself. Because I will tell you something, you see those gays in Port of Spain? I don't know, but they don't really like me because . . . the reason they don't like me, to tell you the truth, is because of how I move. They like to fight a lot and I am not that kind of person. You understand? I am cooler. I don't go anywhere looking for a fight. If I see something, I would leave. If someone says something about me I pretend that I don't know what they are saying. (November 2016)

Sandy's reflection above shows that she has accepted these gendered assumptions of her trans femininity, but also reveals how she navigates the space by

144   DEFIANT BODIES

adopting similar mores of respectability held by the wider society. She ensures
that she "eh disrespecting nobody," and thinks that "the way yuh carry about
yourself" is an important trait that members of her community, and wider queer
community, should emulate. But adopting these feminized roles also has consequences for her more intimate interactions with the men around her. Sandy
also reminisced about a recent relationship that she had with a young man in
her neighborhood, stating that on the surface many men appeared to be homophobic and transphobic, when in fact they aimed to get her attention:

> I will tell you something eh. It have some of dem men. Cause this happen to
> me plenty times. Some of dem men who does be getting on when they see a
> gay . . . oh a go beat yuh and ah want to kill yuh . . . yuh see these men, is dem
> yuh have to watch. These is de men who does do thing with the gays. They
> does be using it as cover up but when you see dem alone is a cool scene. It hap-
> pen to me plenty times . . . it had the fella who living right down on de corner.
> A young fella. This boy always harassing me. The boy want to . . . I end up
> putting him in court all kinda ting cause the boy harassing me all in the
> road. He was the only person who harassing me and want to pelt me down.
> You know in the ending up, ah does have to laugh. Yuh know what is the
> outcome of that? He end up by me. Well hear what go on: the mother beg me
> to drop the case and he say he wouldn't do it again. Afterwards now, the back
> there (points to her back yard) was open to come home from the block. He
> come "oh Sandy, wais de scene." I say I cool. He say I going and use yuh
> latrine dey. I say go ahead nah and free up. Right here I did sit down (on
> the step leading to her house) . . . next ting I hear "aye Sandy come na." I was
> like wa? He say "come nah boy wham boy?" I say wa de f-ck, I know me and
> de man eh good. Well I get up and go and he was like . . . come and see what
> I have nah . . . ah say "so wait nah, wais de scene? You always harassing me."
> He say "leh we forget that nah." And since after that I remain dealing with dat
> boy right through. That is just the other day I talking about [LAUGHS
> HYSTERICALLY].
>
> *I will tell you something. There are some men, because this happened to me*
> *a lot of times. Some of those men would be aggressive when they see you . . . oh*
> *I will beat you and I want to kill you . . . those are the ones you have to watch.*
> *These are the men who do things with the gays. They use their aggression as a*
> *cover up but when they are alone they are cool. It happened to me plenty of*
> *times . . . There was once this guy who lives around the corner. A young guy. This*
> *boy is always harassing me. The boy wants to . . . I ended up taking him to court*
> *already because he used to harass me on the road. He was the only person who*
> *would harass me and would want to throw stones at me. Do you know that in*
> *the end, I always laugh . . . Do you know what is the outcome of our interac-*
> *tions? He ended up with me. Well hear what happened: His mother begged me*

to drop the court case and he promised that he wouldn't do it again. Afterwards, the back there (points to her backyard) was opened to come home from the block. He came and shouted "oh Sandy, what's up?" I replied "I cool." He asked to use my outdoor toilet. I said sure, free up. I was sitting right here (on the step leading to her house) . . . next thing I hear "Sandy, could you come?" I was like what? He said "come nah boy what happen?" I said what the f-ck, I know we weren't on good terms. Well I went and he was like . . . come see what I have here . . . I said "so wait, what's up? You always harass me." He replied "let's forget that please." And since that I remained dating that boy right through. That was just recently [LAUGHS HYSTERICALLY]. (November 2016)

While Sandy feels safe in these spaces, what does it mean for her, as a working-class trans woman, to be accepted under hypermasculine circumstances that gender and fetishize her body? I think about her location in these public and domestic spheres in relation to Ghisyawan's (2013, 3) succinct theorization that in Indo-Caribbean families, queerness and gendered categories are constructed in relation to a heterosexual man, where female sexuality is seen as a male thing, which links "female pleasure and the 'making of a woman' to penile penetration." This is clear in Sandy's interactions here, and with the police in the introductory chapter, where her legibility depends on her fulfilling particular roles in the various spaces she occupies. At the bars she performs stereotypical hyperfemininity to the amusement of the men; the police use their baton to physically and symbolically penetrate her by forcing her to suck it; and at home she is domesticated, even fulfilling men's domination by satisfying their sexual desires to penetrate her fetishized body, and by performing the feminized task of childcare.

Indeed, Sandy's transgressive femininity disrupted the heteronormative spaces that she co-opted. One Friday night in November 2016, we met at Savannah Bar for her to show me the "scene." "Here too dead!" she exclaimed after we had a few drinks, and we proceeded to another spot just a five-minute drive away, where, as she explained, "de butch boys does lime"[6] (Diary entry, November 18, 2016), referring to the hypermasculine, working-class men who frequented the venue. Dressed in a pair of tight-fitting blue denim pants and a body-hugging black tee, she was unbothered by the crowd dancing to the dancehall tunes being played by the deejay. After about an hour of drinking and dancing she wanted to go to another spot, Pablo's, to see what "action" she could get there (Diary entry, November 18, 2016). Most weekends, she would end her barhopping there as it was open for twenty-four hours and she could stay until public transportation was again available to go home around five or six o'clock in the morning.

Pablo's, although also very heteronormative, was also a transgressive space because of its upper-level guesthouse that attracted a wide-ranging (mostly heterosexual) clientele who paid hourly fees to rent rooms for sex. Although Sandy rarely did sex work there, she tried to "pick fares" with the men who patronized the bar. She liked dancing and would dominate the small dance floor, typically dancing alone or with other women. Most nights Sandy met her friend Big Redz at Pablo's and they would both plot strategies for attracting potential suitors. Patrons were generally friendly with them, except for the occasional taunting or gossip from men and women who partied there. One Saturday night in December 2016, a group of three women and two men were laughing among themselves about Sandy and Big Redz. I engaged them and they explained that while they were a bit uncomfortable by their (Sandy and Big Redz's) presence in the bar, they were actually quite amused at how openly they danced and interacted with everyone else. Later that night, Sandy and Big Redz accused each other of encroaching on each other's territory since some of the men seemed interested in paying for sex. At around 4 A.M., after Big Redz decided to leave, Sandy sat in a corner smoking a cigarette. She explained that they would always fight "because Big Redz too greedy. Every time she see me linking a scene she does come and block de fares. Ah know the ting hard these days but oh f-ck man!" (*"because Big Redz is too greedy. Every time she sees me talking to someone she would intervene and block my work. I know that things are hard these days, but oh f-ck man."*) (Diary entry, December 10, 2016).

While the men around Sandy and Big Redz fetishized them, their interactions with female-bodied women reveal contentions about how their bodies are understood as appropriating femininity. But what is it about their femininities that make these women at Pablo's so uncomfortable? Martha, one of the three women I met that night, told me a bit about this discomfort in a short interview after we saw each other at the bar on a few occasions:

I doh have no problem with gay people doing dey ting yuh know, but yuh see when they want to put on woman clothes and come out in we spaces I does feel lil uncomfortable. I mean, I know plenty bullerman. It have a few living down by me, but dem does work and ting and not too flashy and I okay with that. Like I wouldn't do dem anything here, cause if you remember, we was dancing with dem and ting and laughing that night, but is really out of amusement eh. Dem real brave inno! Imagine how dem does come out here and not be bothered with what we so go tell dem. And on top of it dem is more woman dan we, dey dress to kill in dey tight clothes and makeup and tracking the few ole men it have here too!

I have no problem with gay people doing their thing, but I feel a little uncomfortable when they want to dress in women's clothes and come to our spaces. I mean, I know a lot of bullermen. There are a few living in my community, but they work and are not too flashy, and I am okay with that. I won't harass them here because if you remember, we were dancing with them and laughing that night, but it is really out of amusement. They are really brave.

Imagine that how they come out here and are not bothered by what people like us will say to them. And on top of that, they are also more feminine than us, they are dressed up ad made up and are hitting on the old men here too. (December 2016)

Martha provides some valuable insight into how Sandy and Big Redz's trans femininities disrupt the normative understandings of gender and sexual autonomy. Sandy actively claims space in the rumshop to own her sexual and gender praxis through her engagement with those around her even though it made some of the people around her, like Martha, uncomfortable. This is evident in what Martha was saying to me where she mobilizes a respectability politics that privileges an acceptable gay man who performs legible masculinity, or in her words "dem [who] does work and ting and not too flashy" (*"those who work and are not too flashy"*). She also reads them as bullermen rather than trans women because of their failed masculinities, and her regard for their femininities as comedy, a show, a farce, even a parody of "woman," in its overstated femininity. Martha's claim that "dem is more woman than we" emphasizes the ways that these performances threaten her femininity, especially when they grab the attention of the men in the space. Furthermore, Sandy and Big Redz defy an expectation that they should be relegated to nonheteronormative spaces instead of "put[ting] on woman clothes and com[ing] out in we spaces" (*"dressing like women and coming to our spaces"*), read by Martha as exclusively heterosexual.

These disruptions and navigations can be understood as creating other ways of being and existing in spaces not necessarily meant to accommodate queerness. I therefore offer Sandy's transgressiveness as disruptive and world making, agential and autonomy seeking. Her performances traverse real spaces and move across geographies to unsettle and disrupt dominant ideas of legible gender and sexuality, and therefore give the trans subject vital opportunities to claim space from the periphery at the periphery. While these peripheral locations are important and sometimes necessary for trans people like Sandy, other kinds of spaces are also being created for and by trans women to explore and claim their sexualities and identities.

SAUCY POW: A NATIONAL ICON

Another trans person from East Trinidad, Kelvin "Saucy Pow" Darlington, was a prominent trans figure of iconic status in Trinidad and Tobago from their teenage years in the 1990s until their death in 2021 during the COVID-19 pandemic. They demonstrated how trans people created space in radical and deeply contested ways, while holding the (metaphorical) baton for the queer community, despite public outcry, shaming, violence, and ostracism. Saucy Pow was an iconic figure whose visibly transgressive gender practices brought notoriety, but also created space for other queer and transgressive persons. Unlike Sandy, who attempted to present as feminine as possible, Saucy Pow's manly physique was barely concealed by their slender but muscular body, scanty clothing, and rough makeup. Their hyperfemininity would shine through their dress and mannerisms, even evoking an erotic gaze from their audiences at bars and rumshops across the country, through their sensual dancing and body language. Their performances fluidly shifted between different tropes of femininity, at the snap of a finger, morphing from what may considered to be a lewd dancer who would do headstands on beer bottles into a dainty damsel strutting their stuff through a crowd. As a spectacle, however, Saucy Pow was problematically framed as "exceptional"—not the heterosexual norm, but also not the queer norm. Often, they would be ridiculed or gaslighted for mere entertainment by amused audiences.

Saucy Pow was known for their dancing and sexualized performances in bars and rumshops across the country, especially in the capital city, Port of Spain, at annual Carnival parades, and at the popular Sunday evening limes at Maracas Beach on Trinidad's north coast. They gained increased popularity with the advent of social media platforms like Facebook, YouTube, and WhatsApp, despite not actively controlling much of the content being shared worldwide. A quick YouTube search for "Saucy Pow," for instance, produces at least forty uploads of their public performances at various sites across Trinidad and Tobago. Recorded from as early as 2009, they have done many impromptu performances on the sidewalk for the amusement of local and international limers and passersby. One of Saucy Pow's more iconic appearances on social media has been their entertaining dances in front the Smokey and Bunty rumshop in St. James, Port of Spain. In a YouTube upload on February 17, 2009, Saucy Pow dances in circles to Fay Ann Lyons's soca song "Meet Super Blue" (2009), and gradually tears off layers of their feminine attire to eventually reveal their male body. People flank them during this performance and cheer at various points, with the YouTube blogger providing valuable commentary throughout. For example, just as Saucy Pow begins stripping, he states: "Only in Trinidad and Tobago can a drag queen strut her stuff like this outside a famous bar in St. James, Smokey and Bunty. No bum [sic] bye bye kill no batty man dead here" (Rositaandclementina 2009). Commentaries are not always as welcoming, with some expressing disgust and anger at their audacious appearances in typically hypermasculine spaces like the Smokey and Bunty rumshop in St. James, Port of Spain; at Uncle Sam's bar at Maracas Bay on the island's north coast; or at various street festivals across the country. Other commenters are fascinated by Saucy Pow's dancing abilities, as in a more recent upload on February 12, 2015, where they were filmed wining[7] to Denise Belfon's "Saucy Baby" (2003) and doing cartwheels during the Port of Spain Carnival celebrations. With the title "Trini Drag Queen Saucy Pow," the uploader exclaims, "Saucy Pow was there before Caitlyn Jenner and [popular

RADICAL PRAXIS OF INTERNAL EXILE

local trans women] Jowelle de Souza and Kia Rankin Boss" (Shemika De Trini 2015), reminding viewers of the fact that trans women have been claiming local public space for decades.

In 2012, Saucy Pow was featured on the local television news capsule "CNC3 In Depth" The LGBT Special Report, a series of short segments meant to highlight the LGBT community and issues they may be facing. The host's voice-over narrative frames Saucy Pow's experiences as a trans person in Trinidad and Tobago as hardship, with a somber tone:

> HOST: He's recalling the amount of time it took for him to receive help after an attack as he lay on the ground waiting for an ambulance after a stabbing attack last year.
>
> SAUCY POW: Nobody eh come and save meh inno. About 4 O'clock they call the ambulance, and that was in the morning . . . I was going and dead that night.
>
> *Nobody came to my rescue you know. About 4 O'clock they called an ambulance, and that was in the morning . . . I was going to die that night.*
>
> HOST: Kelvin doesn't hide the fact that he is a transgender man, and as a result he's been the victim of a range of discriminatory acts—from derisive laughter to violence . . .
>
> SAUCY POW: Dey driving, they watching meh cut eye like they want to shoot me, and this and that right, and I just say, "look Saucy just kill yourself."
>
> *They drive by and watch me cut eye like they want to shoot me, and this and that right, and I just decided, "look Saucy just kill yourself."*
>
> HOST: Saucy's experience is one of the extreme instances of prejudice that exists in our society . . . (CNC3 2012)

In this segment, Saucy Pow is misgendered as a transgender man and their reality is bookended by their experiences of hardship not only as a public trans figure but also as a victim of homophobic attacks and an orphan who was repeatedly sexually abused as a child, resulting in their contracting HIV (Seebaran 2012). As I emphasize in earlier chapters, this image of the "at-risk" trans person has saturated popular discourse, and this segment failed in its articulation of LGBT realities by focusing on this narrative of abuse as a teleological tale exemplifying the trans experience. As Gossett et al. (2017, 2) assert, visibility and representation are limited and partial strategies for transgender people of color that do not challenge structures and systems of violence and oppression, meaning that merely seeing trans people in the media is not enough for the public to get a whole or balanced image of trans people and their issues, and that despite representation, trans people still face record levels of violence. However, people like Saucy Pow have shown us how to deploy these very unruly embodiments and performances to unsettle seemingly rigid boundaries of gender and sexuality.

Saucy Pow continued to be in the limelight, and in September 2013 they took control of how they were portrayed through a self-directed video titled "A Day With Saucy Pow," posted to YouTube. In the video, they sashay across the busy street and make their way to the crowded Chaguaramas Boardwalk, and as they approach the camera, their waistline and black bikini glides from side to side in tune to Konshens's (2013) "Walk and Wine." Saucy Pow sips from a plastic cup and dashes past the camera onto the boardwalk while speaking on their phone. "Gyal yuh too hot fi stand up inna one spot, walk out mek everybody see"—they wave at their amused audience and dance up to the bandstand, which is embellished with red, white, and black bunting, presumably decorated for annual Independence or Republic Days celebrations. After a few modelesque contortions, they walk along the water's edge obeying Konshens's call: "Yuh body fit like Shelly, Olympic time, walk up and down and wine." Here, Saucy Pow's gendered performance operated on many discursive levels. Firstly, they inserted themself into the heteronormative public sphere of the weekend beach lime—as Pow saunters across the beach, they impose their unruly trans body on the heteronormative families as they socialized on the shoreline. Secondly, their clever use of the national buntings decorating the bandstand serves to actively claim citizenship by defying what Alexander (1994, 6) calls "technologies of control" implied by Trinidad and Tobago's national colors that produce and reproduce state power. Finally, their body stands out in stark contrast to their hyperfeminized performance—one foot in front of the other, hips exaggeratedly swinging left-right, left-right—as they wade in the gentle crests at the water's edge.

This physical site at which Saucy Pow deploys their transgressive trans femininity and invites their virtual audiences to participate, bears special historical significance in the context of their criminality as a trans woman in a country that deems such bodies as "not productive enough for the nation" (Alexander 1994, 20). The Chaguaramas peninsula has been a historically highly militarized space, with the decimation of indigenous populations during colonization and numerous political treaties being signed between world powers over the years. For instance, the 1941 base agreement saw Britain granting the United States occupation of eleven square miles of land on the peninsula for eighty-two years (Neptune 2007, 8, 192). This agreement was hotly contested by those fighting for independence from British rule at the time, like CLR James, who wrote extensively against America's detention of Chaguaramas, and Dr. Eric Williams, who issued a call to action for people to "repudiate their colonial past, to close a chapter of history in which they traditionally featured as 'passive agents'" (ibid., 193). Remnants of this history are still present as the national regiment and coast guard continue to control most of the Chaguaramas peninsula, and people are prevented from occupying particular places in the area. The latent drum line of

Konshens's (2013) song, reminiscent of military parade, is further cemented by his marching lyrics interspersed between the lines of the chorus:

Gyal,
left, right
watch di gyal dem
left, right

The rhythm evokes the history of control that defines Chaguaramas, while taking us to a place from which to read a disruption of the space. The families socializing on the shoreline also remind the viewer of the heterosexual conditions that define the nation. However, Saucy Pow, as the antithesis, intervenes despite their outlawed existence to "reverse, subvert, and ultimately demystify" the heterosexual gaze that ultimately criminalizes forms of nonproductive sex and gender in that moment (Alexander 1994, 5). Their occupation of this regimented space underscores how their unruly trans femininity responds, quite sarcastically, to these histories. It is from this performance that I name this section, declaring Saucy Pow a national icon, not so much as a figure of adoration within the nationscape but rather as a symbol of the postcolonial homophobic nation with their contradictions that are embodied and revealed through their transgressions.

Navigating Georgetown at Night: Experiencing Queerness in Guyana

In Guyana, queer people are still criminalized, especially working-class trans women who do sex work on the streets at night. When I visited Georgetown, I was able to participate in and witness some of the various ways that queer people were indeed negotiating and navigating not only criminalization but also other sociocultural dynamics in the city. Jeremy, my main contact in Georgetown, informed me that one of the most recent controversies among people in the city was the curfew imposed by the government, aimed at controlling people's movements and their consumption of alcohol. In 2015, the country's public security minister, Khemraj Ramjattan, ordered nightclubs, bars, and restaurants serving alcohol to close at 2 A.M., in response to an upsurge in traffic offenses, decreased work productivity, and a call by women's organization to regulate alcohol consumption due to increased domestic violence by drunken male perpetrators (Stabroek News 2015), a long-documented correlation (Chevannes 2001; Lewis 2003; Crichlow 2004).

In 2013, the organization Help and Shelter produced a compelling documentary about the experiences of survivors and families of domestic violence victims, noting that alcohol and substance abuse often played a significant role in exacerbating the violence that (mostly) women receive. As one advocate explained in this piece, "In communities where alcohol is present, communities should really work hard to remove alcohol. Alcohol and other drugs are entering communities, and this is present in a lot of violence" (Help and Shelter 2013). Much of this discourse centers on Indo-Caribbean populations where men are perceived to engage in excessive alcohol consumption that influences their abusive behavior. Basmat Shiw Parsad (1999, 46) notes in her study of marital violence in Indo-Guyanese households that many women "attribute[ed] their husbands' violent behavior to the debilitating effects of alcohol which appear to cause their husbands to 'lose control' and do things they would not have done under 'normal' circumstances." More recent research on Indo-Caribbean masculinities by Dave Ramsaran and Linden Lewis (2018) has substantiated this observation where they argue, "Among the stereotypes associated with Indian men is their alleged love of alcohol. Indian men indeed have a reputation for consuming significant amounts of alcohol, but more important in the macho Caribbean culture is the accusation that they are unable to manage their consumption. Such perceptions are often combined with another stereotype of Indian men being prone to violence, especially that which is alcohol induced and directed at women" (106). While the authors note this troubling perception, they also argue that the problem of alcoholism is not exclusive to Indo-Caribbean men but rather "alcoholism is both a national and regional problem in the Caribbean" (107).

Likewise, recalling my discussion in chapter 4 of sex in Barbados, it is not only a problem among heterosexual communities.[8] In fact, Preity Kumar (2018) has also noted similar trends among same-sex-loving women in Guyana, where alcohol played in role in their enactment of violence on each other's bodies when women learned and mobilized violence in their intimate partner relationships. One participant in Kumar's (2018) study, Anna, used alcohol—cheap, readily available, and a normal feature of social interaction in Guyana—to cope with trauma, "to numb their pain and silence their suffering in a culture that offers them nothing else" (225). Another participant, Amanda, had been widowed young, and, without emotional and psychological resources, became dependent on alcohol. Kumar details instances when these and other women acted out violently against their partners, or had partners act violently toward them, privately at home and in public spaces where alcohol and other patrons were present. Kumar notes that public arguments often stem from feelings of insecurity and anger.

Alcohol's insidious hold on Caribbean communities is true, not only in Guyana, but here I focus on Guyana's response to alcohol consumption by using a curfew and ordering establishments serving it to remain closed during certain hours. The curfew necessitated new and creative ways of navigating the space. When I arrived during the Christmas season in December 2016, it was still in effect, but I learned quickly that the bars' locations, owners' connections with the police, and the type of crowds they attracted determined an ability to disobey this control. I was able to visit and participate in five spaces across the city to observe firsthand how people have been negotiating gender, race, and class boundaries in the different sites. Below I provide brief accounts of these sites.

OLD TIME CELLAR LOUNGE

After settling in at my hotel, Jeremy invited me to visit Old Time Cellar Lounge, a popular upscale lounge in Georgetown, to get dinner and some drinks. We arrived there at around 12:30 A.M., and although I anticipated that the crowd would have begun dispersing because of the impending curfew, it was still pretty full. Jeremy explained that while the bar can be considered to be a "straight" establishment, Thursday night, karaoke night, attracted a gay crowd that typically came out to sing their favorite R&B, reggae, and pop songs. Groups of men sat in lounge chairs in dark corners of the bar or outside on the enclosed veranda, visible from the street below, while women stood and sat in the middle of the dining area and took turns singing karaoke. Jeremy and I sat at the bar having dinner and drinking local beer and took that time to talk about my plans for the research trip. One Afro-Guyanese lesbian woman, dressed in baggy jeans and a black t-shirt with a pair of silver chains strung from her pant loops, initiated conversation with us a few times and prompted us to dance with each other during one of the breaks from karaoke when the deejay played music, even though we insisted that we were comfortable relaxing by the bar. At various times she kept teasing us to join her on the small dance floor with her friends and shouted to us over the loud soca music, trying to get us out of our seats. Every time we declined her offer, she retreated to her group, but eventually, after realizing that we were not giving in, she came across and spoke to us. This time, in addition to reminding us of how proud she was to be a lesbian, she let us know how disappointed she was that Jeremy and I weren't dancing with them and with each other. She said that she "doh give a skunt[9] about them," referring to the other gay and straight persons in the bar; she thought our hesitance to dance was because we are ashamed of being gay, even though we kept trying to assure her that this was not the case. I noted in my diary, "I see here how gays and lesbians are expected to wear their sexuality on their sleeves, and in their waistline as they dance to the music in order to gain legitimacy among each other in the space" (December 16, 2016).

At 2:00 A.M. the bar was still open and other people were being admitted to purchase drinks and food. Anxious about this arrangement, and a bit scared that the police would appear anytime to shut down the session, I asked Jeremy how common this practice of partying past the curfew was. He pointed out to me that it was actually very common, especially when bar owners make connections with police officers in the district, sometimes paying them off to allow them to continue operating well into the morning. He also highlighted a few subtle changes that occurred since the curfew had started, and that I had not noticed. All the patrons who were occupying the veranda had moved inside the lounge. The karaoke session had finished and instead of playing music from the lounge's speakers, the bartender played from his laptop and a smaller speaker that was loud enough to keep the party atmosphere upbeat. Finally, although people were allowed to enter the bar, there was now a security guard standing behind the locked door at the main entrance to let people enter or leave. By this time mostly gay men and lesbian women were inside. We left at 3:00 A.M. in a taxi; many were parked along the street below the lounge waiting to whisk patrons away quickly in the dark and still early morning air. Although this space used its status to disobey state control, it also became a place for queerness to flourish.

Sally's Rum Shop

The following day, Jeremy and his friends took me to another party happening in the city because he wanted me to experience another queer vibe in Georgetown. Getting around the city by taxi was affordable (only US$2), and after a short ten-minute taxi ride to Kitty Village, we arrived at one of Georgetown's most popular bars, Sally's Rum Shop. There, a large crowd of patrons drank beers and rum and danced on the covered dance floor, on the sidewalk, and in the street, which became impassable due to the thick crowd of people at the venue. This site attracted a large Indo-Guyanese crowd that exhibited hypersexual performances in their dancing with each other. While the homoeroticism here seemed typical of a bar lime in Guyana (or even Trinidad), where it is not uncommon to see women dancing with each other, or Indian men trying to outdo each other's dance moves by gyrating together, it was Jeremy's introduction to his bisexual cousin and her two gay and two lesbian friends that alerted me to its queerness.

Jeremy's cousin, Sasha, who identified as mixed race, had arrived there before us to meet her friends for their usual Friday evening after-work lime, and they had claimed a spot on the dance floor to dance and drink well into the night. Noticing the amount of freedom they had in the space, I asked her what she thought of the gender dynamics that allowed this. In between some drinks, she and her friends, who were also mixed race, explained that the appeal of two women dancing together was attractive to the men in the bar and so they took advantage of that. They also thought that their race made them more exotic and alluring to those watching them. This sentiment captures the popular politics across the region where women's bodies and behaviors satisfy men's fetishistic ideas of femininity. Additionally, their lighter complexions, or "exotic" appearance, helped to sanitize and make their presence in space attractive. According to Kumar (2018, 211), "Red women or mixed-race women occupy a unique history in Caribbean societies with these beauty ideals and stereotypes continuing to impact other women's idea of femininity and desire," with even woman-loving women fetishizing the mixed-race woman for her beauty and appeal. Additionally, Kumar notes that mixed-race women felt they were subject to violence because of the stereotypes associated with their race. Although these tensions continue to encourage problematic interactions in the region, it is interesting to note how Sasha and her friends were able to use their location as exotic and alluring, to instead carve a space for their queerness to thrive. By doing so they acknowledged that although their performances existed for the consumption of the spectator, they can also use this fetishization to embody and perform their queer erotic autonomy in a space that can become hostile for some.

The two gay men who were with Sasha, one Afro-Guyanese and the other Indo-Guyanese, were more cautious about how they interacted with each other, having expressed to me that they felt as if their shows of public homosociality while dancing may have encouraged unwanted stares and comments from other patrons. Although they weren't afraid of this, they felt it necessary to micropolice their movements to avoid the possibility of any unwanted interaction with the people around them. Both men danced close to each other, and with the women on the dance floor; however, their hypervigilance stood in contrast to the homoerotic performances happening in the space between Sasha and her friends, and between other men and women on the dance floor. I wondered why these two gay men felt that they could not participate. Was it because of their sexuality? Was it because of their race? Both? On these registers, I wonder how the interaction would have been if both men were Indo-Guyanese or Afro-Guyanese. Would two Indo-Guyanese gay men feel a need to police themselves as much even though they are "allowed" or "expected" to dance with each other under the influence of alcohol? Would two Afro-Guyanese gay men police their performances even more to prevent emasculating themselves? I think about these questions in reference to the experiences of gay men like Kenty Mitchel who I discuss earlier on, where their nonvirility posed a threat to patriarchal and heteronationalist notions of Black masculinity. In this scenario I saw that both men were performing what was expected of them in the space. I push this idea even further, thinking through Ramsaran and Lewis's (2018) exploration of racial tensions between Indo- and Afro-Guyanese men, where Indo-Guyanese men often draw sometimes derogatory references to characteristics of their Afro-Guyanese counterparts in their claiming of belonging in the social, cultural, and political landscape. They argue:

> Defining Indo-Guyanese masculinity necessarily occurs in a racially charged environment in which race plays an inevitable role in how men view themselves and what claims and expectations society places on them. Any consideration of Indo-Guyanese masculinity operates on a mindscape of the perceived hegemony of African Guyanese and, more generally, African

Caribbean masculinity. African Guyanese and African Caribbean masculinity simultaneously set the parameters for Indo-Guyanese masculinity as well as its point of departure. Whether explicitly or implicitly, Indian men in Guyana almost always refer to some characteristic of African Guyanese male behavior in describing who they are or what they consider important to do as men. (109–110)

Based on this logic, then, could these interactions between the gay men be read as of them sizing up each other, and the other men around them to ensure that their claim to masculinity, albeit queer, remains a safe distance away from each other? I did not have the opportunity to speak with these men outside of this context to inquire about their behavior. Maybe they did not like to dance, or maybe they chose not to dance because of the politics at play in this space and the stakes of losing their masculinity by performing homoeroticism as queer men. It is important to note, however, that these kinds of homoerotic and homosocial displays are often acceptable between perceptibly straight men but not for those perceived as transgressive simply because such "straight" performances do not destabilize hegemonic masculinity and virility, especially when performed in hypermasculine spaces like the rumshop and in sports. While I have only scratched the surface in thinking about these possibilities here, it will be illuminating to interrogate these interactions further to better understand how gay men interpret the gender and racial dynamics of their relationships in spaces like these in Guyana and across the Caribbean.

CHRISTMAS PARTY

Jeremy then invited me to a small Christmas party in Georgetown on Saturday, December 17, 2016. A popular gay Indo-Guyanese fashion designer hosted about forty queer persons from the city, ranging from other designers, NGO workers, and gay men from the community. We arrived at this modest gathering, which happened in the driveway between two buildings, at about 9:00 P.M. Although the guests were predominantly gay Afro-Guyanese men, four trans women made a fashionably late entrance at around 11:30 P.M. One of them, a Filipina trans woman who migrated to Guyana in 2015, joked about having to prepare herself for a long night on the streets after the party finished. She showed us her tall boots that complemented her Black kimono outfit, saying that they were easy to run in if necessary, alluding to the possibility of police raids and the chance of her having to run from drunken men who would heckle sex workers on the street. Another group of guests, some white U.S. Peace Corp volunteers, stood out as they sat among everyone else in this small gathering. In one of the buildings, the host laid out a wide array of local dishes for a buffet-style dinner. Guests added drinks to large coolers positioned alongside the other building and we sat

Figure 25. Sally's Rum Shop in Kitty Village, Georgetown, Guyana, December 2016. Photo by author.

on chairs and benches, forming a large circle while we drank and chatted with each other. Just beyond the small kitchen was what the host called his Christmas fantasy room, extensively decorated for the season, topped with Christmas carols playing softly in the background. He kept reminding us to go in and take pictures, as this was one of the highlights of his party every year.

Figure 26. Christmas fantasy room, Georgetown, Guyana, December 2016. Photo by author.

The location of this event was quite interesting, as it was at a relatively public venue easily accessible from the roadway, and located in the city center, just a short distance away from the busy commercial streets. It was the caliber of guests, perhaps, whose respectability protected them from unwanted harassment from the public or police made the location possible. There were no visible racial tensions among those present, so unlike the scenario I experienced at Sally's, I do not attempt to read interactions here based on perceptions of race, but instead consider how the racial composition of the guests may have acted as a safety buffer. Firstly, as a popular fashion designer, the host was well respected in the city, so he was not exposed to the type of treatment that others may experience. Secondly, the trans women's proximity to him in that moment could possibly mean that they were temporarily spared from potentially dangerous interactions with the police and public that they would ordinarily face as illegitimate persons prevented from occupying public space in the city. For Sandy in Trinidad, Savannah Bar's working-class clientele and their acceptance of her and Big Redz's gender transgression created a safe space for them to socialize, dance, and even "pick fares," despite it not being an exclusively queer space. While Sally's working-class atmosphere was not as accepting, this Christmas party was an exclusively queer event, occurring in the usually unwelcoming urban space, yet protected through respect given to middle- and upper-class persons, celebrity status and the "foreign" rank of the white U.S. Peace Corp volunteers, who had the luxury of being "safe" in Guyana because of the protection they receive as outsiders. This kind of presence and safety has a long, tenuous history in the region where "third-world states like Guyana are generally only recognized by the United States after tragedies like Jonestown, or when there are ideological or geo-political imperatives that elicit their concern" (Westmaas 2008).[10] I was unable to engage with these volunteers, other than briefly at this party, but their presence testifies to their complicity in the neoliberal impetus for their helping imperative. While this discussion lies beyond my focus in this project, I point this out to signal the historical positioning of white Americans in the region to help, to provide guidance, and to rule. It must be considered alongside the queer liberatory interventions explored in previous chapters, as they are rooted in the same colonizing discourses and institutional infrastructures. They symbolize progress, acceptance, and the superiority of first-world narratives, even at the expense of local communities who view their needs differently. This event interestingly juxtaposed social groups representing opposite ends of the social continuum of respectability: the transgender sex workers on one extreme as societal outcasts, outlaws, and unapprehended criminals, and the foreign aid workers on the other, respected and glorified in this contested urban space.

Villa Court

Jeremy, some of his friends, and I left in a hired taxi at around midnight to head to a soca party and Mashramani[11] band launch close by, at Villa Court. We arrived at approximately 12:15 A.M., just in time to get a good spot in the courtyard of the fancy restaurant and lounge that was transformed into a party space with a large stage for soca performances and models showcasing a selection of costumes for Mashramani 2017. This space, like the typical soca fête in Trinidad and Tobago, was hypersexualized through men and women's dancing and responses to the wide selection of music being played by the deejay and soca artistes who instructed the audience on how to claim space at the venue. At one point during the night, one of the persons in my group directed my attention to a group of fashionably dressed women wearing elaborate makeup and flanking a tall Indo-Guyanese person as they walked through the crowd. The person at the center of the group was a well-known trans celebrity makeup artist who was quite popular in the city. I inquired about how they were allowed in the space without much awkward interactions from other patrons, and Jeremy simply explained to me that Guyanese people are not necessarily concerned about that when they are partying. He also pointed out that the crowed was largely middle-class Indo- and mixed-Guyanese, alluding to an assumption that these populations are more accepting of queerness than Afro-Guyanese people. I again recall Ramsaran and Lewis's (2018) work on these perceptions and some of the tensions about race among Indo-Caribbean people, where they recognized, "In our experience interviewing Indo-Caribbean men, statements about 'other men' and 'other races' are very often indirect references to African Caribbean or African Guyanese men. Indians in fact seem unable to avoid making such comparative references, however indirectly. Once 'other races' have been thus identified, one must point out their differences, or shortcomings, in relation to Indian men. Some behavior or characteristic must set Indian men apart from men of 'other races.'" (101).

In this instance, Jeremy was probably pointing to the idea that Indo-Guyanese people were more accepting of sexual and gender transgressions, and this further helped to situate them as less aggressive or dangerous than their Afro-Guyanese counterparts. Or as Ramsaran and Lewis argue further, these stereotypes are used to produce Indo-Caribbean people as morally superior (126). Because the patrons attending the party that night were perceived to be from middle-class backgrounds, they were also positioned to be less aggressive, and as Belinda Edmondson (2009, 8) argues in her work on "middlebrow" politics in the Caribbean, they are seen as "genteel" and "respectable."

In addition to the race and class politics happening in the space, Jeremy hinted that it was more accommodating since the crowd consisted of people who were concerned about "who's who" in the community. So, because this trans woman was quite famous, her celebrity status protected her gender policing by other patrons and arrest from the mob of police officers guarding the entrance and directing people in front the venue. This moment, in relation to my earlier interaction with the trans women at the Christmas party and with the lesbian/bisexual women and gay men at Sally's Rum Shop, was poignant as it reminded me of the realities that Black working-class trans women face in Georgetown due to the (then) criminalization of cross-dressing, and the policing of their movement within the city. I was also able to maximize on the perks of these "who's who" dynamics in this space because of Jeremy's popularity in the city. At various points during the fete, our group of four men danced with each other, though discreetly, while watching the live performances and costumes during the band launch segment. Even though I was a bit nervous at points, Jeremy reminded me that "nobody won't f-ck with us because they know who I am."

Like the Old Time Cellar Lounge, this party went way past the curfew, which was probably possible because it was at a big, popular venue with the necessary authorization. There was also another interesting moment in the party that facilitated erotic homosocial bonding between men when a male patron was invited on stage and, as a Guyanese entertainment blog review stated, "he showed how the Indian Guyanese men can really perform on the dance floor" (Khatoon 2017). When a popular Guyanese soca artiste was called onto the stage for a wining competition, the men were called to display their competitive virility through highly homosocial and sexualized dancing for an eager audience.

STYLE CAFÉ

We visited Style Café after leaving Villa Court for more hours of partying at a queer event hosted by community members, but this time the environment was much different than the other queer spaces that Jeremy had taken me to. While the other three sites were largely middle class and had a mixture of Indo-, Afro-, and mixed-race Guyanese people, the crowd here was mostly Afro-Guyanese working-class gay men and trans women. The wooden colonial-style building was dimly lit, with patrons cramped into the small dining room area, which was converted into a dance floor. Other people who preferred a bit more space hung out in small groups on the spacious balcony spanning the front of the entire building and overlooking the Promenade along a popular strip running through the center of the street. After a while of partying, the already-dark café was shot into further darkness as one of the usual power outages, or "blackout" as residents called it, struck. Luckily, the deejay was prepared with his battery-powered music system, so the music was not affected. The already-hot room became hotter as sweaty bodies rubbed against each other in time with the soca and dancehall tunes that he played. Trans women claimed a central space in the party and danced very energetically and competitively, trying to outdo each other's best moves. Although visibility was minimal, I could see their silhouettes flipping and contorting in time with the music, and I even had to dodge a few limbs that came my way in the process. This experience immediately reminded me of Sheller's (2012, 35–36) theorization of citizenship from below, where such performances happen "literally 'below' the mainstream public in that they gather in hidden places, in the night-time, in the dancehalls and jook joints, in the sexually suspect cultural spaces beneath the radar that occasionally emerge into a broader public space." It also provided me an opportunity to experience firsthand what Audre Lorde meant when she theorized the centrality of the erotic in queer lives. These queer people created space through a honing of their creative energies to reclaim a knowledge and language about their queer lives (1984, 112). These moments I believe help to share queer joy in ways that lessen the threat of difference in homophobic and transphobic situations (114).

In Style Cafe, there was very little policing of people's gender performances as they partied into the night. This was unlike what I experienced at Sally's Rum Shop the night before, where the two gay men seemed to be hyperconscious of their bodies in relation to those around them. Such inclusivity and comfort are important to note based on Style Cafe's past experience with violence where, in 2011, the establishment's owner was victim to a horrific robbery that resulted in the death of one of the attackers, the establishment's closure, and its eventual reopening with drastically reduced visibility (Guyana Chronicle 2012). Since reopening, it has developed an ongoing working relationship with SASOD, which would host many of its events like its annual film festival there. I draw attention to these developments not only to signal a need to document these histories but also to highlight the ways that civil society organizations like SASOD continue helping to make space for queer people despite the baggage of their largely male-centered, middle-class organizing in the past. It is through relationships like these that urban spaces gradually become queer-friendly and safe for people who may otherwise feel unsafe as they occupy urban space in Georgetown. At Style Cafe, we see the large-scale transnational politics of activist work colliding with the everyday praxis of trans women and queer people in Guyana, allowing for connections across social class. Sites like these function as contact zones that allow us opportunities to think carefully about how exchanges across race, class, and gender foster relationships that are more accessible and relatable to persons who may not necessarily have access to formal activist interventions. They allow us to experience how people at the margins negotiate these intersections on their terms and with their creative and transgressive methods. These dynamics present fruitful opportunities for a more in-depth investigation of queer realities "on the streets" of Georgetown.

By getting a glimpse into how queer and trans people occupied space in Trinidad and Guyana, I was able to access a subculture in which they were exercising agency by negotiating race, class, gender, and economic geographies within the city. While, like the rest of the Anglophone Caribbean, issues of nonhegemonic gender and sexuality continue to define legibility in these countries, each site provides clear examples of how various persons were able to queer the spaces they occupied. By publicly occupying the rumshop or partying more inconspicuously in the darkness of the night and creating a sense of home, they were able to claim a queer presence in the cities and towns in ways that both reinforced and disrupted the hegemonic notions of race, class, and gender. I think about these possibilities in relation to Krystal Ghisyawan's (2016, 181) conceptualization of "transitory spaces" that are co-opted by queer subjects whose performances traffic through dominant spaces creating a web of relations." Or, as Sheller (2012, 23) argues further, such space-making praxes provide "hints of an alternative Caribbean ideology of freedom, one grounded in the living sensual body as a more fully rounded, relationally connected, erotic, and spiritual potential."

Queer and trans people continue to navigate their alterity within the confines of colonial laws that legislate sexual and gendered legitimacy. They also confront the exile they experience within the region and the prescriptive forms of conditional queerness that work to structure their existence, and while understanding them intimately, they craft strategies to weave their transgressive lives through them. When queer and trans people are creating and claiming space, they do so with keen attention to the region's lingering buggery laws and their moral baggage. They understand how cross-dressing laws are closely linked to regulations in public spaces. They know well how loitering laws are used to apprehend them when police officers have insufficient evidence to arrest them for sex work, which is still illegal in many jurisdictions across the Anglophone Caribbean. Still, they can navigate complicated geographies, sometimes in the literal darkness of the night to survive and foster thriving communities.

Coda

A DEFIANT POLITICS OF HOPE
IN THE QUEER CARIBBEAN

The sites I explore in this book provide immense opportunities to learn more about the nuances and vibrance of queerness beyond human rights, transphobia, homophobia, and discrimination in the Anglophone Caribbean. Through my interlocuters, I spend time thinking carefully about how queer people are negotiating, navigating, resisting, and co-opting space, despite their realities of being heavily policed where they live, and indeed, thrive. It is critical to note that queer and trans geographies across the region foster a culture of possibility and provide alternative references for expansive experiences of gender and sexuality. While trans people often experience a sense of displacement and unbelonging within queer community, their radical gendered praxes in internal exile take us to a place outside of homonormativity to "offer a critique of the present . . . by casting a picture of what can and perhaps will be" possible (Muñoz 2009, 35). I position queer people, and especially working-class trans and gender-nonconforming people, as the vanguards of disruptive change across the region, and as Jose Muñoz reminds us in his theorization of the utopian futurity that queerness represents, we can turn to them to simultaneously critique the present while recognizing viable alternatives for the future. He offers that we must "insist on a queer futurity because the present is so poisonous and insolvent" (ibid.). Indeed, we must critically recognize that queer and trans people are still subject to policing through laws and societal norms that continue to restrict same-sex intimacy and expansive gender identifications and expressions, forcing them to "occupy relative rather than absolute citizenship, or rather none at all" (Alexander 1994, 52). However, as I have demonstrated, while socioeconomic status, race, gender, and sexuality all intertwine and often work to define the roles and expectations to which everyone is pressured to conform, queer and trans people are negotiating these intersections in interesting, disruptive and exciting ways.

CODA

The divide between international human rights defenders, community-based activists within the region, and nonpoliticized queer and trans people remains too deep, rendering the needs of those at the margins largely unattended. This is not to say that critical and deeply complex work isn't being done. In fact, since I did this research, this landscape has changed significantly, with queer and trans activist organizations strengthening their mandates and community reach. The Sexual Culture of Justice project in Trinidad and Tobago opened many doors for organizations beyond the European Union Funded grant, with members of the Alliance for Justice and Diversity expanding their work. For instance, the Silver Lining Foundation eventually registered formally as a civil society organization and has produced several community data–driven outputs like its National Schools Climate Surveys in 2016 and 2019, which reveal the issues faced by LGBTQI+ secondary school students in the country. Friends for Life and Womantra have also expanded their work, and the Trans Coalition of Trinidad and Tobago, which comprises mostly working-class trans people doing work at the grassroots level, was also able to formally register and establish bank accounts. Groups like CAISO have also been able to negotiate more appropriate support models with funders like ASTREA Lesbian Foundation for Justice to aid women-led organizations that respond to the direct needs of lesbian, bisexual, and trans communities. This arrangement has made small grants of up to US$10,000 available to groups across the region to do their work in ways that are flexible, with easy reporting requirements and the freedom to change focus as necessary while doing the work.[1] Another important development is the Women's Voice and Leadership—Caribbean project between the Equality Fund and various Caribbean organizations that was made possible through responsive aid to bring together women, including trans women, to advance their own activism and to share resources for transformative work on women's and queer rights, economic justice, sexual and reproductive health rights, and climate justice. This has seen strengthening solidarities among Caribbean countries like Antigua and Barbuda, Belize, Dominica, Grenada, Guyana, Jamaica, Saint Lucia, St. Vincent and the Grenadines, and Suriname.[2] This kind of change is signaling that groups are, indeed, constantly grappling with the evolving contexts within the region. They are also finding ways to ensure that international aid responds more accurately to their needs. The hope is that this kind of work will continue to grow and that activist organizations across the region continue to inform queer human rights work in ways that reflect queer and trans people's nuanced experiences.

All too often, these stories of defiance and resilience from within the region are rendered invisible by the powerful gay international and those controlling financial investments in the queer Caribbean. Global North narratives continue to write a colonizing and revisionist history, painting a one-sided picture of the region and distorting legacies of defiance and resistance. Further, they diminish the critical advocacy work being done by civil society organizations within the region as they advocate and build bridges with allies in a politics of hope that queer and trans realities would continue changing. In *Silencing the Past*, Michel-Rolph Trouillot (1995, 21) theorizes that these kinds of narratives "distort life whether or not the evidence upon which they are based could be proved correct." He asks, "But what makes some narratives rather than others powerful enough to pass as accepted history if not historicity itself? If history is merely the story told by those who won, how did they win in the first place? And why don't all winners tell the same story?" (21–22). We must sit with these provocative questions as we collectively think about what knowledge takes precedence despite the work being done across queer historical moments in the Anglophone Caribbean. The experiences captured in this book demonstrate the need for us to intervene and disrupt such popular narratives of queerness to call attention to the silenced (but not silent) and untold stories of resilience and resistance enacted by queer and trans people. Activists and funders outside the region, especially those with limited knowledge or embodied experience, must take an opportunity to learn from these stories. They must find ways to listen intently to those doing the hard work from within the region and within communities. This will certainly demand deep introspection and an acknowledgment of how they are implicated producing a one-sided understanding of the Caribbean. It will also require the hard work of healing broken relationships with activists within the region and an acknowledgment that queer human rights activism as a stand-alone framework is severely insufficient for effecting change.

A fight for queer autonomy and freedom can only be possible when unlikely solidarities are fostered among all of us who desire this change. As the stories told in this book demonstrate, we need to continuously learn from the persons occupying and co-opting "the streets," as they hold the wisdom and power to truly destabilize hegemonic power as they actualize alternative forms of agency. This will allow us to simultaneously advocate and celebrate queerness while centering experiences from the margins. We will learn more about how queer and trans people are managing to destabilize hegemonic power, and how they exercise erotic autonomy when they choose to move about in the world in the genders they identify with, to perform sex work, to engage in casual sex, to form communities of belonging, and to engage in outreach and advocacy work. Returning to Alexander's (2005) argument, queer and trans people are indeed showing us that their lives "destabiliz[e] that which hegemony has rendered coherent or fixed; reassembl[e] that which appears to be disparate, scattered, or otherwise idiosyncratic; foreground that which is latent and therefore powerful in its apparent absence" (192). Inspired by this radical idea of actualizing alternative forms of citizenship through sexual and erotic intimacy, I call attention to these modes of survival employed by queer and trans people in the trenches as they continue to work toward creating new meanings and understandings about gender and sexuality within the region.

I deem this unruly and disruptive praxis a queer politics of hope and I look forward to continue witnessing the worlds that are being created by queer and trans people as they negotiate internal exile, create and co-opt space, and make community to defy the shackles of compulsory heterosexuality and compulsory binary gender identification. Queer and trans people refuse to be bound. As I put a full stop on this project the very day Queen Elizabeth II departed this world, on September 8, 2022, I continue to reflect the valuable lessons that queer and trans people located across the Caribbean could teach us about the ongoing effects of British (and European) colonization. While the monarchy and its benefactors mourn and change guards to keep their power intact, oppressed people around the world are still navigating the long shadows that this institution of British and other European empires cast on us. If we sit with the stories of resilience that I explore, if we truly listen to the silenced (but not silent) lessons contained within these covers, we will receive a valuable blueprint for negotiating our deeply complicated experiences as a people constrained by the sugarcane plantations.

Queer and trans people teach us how to deliberately negotiate everyday oppression.

Queer and trans people show us how to engage praxes of defiance to foster self-actualization and resist silence.

Queer and trans people reveal how to ensure our enduring presence.

Acknowledgments

I could write a book about my experiences you know! You will put it how I say it?
—Sandy, Trinidad and Tobago, 2016

In reflecting on my journey with this book, I often return to the stories that Sandy, my trans interlocutor from East Trinidad, shared so generously and graciously with me. I continue to hold the accounts that you will engage closely and protect its wisdom as I seek to tell some of the difficult yet exhilarating stories about queer and trans experiences in the Anglophone Caribbean. Writing this book was indeed a long and emotionally taxing but fulfilling journey! I am amazed that my little brain has been able to write these words, inspired by the radical queer and trans people doing work in the trenches across the Caribbean. Thank you to the brave people from Barbados, Guyana, Jamaica, and Trinidad and Tobago for trusting me with your knowledge. Without you, this would have been impossible.

Thank you to everyone who supported me with this research. Mummy, Blair, Melanie, and Meshach, you continue to invest in me emotionally, financially, and otherwise. Thank you for helping me throughout this colorful journey to achieve all my goals. Warren, Dr. Harding, your unwavering love and support melts my heart—is a Doubles and Ting kinda vibes! To my friends and colleagues at the University of the West Indies, thank you for giving me an opportunity to expand this work from a somewhat naïve project into what now stands on these pages. A special thank-you to the Institute of Gender and Development Studies for providing me a space to work and to engage with your brilliant scholars over the years. Marcia Howard, you gave me an opportunity to visit Toronto and provided access to a world of opportunities that was otherwise unavailable to me in Trinidad. My friends from *the sweetness and light* crew, we started this journey together. Aduke Williams, Rhoda Bharath, and Michael Norgriff, our days at UWI were eventful. Without your support and encouragement, this project may have never been completed. Special thank-you to Darrell Baksh for spending countless days listening to my crazy ideas and supporting me through my growing pains. And Melissa Maraj, I will always cherish the memories of our outings across Toronto in search of the next best comfort food joint to relax and revive our souls in those unlivable Canadian winter temperatures.

To my mentors, thank you for supporting me and pushing me to the limit, even when I ran out of steam and felt like giving up. A special thank-you to Rinaldo Walcott for seeing my potential long before I realized it. Thank you for all the opportunities you have provided me and for your endless support. Thank you, Alissa Trotz, for going beyond the call of duty as a member of my doctoral committee, and as my postdoctoral fellowship mentor, at the University of Toronto's Women and Gender Studies Institute. You continue to provide me with the intellectual support and encouragement that I need to do my work. I am forever grateful for having an opportunity to learn so much from you, and I aspire to one day be as great an educator as you are. Kamala Kempadoo, you continue to challenge and push me to excel, and this keeps me inspired. Marieme Lo, your encouraging words always lifted me up while I was a lonely student writing my life away, and for that I am grateful. To the administrative staff at UofT's Women and Gender Studies Institute, thank you for all your support and for helping the space become more welcoming. Joanne Saliba, Marian Reed, and Paul Tsang, your support while I was a grad student, postdoctoral fellow, and even after I left has been tremendous, and I promise to pay it forward.

To the many scholars of color I've met along the way, thank you for fostering spaces for us to share our energies with each other. I will always cherish our enriching conversations and the solidarities we are building as we navigate our way through academia and often-hostile environments wherever we are located. Nicole Charles, R. Cassandra Lord, Cornel Grey, and Preity Kumar, thank you for being in my corner. Susan Narain, Patrice Allen, J. Josel Grant, Shenella Charles, Chevy Eugene, and all the other doctoral candidates with whom I have spent precious time, I see you crossing the finish line, and you will surely see me cheering the loudest. I am happy that we continue to build community together across geographies. Sonny Dhoot, I keep smiling because of the great days we had in our office together, even when we weren't sure what would be our next move in this whole process. I am even happier to reconnect with you as we continue our academic journeys in Colorado. You have already made my transition manageable. Fatimah Jackson-Best, you came back to Toronto in the right time to continue to give me all the motivation I need to keep pushing, with just the right amount of Bajan wotlessness to complement my Trinbago bacchanal. You gave me the inspiration to write chapter 3 on queer sex in Barbados while we met for that sweet *Mofer* Ethiopian Coffee at Oakwood and St. Clair!

Completing this project would barely be possible without valuable funding and scholarship opportunities. Thank you to the Women and Gender Studies Institute, the Mark Bonham Institute for Sexual Diversity Studies and its ground-

ACKNOWLEDGMENTS

breaking Queer and Trans Research Lab, and Massey College for providing me with valuable financial, administrative, and intellectual support for this project. A special thank you to my colleagues at the Institute for Gender and Development Studies at the University of the West Indies St. Augustine Campus, especially Angelique Nixon, Sue Ann Barratt, and Gabrielle Hosein, Rhoda Reddock and Patricia Mohammed, for supporting me and pushing me to interrogate queerness and Caribbeanness critically. To my new colleagues at Colorado State University, thank you for embracing me so quickly, for cheering me on and supporting my professional development as I made such a big transition. I look forward to finding intellectual community with you.

Angelique, your motivation, guidance, and intellectual and emotional support are beyond amazing. Your insight into critical queer and trans organizing dynamics in the region remains necessary in helping me contribute, in my own little ways, to a vision of defiant queer freedom. That last push you gave me was just what I needed at the end. I am happy to have so many opportunities to think with and learn from you. Krystal Ghisyawan, I can't begin to quantify the love and admiration I have for you with your brilliant self. You showed up for me in so many unimaginable ways. You held my hand and steadied my pen (well, really, my typing fingers) when I ran out of steam and gently urged me to push through. I appreciate all the ways you inspire me to think and explore my ideas. Angelique and Krystal, I look forward to continuing thinking and co-conspiring with you as we work with queer and trans communities and theorize our experiences. Shay, I am honored to have your amazing artwork as my book cover—you have mad skills and I'm happy that the world will get to feel the same warmness I feel every time I look at it!

To my family, the Attais, Castillos, Gulstons, and Musewes, thank you for all your support over the years and for cheering me on. Thank you, Uncle Clement, and Aunt Sandra for connecting me with Sandy; she changed my outlook on this project and my scholarly/ activist work. A special thank-you to Uncle Felix, Aunt Lennor, and cousins Judith, Kwame, and little Read Delfish for providing me with a safe, comfortable, and nurturing home in Scarborough over the years. To my family members who have gone—Granny Phillis, Grandpa Cufan, Grandpa Tony, Uncle Freddy, Uncle David, Uncle Richard, Uncle Nello, Kathy-Ann, Lana, Uncle Bethel, Aunty Yvette and Daddy—I am sorry that you aren't here in the flesh to see me finish, but I walk on your shoulders. My Torrecilla Gardens Arima family, thank you for helping me embrace every part of this journey. My expats crew Adam, Keon, Lisa, Rosalie, Rob, and Sandra, thanks for the encouragement, support, and great memories during the most frustrating days. To my fellow corruptors Jamila, Adrian, Laverne, Carlos, Alyah, Aronne, Ryan, and Matthew, thank you for giving me my daily laughs and just the right dose of bacchanal to keep me afloat. Special thanks to Jamila and Laverne for accepting my random phone calls and for being the ears to my ideas and frustrations. You made Canada, Trinidad, and now the United States seem closer than they really are. To all those whose names escape me, to those of you who lift me up without either of us knowing, cheers!

To the voices in book, without you this project would have been impossible. You have taught me so much about resistance and community making, even when the odds are stacked so high against you. I hope that I do you justice in this project. I look forward to working with you as we continue to resist and create community in a defiant politics of hope across the region.
Sweetness and Light!

Notes

INTRODUCTION — QUEER LIBERATION IN THE ANGLOPHONE CARIBBEAN?

1. A person of mixed African and Indian descent. See Barratt and Ranjitsingh (2021) for their discussion of Dougla politics in the twenty-first century, in which they theorize the emergence of mixed-raced identities because of material, ideological, and linguistic conditions of the colonial and contemporary Caribbean.

2. Another interviewee, Sariah, described this type of behavior as "obnoxious," noting that while it is a deliberate form of queer performance to embody the unrespectable rebel, it also draws the wrong kind of attention and scrutiny from others who might call them "ghetto and disgusting" (October 2016).

3. The word "lime" is a Trinidad and Tobago English term for hanging out with friends.

4. "Macoumé man" is a term used to refer to gay men in Trinidad and Tobago and other Caribbean countries once colonized by the French. Vanessa Agard-Jones notes that the term "Macoumé" is typically uttered pejoratively toward men who express gendered traits typically considered feminine. For more discussion on this topic, see Agard-Jones 2013.

5. "Bullerman" is a derogatory term used to refer to gay men in Trinidad and Tobago. Incarnations of these terms evident across the region include "Buller" (Barbados); "Antiman" (Guyana/ Antigua); "Battyman" and "Fish" (Jamaica).

6. "Awa" is Trinidad and Tobago English for "or what."

7. I offer translations, where possible, to some Caribbean slang and language in italicized sections below interview excerpts throughout the book to provide some clarification for persons who may be unfamiliar with Caribbean orthographies.

8. Queer Caribbean scholar Amar Wahab (2012, 493) reads these kinds of acts by the police as "a way to understand homophobic policing that is at once a form of state rational practice even as these practices are systematically erased from truth-seeking inquiries that attempt to critique state reason." Hawkey et al. (2021) also note that trans women of color may experience additional prejudice, discrimination, and sexual violence due to the intersection of gender, sexuality, race, and social class.

9. At the time of my research at least two activists I knew left Trinidad for Canada and the United States and another from Jamaica left for the United States shortly after our interview.

10. In all the (independent) British Caribbean (besides the Bahamas, which repealed its sodomy laws in 1991), legal sanctions still remain on the books under various sexual offenses acts, carrying varying penalties for engaging in same-sex activities, ranging from between two and ten years imprisonment in Guyana to ten years in Jamaica. Until 2018 in Trinidad and Tobago, offenders could have served a lifetime sentence (Carrico 2012, 8). Many constitutional challenges to colonial buggery laws have been launched across the Anglophone Caribbean since completing this research. Rulings in Belize, Trinidad and Tobago, and Guyana have begun changing this legal landscape. In the most recent ruling, Antigua and Barbuda's Sexual Offences Act of 1995 was deemed unconstitutional by Honourable Marissa Robertson on Tuesday, July 5, 2022, who ruled that Sections 12 and 15 of the act contravened citizens' constitutional protection from discrimination on the basis of sex. She also pronounced that Sections 12 and 15 of the act were "inconsistent with the rights of persons sixteen years and older to engage in consensual sexual intercourse" in private. See https://antiguaobserver.com/antigua-court-rules-anti-buggery-law-unconstitutional/ for more information.

11. On another note about naming practices in this work, it is also important to make clear my decision to name some participants as opposed to others in order to maintain confidentiality and protect their anonymity. It is of utmost importance for me to ensure that I respect my participants' wishes by referring to them as they have permitted. To maintain confidentiality and anonymity where necessary and possible, I use pseudonyms for most participants. The same was not necessary or possible for public venues, prominent activist groups, and community leaders who are already known for their work and for whom visibility is essential if they are to continue reaching the groups and individuals in need of their services. They have received recognition through the increased attention given to queerness across online blogs and news media. Participants were excited about having their experiences documented by a Caribbean researcher who understood many of their cultural nuances (Carty and Gupta 2009, 125) rather than the typical white scholar doing similar research but who was usually far removed and unaware of the inner workings of the region. To improve the legibility of Caribbean queer culture, I translate some parts of our conversations from the various forms of Caribbean English to "standard" English, so that Caribbean language and nuanced narratives are not misconstrued.

12. Similarly, Marlon Bailey (2013, 4) examines how the Black queers in the ballroom community in Detroit reimagine gender identity, create kinship, and forge community despite their marginalization. As Bailey posits, Black queers "rely on cultural labor not only to survive but also to enhance the quality of their lives" (16).

13. Jafari Allen's 2011 work focused on Cuba.

14. In her work on active presence of queerness in the region, and women's claiming of visibility and disrupting the expected order of things, Rosamond King (2014) theorizes that *sexual agency* describes "the activity of women voicing, advocating for, and/or pursing control of their own sexuality or erotic pleasure on their own terms. The inclusion of pleasure is key to sexual agency because women's sexuality is traditionally mandated to be in service of men, procreation, and the nation. Agency can take many forms, including engaging in extramarital or nonmonogamous sex, initiating sex, determining whether

NOTES TO PAGES 27–36

or not to have sex and under what circumstances, deciding what kind of sex to have, or display desire . . . sometimes the goal of agency is to defy the expectations of family or culture and to discover and claim one's sense of self or identity . . ." (124).

15. In the book's introduction, Stoler (2013, 11) posits, "By definition, ruination is an ambiguous term, being an act of ruining, a condition of being ruined, and a cause of it. Ruination is an act perpetrated, a condition to which one is subject, and a cause of loss. These three senses may overlap in effect, but they are not the same. Each has its own temporality. Each identifies different durations and moments of exposure to a range of violences and degradations that may be immediate or delayed, subcutaneous or visible, prolonged or instant, diffuse or direct."

CHAPTER 1 — LIBERATING THE QUEER CARIBBEAN

1. Canadian missionaries established the first Presbyterian missions in Trinidad in 1868 and in Stabroek, Guyana, in 1881. Historians Brinsley Samaroo (1975, 42, 46) and Dale Bisnauth (1989, 123) discuss how Canadian missionaries instructed Indian indentured immigrants about how they had strayed from the path of civilization by maintaining their ancestral sacred practices of Hinduism and Islam.

2. This Canadian imperialism can be read through Sylvia Wynter's (2003, 271) provocative theorization of the Human, where an inherent ideology of superiority has informed projects of domination from mass Christianization to imperial expansion in the Caribbean, and where truths of humanness have come to define "objective sets of facts" that are brought into existence, "produced and reproduced." These "objective facts," Wynter argues, are sustained by very specific ideas of order "thereby coming to invent, label, and institutionalize the indigenous peoples of the Americas as well as the transported enslaved Black Africans [and Indian indentured] as the physical referent of the projected irrational/subrational Human Other" (281).

3. I am thinking here with Jasbir Puar mapping of homonationalism in queer times (2007) and her theorization of how queer interventions often work to include homosexuality in imaginations of national inclusion.

4. In 2020, Barbadian prime minister Mia Mottley declared the Government of Barbados intended to pass legislation to recognize sexual orientation as a fundamental human right, which would in effect protect people from discrimination based on their sexual orientation. Two years later, on December 13th, 2022, the Supreme Court of Barbados ruled that Sections 9 and 12 of the Sexual Offences Act which criminalize buggery and serious indecency are null and void. For more discussion on this topic, see: https://barbadostoday.bb/2020/07/23/lgbt-leaders-unimpressed-by-pms-equality-pledge/; https://globalvoices.org/2020/09/17/barbados-declares-intent-to-recognise-same-sex-unions-and-remove-british-queen-as-head-of-state/; https://www.independent.co.uk/news/world/americas/barbados-lgbt-rights-republic-b1972082.html; and https://www.nationnews.com/2022/12/13/buggery-laws-struck-supreme-court/.

5. The local queer groups working in partnership with AIDS-Free World were Community Education, Empowerment & Development; the Latin American and Caribbean Network of Transgender People; the Barbados Gays, Lesbians Against Discrimination; Empowerment, Quality, Unity, Acceptance, Love, Strength; and the Movement Against Discrimination Action Committee. See Atwell 2017.

6. In Guyana, I met with three representatives from the group who provided a comprehensive overview of the work the organization was in the process of doing, which at

the time of this research pivoted on three large program areas. Firstly, its "Anti-Homophobia Initiative," a youth-led social change project sought to sensitize citizens about homophobia and transphobia by engaging prominent stakeholders, included academics, religious groups, the private sector, and government ministers. Secondly, a "Human Services Project" attempted to increase access to basic human services like education, employment, sexual and mental health amenities, and housing. SASOD's third, and most prominent, focus area was its human rights program, which sought legal and policy reform through strategic litigation—for instance, a law and policy reform campaign, done in partnership with the US State Department, sought to "amend the Prevention of Discrimination Act 1997 that exists particularly for employment and governs improvement, pension, access to and membership in various associations. There are a number of grounds listed in this Act but sexual orientation and gender identity are not. So, part of the project is working toward the amendment of that Act to include sexual orientation and gender identity as grounds so LGBT persons could be protected in the workplace" (SASOD's Advocacy and Communications Coordinator, December 2016).

7. Envisioning, led by Nancy Nicol, professor of visual arts at York University in Toronto, was part of a larger project titled Envisioning Global LGBT Human Rights. The Canadian subsidiary, which comprised a team of academics, activists, and community groups received CAD$1,000,000 (SSHRC 2011) in funding from Canada's Social Sciences and Humanities Research Council for a five-year (2011–2016) project to investigate (1) the laws that criminalize same-sex sexual intimacy in commonwealth countries, (2) movements to decriminalize these laws, (3) the relationship between United Nations human rights mechanisms and LGBT rights initiatives, and (4) issues affecting asylum seekers in Canada (Nicol, Gates-Gasse, and Mule 2014, 2). To this end, it has worked with partners in India, Uganda, Kenya, Botswana, Saint Lucia, Jamaica, Belize, and Guyana to produce video shorts, documentaries, a Toronto World Pride 2014 conference, and an exhibition titled *Imagining Home: Migration, Resistance, Contradiction* at the Canadian Lesbian and Gay Archives (CLGA). These outputs have similarly framed Caribbean queers as needing to escape a violently homophobic region in order to fully actualize their queerness.

8. Its first report, Envisioning LGBT Refugee Rights in Canada: Exploring Asylum Issues, identified a number of areas where research was needed on LGBT refugee issues, including (1) the experiences of LGBT refugees and obstacles that they encounter; (2) the legal and social service contexts that affect LGBT refugee claimant; (3) the impact of changes to Canada's immigration and refugee policy and law during this period; and (4) the need to raise awareness about the impact of these legal and policy changes with refugee claimants, service agencies, the general public, and public policy administrators (Nicol, Gates, and Mule 2013, 13). Its second report, Envisioning LGBT Refugee Rights in Canada: The Impact of Canada's New Immigration Regime (2014), focused "specifically on the implementation of Bill C-31 and the impact of the resulting Protecting Canada's Immigration System Act on LGBT refugees in Canada." Its final report, Envisioning LGBT Refugee Rights in Canada: Is Canada a Safe Haven? (2014), "presents an analysis of the data collected between June 2012 and May 2014 in focus groups with LGBT refugees on their experiences and the obstacles they face" (13).

9. Nancy Nicol, professor of visual arts at York University in Toronto.

10. Viviane Namaste's (2011, 42) argument that "certain kinds of speech are not allowed, while others can only occur in select contexts" provides useful context here to

NOTES TO PAGES 46–57

emphasize the silencing of numerous other identities, sexualities, and praxes that share spaces of queerness in the region.

11. The funding landscape has been changing since completing my fieldwork. The Women's Voice and Leadership-Caribbean partnership with the Astraea Lesbian Foundation for Justice, started in 2019/2020, offers responsive grants to organizations doing work with women and LBTQ+ communities, where community-informed initiatives are prioritized for funding and support. Likewise, CAISO also partnered with Astraea in 2021 for a Caribbean responsive grant mechanism to provide funding and support for community organizations that prioritize the needs of Lesbian, Bisexual, and Trans (LBT) communities. CAISO also launched its wholeness and justice program in 2020 with funding from Arcus and Astraea. Unlike much of what was happening while I conducted research, these collaborations have allowed these groups to build relationships with the funders and get operations support while prioritising trans and intersex people, especially those who are working class.

12. They used the term "Amerindian" to identify their indigeneity.

13. Or as Jasbir Puar (2007, 9) discusses of homonormative queer politics, these kinds of interventions fail to "necessarily contradict or undermine heterosexual exceptionalism; in actuality [they] may support forms of heteronormativity and class, racial, and citizenship privileges they require."

CHAPTER 2 — ON THE GROUND

1. As M. Jacqui Alexander (1997, 83) expounds, "No nationalism could survive without heterosexuality—criminal, perverse, temporarily imprisoned, incestuous or as abusive as it might be, nationalism needs it. It still remains more conducive to nation-building than same-sex desire, which is downright hostile to it, for women presumably cannot love themselves, love other women, and love the nation simultaneously."

2. See Alexander 2005, Ghisyawan 2016, Gill 2018, and Tinsley 2018 for discussions on sacred practices among queer people in the Caribbean.

3. See https://tt.vlex.com/vid/mitchell-v-attorney-general-793513433 for more information on this ruling. Amar Wahab (2012, 483) reads this event as "a way to understand homophobic policing that is at once a form of state rational practice even as these practices are systematically erased from truth-seeking inquiries that attempt to critique state reason." He argues that the strip search represented "the state's capacity to calibrate its coercive force, especially when noncompliant subjects question the limits of its coercive power" (492).

4. In analyzing the Colywn Harding case in Guyana, Alissa Trotz (2014, 355) argues that such state-sanctioned violence by the police "underlines the authoritative status accorded to violent, predatory and heteronormative masculinist norms, in which the act of penetration with a police baton operates as an instrument of emasculation and violent subordination" of the nonheteronormative other.

5. Many other constitutional challenges have been filed across the Caribbean since completing this research. The latest ruling to remove colonial buggery laws in Antigua and Barbuda was proclaimed in June 2022.

6. It is interesting to note that archbishop reverted to some problematic statements about sexual orientation and gender identity, claiming that gender ideology is a "diabolical" social construct that is a lie and should not be supported by Christians." See https://

newsday.co.tt/2021/07/04/rc-archbishop-gordon-gender-ideology-a-diabolical-lie/ for more context.

7. See Joseph Massad's *Desiring Arabs* (2007).

8. Guyana's Summary Jurisdiction (Offences) Act 10 of 1998, Chapter 8.02 Act V Section 143(b) titled Offences Against Religion, Morality and Public Convenience states that anyone who "wanders abroad, or places himself in any public way or public place, or intrudes in any private premises after being lawfully ordered to depart, and uses any solicitation, means, or device to induce the bestowal of alms upon him, or causes, procures, or encourages any other person to do so . . . is liable to a fine of not more or less than seven thousand five hundred dollars nor more than fifteen thousand dollars or to imprisonment for two months."

9. https://caisott.org/add-all-three-campaign.

10. https://caisott.org/responsive-grants.

11. See AJD's website for more information: https://justicediversitytt.wordpress.com /about-2/.

12. In its inaugural documentation, the AJD explained that it aimed to "pursue a suite of linked activities (with families, teachers, counsellors, men in local communities, police, scholars, students, community organizers, media, and legislators)" aimed at influencing "a sexual culture of justice" in Trinidad and Tobago through change in societal thinking. We envision this "sexual culture of justice" as advocacy for social change to gender norms and sexual rights, which is grounded in local analysis and action-based research" (Alliance for Justice and Diversity 2017).

13. To make a sound of disgust or displeasure by sucking air and saliva through the teeth. See Lize Winer's (2008) *Dictionary of Trinidad and Tobago Creole English* for more context.

14. The Alliance for Justice and Diversity's approach to their Sexual Culture of Justice (SCJ) project was an attempt to do this as organizations were able to utilize money received from the European Union grant to do their work. Further, many members of the alliance were able to produce research and outputs that have since been used to strengthen regional organizations and become more sustainable and rooted in local and regional needs. For example, CAISO's 2020 Policy Agenda (see: https://gspottt .wordpress.com/what-we-do-2/2020-lgbti-policy-agenda-2-0/) and the associated community engagements, and its life histories research with working-class LGBTQI+ people was funded by the SCJ project but was completely designed and facilitated through a local team and rooted in a regional queer praxis. I am keenly aware of the complexity of my own ongoing engagement with CAISO and queer and trans communities while I analyze the work that is being done. While conducting fieldwork, I was part of the CAISO team working on the EU grant, and since completing this research, I volunteer with the organization on various projects. As a scholar interrogating the stakes of activist work in the region, then, I am also implicated in offering knowledge about regional queer politics that is produced and contextualized a particular moment, but I must underscore that this discussion needs to be understood within broader constantly evolving contexts beyond this project.

CHAPTER 3 — BETWEEN THE WALLS

1. While this chapter does not address trans people specifically, and only suggests their potential presence within these kinds of abandoned spaces, "trans" offers a modality,

NOTES TO PAGES 94–124

a way of being and operating in normative space as a gender- or sexually nonconforming person. Transness "attends to the generative force embedded in the desire for destruction. Transness models an anarchist modality" wherein the passion for destruction is also a creative passion (Bey 2021, 198). Trans entails the tearing down of epistemic and institutional structures and the building up of new ways of being within these spaces. Likewise, the abandoned hotels are not necessarily as unproductive as they are imagined to be in nationalist and heterosexist discourses of respectability; rather, they are transgressive and allow us to be attentive to the ways that queer people are envisioning alternative ways of belonging within contexts of hostility, homophobia, transphobia, and discrimination. The hotels represent a breakdown of the normative social order and the recreation of new modalities of being.

2. The Rastafari way of life guided by principles of purity, anti-secularism and an avoidance of worldly pleasures.

3. It is important to note that not all people with locs are Rasta or ascribe to Rastafari livity. However, it is not uncommon in the Caribbean to refer to people who wear locs as Rasta. Therefore, because we are unaware of who is writing here, we are also unaware of which "Rasta" is really being referred to. This, however, opens up an important conversation about the kinds of baggage that labels carry in the Caribbean.

4. Mia Motley's political party was successful in two successive national elections in 2018 and 2022, winning all thirty electoral seats in Parliament. She also successfully removed the queen of England as Barbados's head of state in 2021, a move that previous leaders have shied away from over the years.

CHAPTER 4 — QUEENS, KINGS, AND KINSHIP NETWORKS

1. A form of dancing in Trinidad and Tobago and the Caribbean, which is characterized by moving one's hip in a circular motion in time with the upbeat tempo of soca and other forms of music.

2. Ballroom is an art form, way of life, and underground queer culture created by Black queers and other queers of color in the United States during the 1970s and 1980s at the height of the HIV/AIDS epidemic. These communities provided a safe space for queer people who were estranged from their families and mainstream society to support each other emotionally, financially, spiritually, and so on. Up until Ballroom culture was co-opted by mainstream popular culture and made popular by icons like Madonna in the 1980s and 1990s, it remained relatively underground and within the realms of the poor, working-class queer people.

3. If they have access to a physical house, which is not always the case. At the time of my research, there were a few physical residences where trans women and other queer people would live together. Others who were unable to afford housing because of a lack of stable income, their careers in sex work, or their trans visibilities often lived in abandoned houses in the city. These houses would generally have no electricity, running water, and other basic amenities.

4. Refers to someone who was assigned female at birth, but identifies their gender as masculine, but not necessarily as male. Can also include nonbinary persons, genderfluid people, genderqueer people—anyone assigned female at birth whose gender falls in the more masculine range.

5. I use a pseudonym here for this organization as it was just being formalized at the time of my research and held limited public presence.

NOTES TO PAGES 136–165

CHAPTER 5 — RUMSHOPS, NIGHTLIFE, AND THE RADICAL PRAXIS OF INTERNAL EXILE

1. A traditional gambling card game inherited from England in Trinidad and Tobago. It involves four players forming two teams who compete against each other and "hang" the opponent's "Jack." The first team to amass fourteen points wins the game. In Trinidad and Tobago, competitive tournaments are typically held in bars and rumshops for prizes ranging from cash to alcohol and household appliances—and of course, bragging rights.

2. Trinbagonian slang for penis. Other variations include "dick," "wood," "hood," "cockie," and many more terms across the Anglophone Caribbean.

3. Chain store specializing in cosmetics and toiletries.

4. Marc's experiences with cis-gender men are in line with Gloria Wekker's (2006, 73) theorization of Mati work and Afro-Surinamese women's negotiation of intimacy where "erotic and sexual relations between women are public, acknowledged, validated and often openly celebrated."

5. I use a pseudonym for these establishments upon Sandy's request.

6. A term used by many queer people in Trinidad and Tobago to refer to (typically) Black, hypermasculine, working-class men.

7. A form of dancing in Trinidad and Tobago and the Caribbean, which is characterized by moving one's hip in a circular motion in time with the upbeat tempo of soca and other forms of music.

8. I am not repositioning the type of alcohol use explored in chapter 4 as influencing violence in the space. Rather, I am deliberately drawing connections to show how deeply rooted and pervasive issues of alcohol consumption is in a region whose history of sugarcane plantation and enslavement birthed a vast industry.

9. Guyanese expletive typically used to express anger or surprise, or to add extra contextual flare to an exclamation.

10. According to the Peace Corp (n.d.), 912 volunteers have visited Guyana since its program was implemented between 1966 and 1971, and then again from 1995 to present. Volunteers currently visit under four major projects—Education, Health, Environment and Let Girls Learn—and work with government institutions, in rural communities, and with community organizations (Westmaas 2008).

11. Guyana's Mashramani festival, which commemorates the country becoming a republic on February 23, 1970, is celebrated annually on that date (Lutchman 1970, 98). The Jaycees of Linden first started the celebrations in 1966 when Guyana gained independence, and it featured masquerade bands performing in the streets as an Afro-Guyanese celebration (*Guyana Chronicle* 2011). After the country received its republican status in 1970, the celebration was adopted on a national scale and moved to the capital city, Georgetown, where large groups parade along the streets dancing to calypso, soca, and other music in elaborate costumes, similar to the Carnival festivities across the region.

CODA

1. https://caisott.org/responsive-grants.

2. https://equalityfund.ca/what-we-do/womens-voice-and-leadership-caribbean/.

References

Agard-Jones, Vanessa. 2012. "What the Sands Remember." *GLQ* 18 (2–3): 325–346.

———. 2013. "Bodies in the System." *Small Axe: A Caribbean Journal of Criticism* 17 (3 [42]): 182–192.

Ahmed, Sara. 2006. "Orientations: Toward a Queer Phenomenology." *GLQ: Journal of Lesbian and Gay Studies* 12: 4.

AIDS-Free World. 2013. "Police Attend LGBT Human Rights Training Sessions in the Caribbean." Accessed February 3, 2016. http://www.aidsfreeworld.org/Publications-Multimedia/Countdown-to-Tolerance/2013/May/Suriname-Police-Training.aspx.

Alexander, Jacqui M. 1994. "Not Just (Any) Body Can Be a Citizen: The Politics of Law, Sexuality and Postcoloniality in Trinidad and Tobago and the Bahamas." *Feminist Review* 48: 5–23.

———. 1997. "Erotic Autonomy as a Politics of Decolonization." In *Feminist Genealogies, Colonial Legacies, Democratic Futures*, edited by M. Jacqui Alexander and Chandra Talpade Mohanty, 63–100. New York: Routledge.

———. 2005. *Pedagogies of Crossing: Meditations on Feminism, Sexual Politics, Memory, and the Sacred*. Durham, NC: Duke University Press.

Allen, Caroline F., and Juliette Maughan. 2016. *Country Gender Assessment (CGA) Barbados*. Barbados: Caribbean Development Bank.

Allen, Jafari S. 2011. *¡Venceremos?: The Erotics of Black Self-Making in Cuba*. Durham, NC: Duke University Press.

———. 2016. "Black/Queer Rhizomatics. Train Up a Child the Way Ze Should Grow . . ." In *No Tea No Shade: New Writings in Black Queer Studies*, edited by E. Patrick Johnson, 27–47. Durham, NC: Duke University Press.

Alliance for Justice and Diversity. 2017. "Take Care of Each Other's Safety, LGBTQI NGOs Urge Community, Launching First Phase of Campaign," March 23, 2017. https://justicediversitytt.wordpress.com.

———. 2018. "A Group of Six Faith Leaders Have Lost Their Way." Press Release. June 13, 2018.

Altman, Dennis. 2002. *Global Sex*. Chicago: University of Chicago Press.

Alturi, Tara. 2001. "When the Closet Is a Region: Homophobia, Heterosexism and Nationalism in the Commonwealth Caribbean." *Working Paper* 5:281–325.

Anderson, Fiona. 2015. "Cruising the Queer Ruins of New York's Abandoned Waterfront." *Performance Research: Journal of the Performing Arts* 20 (3): 135–144.

Anglin, Suelle. 2016. "The New Era of Advocacy." *Pride Ja Magazine Issue 1*. Accessed July 10, 2017. https://issuu.com/j-flag/docs/prideja_magazine_issue_1.

Armstrong, Neil. 2017. "PRiDE JA 2017 Invites Canadians to Attend the 3rd Annual Celebrations in August." Accessed July 10, 2017. https://anglescovered.blogspot.com /2017/07/pride-ja-2017-invites-canadians-to.html.

Attai, Nikoli. 2013. *Trans T&T: An Investigation of Transgender Lives and Communities in Trinidad and Tobago*. Master's thesis, University of the West Indies, Saint Augustine, Trinidad.

Atwell, Carlos. 2017. "Cops get LGBTI Sensitivity Training." *Nation News*, March 17, 2017. http://www.nationnews.com/nationnews/news/94675/cops-lgbti-sensitivity-training.

Avery, Dan. 2018. "Trinidad Decriminalizes Homosexuality in Landmark Court Case." *Logo New Now Next*, April 12, 2018. http://www.newnownext.com/trinidad-decrimi nalizes-homosexuality-in-landmark-court-case/04/2018/.

Bailey, Marlon M. 2013. *Butch Queens Up in Pumps: Gender, Performance, and Ballroom Culture in Detroit*. Ann Arbor: University of Michigan Press.

———. 2016. "Black (Gay) Raw Sex." In *No Tea No Shade: Hew Writings in Black Queer Studies*, edited by E. Patrick Johnson, 239–261. Durham, NC: Duke University Press.

Barbados Tourism Investment. (n.d.). *Tourism Profile*. https://www.barbadostourism investment.com/tourism-profile/.

Barbera, Rosemary A. 2008. "Internal Exile: Effects on Families and Communities." *Refuge* 25 (1): 69–76.

Barratt, Sue Ann, and Aleah N. Ranjitsingh. 2021. *Dougla in the Twenty-First Century: Adding to the Mix*. Jackson: University of Mississippi Press.

Bedasse, Monique. 2017. *Jah Kingdom: Rastafarians, Tanzania, and Pan-Africanism in the Age of Decolonization*. Chapel Hill: University of North Carolina Press.

Bey, Marquis. 2021. "Trouble Genders: "LGBT" Collapse and Trans Fundamentality." *Hypatia* 36: 191–206.

———. 2022. *Black Trans Feminism*. Durham, NC: Duke University Press.

Bishop, Matthew. 2010. "Tourism as a Small-state Development Strategy: Pier Pressure in the Eastern Caribbean?" *Progress in Development Studies*, 10 (2): 107.

Bisnauth, Dale. 1989. *History of Religions in the Caribbean*. Kingston: Kingston Publishers.

Boduszek, Daniel, et al. 2017. "Victimisation, violence perpetration, and attitudes towards violence among boys and girls from Barbados and Grenada." *Research Report*. Huddersfield: University of Huddersfield. http://eprints.hud.ac.uk/id/eprint/32544/.

Bri Sweetness. 2013. "A Day With Saucy Pow @ The Chaguaramas Boardwalk." https:// www.youtube.com/watch?v=XunkoKurKWM.

Broderick, Jalna. 2014. "Jamaica." Interview by Nanci Nicol. *Telling Our Stories*, n.d. Video, 5:24. http://envisioning-tellingourstories.blogspot.com/p/jamaica-2.html.

Browne, Janine. 2017. "Human Rights Activist Challenges AG On Laws That Impinge On LGBT Rights." *CTV News*, February 23, 2017. Accessed September 13. http://ctvtt .com/ctv/index.php/c-news/news/item/46872-human-rights-activist-challenges-ag -on-laws-that-impinge-on-lgbt-rights.

REFERENCES

Butterworth, Benjamin. 2018. "Amber Rudd Announces Major Fund to Help End Anti-Gay Laws in Commonwealth Countries." *Pink News*, April 19, 2018. https://www.pinknews.co.uk/2018/04/19/amber-rudd-announces-major-fund-to-help-end-anti-gay-laws-in-commonwealth-countries/.

Cabezas, Amalia L. 2019. "Latin American and Caribbean Sex Workers: Gains and Challenges in the Movement." *Anti-Trafficking Review* 12: 27–56.

CAISO. 2010a. "We Take a Pride in our Liberty." *GSPOTTT*, October 17. 2010. https://gspottt.wordpress.com/2010/10/17/we-take-a-pride-in-our-liberty/.

Caribbean Court of Justice. 2018. "CCJ Declares Guyanese Cross-Dressing Law Unconstitutional." November 13, 2018. https://ccj.org/ccj-declares-guyanas-cross-dressing-law-unconstitutional/.

———. 2010b. "The Real Story: Tune In." *GSPOTTT*, October 27, 2010. https://gspottt.wordpress.com/2010/10/27/the-real-story-tune-in/.

———. 2010c. "Christians Declare War on Love: Don't Let Them Outshout You!" *GSPOTTT*, October 10, 2010. https://gspottt.wordpress.com/2010/10/24/christians-declare-war-on-love/.

———. 2015a. "God Hates Folks Who Tell Folks Who God Hates." *Trinidad Express*, February 8, 2015.

———. 2015b. "You Could Cock up Your Foot on Couch if You Want." *Trinidad Express*, February 25, 2015.

Carrico, Christopher. 2012. *Collateral Damage: The Social Impact of Laws Affecting LGBT People in Guyana*. Bridgetown: UWI Right Advocacy Project.

Carty, Linda, and Monisha Das Gupta. 2009. "Solidarity Work in Transnational Feminism: The Question of Class and Location." In *Activist Scholarship: Antiracism, Feminism, and Social Change*, edited by Julia Sudbury and Okazawa Rey, 95–110. Boulder, CO: Paradigm Publishers.

Charles, Dee Lundy. 2013. "Police Schooled in Sensitivity Towards Gays." *St. Lucia Star*, September 2, 2013. https://stluciastar.com/police-schooled-in-sensitivity-towards-gays/?fb_source=pubv1.

Chaudhuri, Soma. 2017. "Witches, Activists, and Bureaucrats: Navigating Gatekeeping in Qualitative Research." *International Journal of Sociology* 47 (2): 131–145.

Chevannes, Barry. 2001. *Learning to Be a Man: Culture, Socialization, and Gender Identity in Five Caribbean Communities*. Barbados: University of the West Indies Press.

Cliff, Michelle. 1987. *No Telephone to Heaven*. New York: Dutton Penguin.

CNC3. 2012. "CNC3 Indepth LGBT Special Report." *CNC 3 Television*, March 19, 2012. https://www.youtube.com/watch?v=BDB6HLCJwbQ&index=6&list=PLj_ePdbwM3j8mS8eUC3NHlEDRfTiyRcOn.

Cohen, Cathy J. 1997. "Punks, Bulldaggers and Welfare Queens: The Radical Potential of Queer Politics?" *GLQ* 3:437–465.

———. 2004. "Deviance as Resistance: A New Research Agenda for the Study of Black Politics." *Du Bois Review: Social Science Research on Race* 1 (1): 27–45.

Crichlow, Wesley E. A. 2004. "History, (Re) Memory and Biomythography: Charting a Buller Man's Trinidadian Past." In *Interrogating Caribbean Masculinities: Theoretical and Empirical Analyses*, edited by Rhoda Reddock, 185–222. Kingston: UWI Press.

———. 2014. "Hyperheterosexualization and Hypermasculinity: Challenges for HIV/AIDS Intervention in the Caribbean Trinidad and Tobago." *International Journal of Sociology and Anthropology* 6 (1): 28–41.

Cumberbatch, Shawn. 2017. "Battle for Millions." *Nation News*, June 23, 2017. http://www
.nationnews.com/nationnews/news/98023/battle-millions.

Daily Express. 2010. "Dealing with Same Sex Attraction." *Daily Express*, October 23,
2010. Accessed March 15, 2016. http://www.trinidadexpress.com/news/Dealing_with
_same_sex_attraction_-105614443.html.

Daily Xtra. 2017. "Inside Montego Bay Pride." YouTube, November 3, 2017. https://www
.youtube.com/watch?v=hg3EOYyVU_4.

DeShong, Halima. 2012. "What Does It 'Really' Mean to Be a Wo/Man?: Narratives of
Gender by Women and Men." In *Love and Power: Caribbean Discourses on Gender*,
edited by Eudine Barriteau, 106–150. Kingston: UWI Press.

De Souza, Janelle. 2018. "Rebuild TT Not Anti-gay." *Trinidad and Tobago Newsday*,
June 16, 2018. http://newsday.co.tt/2018/06/16/rebuildtt-not-anti-gay/.

De Trini, Shemika. 2015. "Trini Drag Queen—Saucy Pow." Accessed August 12, 2017.
https://www.youtube.com/watch?v=YVtaMXeIwwo&list=PLj_ePdbwM3j8mS8eUC3
NHlEDRfTiyRcOn&index=2.

Dovkants, Keith. 2012. "Paradise Postposed." *Evening Standard*, April 13, 2012. https://
www.standard.co.uk/hp/front/paradise-postponed-6826496.html.

Editor. 2018. "Carrington wants Mia to Say if She is Gay." *Barbados Today*, May 23, 2018.
https://barbadostoday.bb/2018/05/23/carrington-wants-mia-to-say-if-she-is-gay/.

Edmondson, Belinda. 2009. *Caribbean Middlebrow: Leisure, Culture and the Middle
Class*. New York: Cornell University Press.

Ellis, Nadia. 2011. "Out and Bad: Toward a Queer Performance Hermeneutic in Jamaican Dancehall." *Small Axe: A Caribbean Journal of Criticism* 15 (2 [35]): 7–23.

Espinet, Ramabai. 2003. *The Swinging Bridge*. Toronto: Harper Perennial Press.

European Union External Action. 2017. "A Sexual Culture of Justice: Strengthening
LGBTQI & GBV Partnerships, Capacity & Efficacy to Promote & Protect Rights in
T&T," May 30, 2017. https://eeas.europa.eu/headquarters/headquarters-homepage/27110
/sexual-culture-justice-strengthening-lgbtqi-gbv-partnerships-capacity-efficacy-pro
mote-protect-ga.

Ford-Smith, Honor. 1989. *Ring Ding in a Tight Corner*. Toronto: ICAE.

Franca, Alida Carloni. 2020. "The Internal Exile of Dalit Women in Andra Pradesh." In
India in the World, edited by Cristina M. Gámez-Fernández. Cambridge Scholars
Publishing.

Garofalo, Piero, Elizabeth Leake, and Dana Renga. 2013. *Internal Exile In Fascist Italy:
History And Representations Of Confine*. Manchester: Manchester University Press.

Ghisyawan, Krystal. 2013. "'Because I'z a lesbian, they feel I have a penis': An analysis of
gender-roles in family work." Presented at the IGDS 20th Anniversary Conference on
"Continuities, Challenges and Transformations in Caribbean Gender Relations."
University of the West Indies, November 6, 2013.

———. 2016. "Queering Cartographies of Caribbean Sexuality and Citizenship: Mapping Female Same-Sex Desire, Identities and Belongings in Trinidad." PhD diss.,
University of the West Indies.

———. 2022. *Erotic Cartographies: Decolonization and the Queer Caribbean Imagination*. New Brunswick, NJ: Rutgers University Press.

Ghisyawan, Krystal, Yasphal Kissoon, and Katija Khan. 2019. "Trinidad & Tobago
National School Climate Survey Report 2019: Bullying and Gender-Based Violence in
Secondary Schools." Port of Spain: *The Silver Lining Foundation*.

REFERENCES

Gill, Lyndon, K. 2012. "Chatting Back an Epidemic Caribbean Gay Men, HIV/AIDS, and the Uses of Erotic Subjectivity." *GLQ: A Journal of Lesbian and Gay Studies* 18 (2–3): 277–295.

———. 2018. *Erotic Islands: Art and Activism in the Queer Caribbean*. Durham, NC: Duke University Press.

Gordon, Todd. 2010. *Imperialist Canada*. Winnipeg: Arbeiter Ring Publishing.

Gosine, Andil. 2005. "Stumbling into Sexualities: International Discourse Discovers Dissident Desire." *Canadian Woman Studies* 24 (2–3): 59–63.

———. 2015. "CAISO, CAISO: Negotiating Sex Rights and Nationalism in Trinidad and Tobago." *Sexualities* 18 (7): 859–884.

Gossett, Reina, Eric A. Stanley, and Johanna Burton, eds. 2017. *Trapdoor: Trans Cultural Production and the Politics of Visibility*. Boston: MIT Press.

Guyana Chronicle. 2011. "The Origin of Mashramani." *Guyana Chronicle*. February 23, 2011. Accessed August 29, 2018. http://guyanachronicle.com/2011/02/23/the-origin -of-mashramani.

———. 2012. "Dutch Bottle Café Re-opening." *Guyana Chronicle*. February 04, 2012. Accessed August 29, 2018. http://guyanachronicle.com/2012/02/04/dutch-bottle-cafe -re-opening.

———. 2017a. "Cross Dressing Ruling Upheld by Appeal Court." *Guyana Chronicle*. February 27, 2017. https://guyanachronicle.com/2017/02/27/cross-dressing-ruling-upheld -by-appeal-court.

———. 2017b. "Appeal Court Upholds Ruling on Cross-Dressing." February 28, 2017. https:// guyanachronicle.com/2017/02/28/appeal-court-upholds-ruling-on-cross-dressing/.

Hawkey, Alexandra J. et al. 2021. "Trans Women's Responses to Sexual Violence: Vigilance, Resilience, and Need for Support." *Archives of Sexual Behavior* 50: 3201–3222.

Help and Shelter. 2013. "Break the Silence, Stop the Violence." *Help and Shelter*. Accessed August 29, 2018. http://www.hands.org.gy/.

Heron, Barbara. 2007. *Desire for Development: Whiteness, Gender, and the Helping Imperative*. Waterloo: Wilfrid Laurier University Press.

Hewitt, Roderick. 2016. "The Influences of Conservative Christianity, Rastafari and Dance Hall Music within Jamaica on Homophobia and Stigma against People Living with HIV and AIDS." *Alternation* 23(2): 169–184.

Hoad, Neville Wallace. 2007. *African Intimacies: Race, Homosexuality, and Globalization*. Minneapolis: University of Minnesota Press.

Hodge, Merle. 2002. "We Kind of Family." In *Gendered Realities: An Anthology of Essays in Caribbean Feminist Thought*, edited by Patricia Mohammed, 474–485. Kingston: UWI Press.

Hong, Grace Kyungwon. 2015. *Death Beyond Disavowal: The Impossible Politics of Difference*. Minneapolis: University of Minnesota Press.

Hudson, Kris. 2010. "Barbados Shores Up a Troubled Four Seasons." *Wall Street Journal*, January 22, 2010.

Hudson, Peter James. 2017. *Bankers and Empire: How Wall Street Colonized the Caribbean*. Chicago: University of Chicago Press.

Hunte, Barry. 2014. "St. Lucia." Accessed July 27, 2017. http://envisioning-tellingourstories .blogspot.com/p/st-lucia-2.html.

Jackson, Shona. 2016. "Sexual Sovereignty in the Caribbean and Its Diasporas." *Theory and Event* 19 (4). https://muse.jhu.edu/article/633274.

Johnson, Patrick E. 2003. *Appropriating Blackness: Performance and the Politics of Identity.* Durham: Duke University Press.

Jones V. The Attorney General of Trinidad and Tobago, CV 2017–0072. Trinidad and Tobago High Court of Justice (2018).

Justice K. S. Puttaswamy (Retd) and ANR v. Union of India and Others. 494 of 2012. D. Y. Chandrachud (The Supreme Court of India, August 24, 2017). https://indian kanoon.org/doc/91938676/.

Kempadoo, Kamala. 2004. *Sexing the Caribbean: Gender, Race, and Sexual Labor.* New York: Routledge.

———. 2009. "Caribbean Sexuality: Mapping the Field." *Caribbean Review of Gender Studies* 3: 1–24.

Khatoon, Bibi. 2017. "Palm Court All Set for a Mind Blowing Mash Parade with Trinity Band." *News Room*, February 3, 2017. https://newsroom.gy/2017/02/03/palm-court-all -set-for-a-mind-blowing-mash-2017-parade-with-trinity-band/.

King, Rosamond S. 2014. *Island Bodies: Transgressive Sexualities in the Caribbean Imagination.* Gainesville: University Press of Florida.

Konshens. 2013. *Walk and Wine / On Your Face (Official Music Video).* Accessed August 15, 2017. https://www.youtube.com/watch?v=xxmYLNroNxM.

Kumar, Preity. 2018. "Women Lovin' Women: An Exploration of Identities, Belonging, and Communities in Urban and Rural Guyana." PhD diss. York University, Toronto.

La Vende, Jensen. 2016. "Saucy Pow Denied Bail on Sex Charge." *Trinidad Guardian*, January 15, 2016. Accessed September 23, 2017. http://www.guardian.co.tt/news/2016 -01-15/'saucy-pow'-denied-bail-sex-charge.

Lang, Nico. 2018. "Theresa May Urges 37 Countries to Repeal Sodomy Laws amid Pressure from LGBTQ Advocates." *Into More*, April 17, 2018. https://intomore.com/culture /theresa-may-urges-37-countries-to-repeal-sodomy-laws-amid-pressure-from-lgbtq -advocates/6cff2c990adb4ab4.

Lazarus, Latoya. 2013. *The Church and the Law: Examining the Role of Christianity in Shaping Sexual Politics in Jamaica.* PhD diss., York University.

———. 2016. "Religion and Rights: Is there Still Room for Christianity at the Table? *Culture and Religion* 17 (1): 35–55.

Lewis, Linden, ed. 2002. "Envisioning a Politics of Change within Caribbean Gender Relations." In *Gendered Realities: An Anthology of Essays in Caribbean Feminist Thought*, 512–530. Kingston: University of the West Indies Press.

———. 2003. *The Culture of Gender and Sexuality in the Caribbean.* 1st ed. Gainesville: University Press of Florida.

Loop TT. 2018. "Pundit Slams Religious Protests: Gay Rights Are Human Rights." April 9, 2018. www.looptt.com/content/pundit-slams-religious-protests-gay-rights-are-human -rights.

Lorde, Audre. 1982. *Zami: A New Spelling of My Name.* New York: Crossing Press.

———. 1984. "Uses of the Erotic: The Erotic as Power." In *Sister Outsider: Essays and Speeches by Audre Lorde*, 53–59. New York: Crossing Press.

Love, Heather. 2014. "Queer." *TSQ* 1 (1–2): 172–176.

Lutchman, Harold. 1970. "The Co-Operative Republic of Guyana." *Caribbean Studies* 10 (3): 97–115.

Massad, Joseph A. 2007. *Desiring Arabs.* Chicago: University of Chicago Press.

REFERENCES

Massey, Doreen. 1994. "A Global Sense of Place." In *Space, Place and Gender*, 146–156. Minneapolis: University of Minnesota Press.

Matthews, Janeille Zorina, and Tracy Robinson. 2019. "Modern Vagrancy in the Anglophone Caribbean." *Caribbean Journal of Criminology* 1 (4): 123–154.

McClintock, Anne. 1995. *Imperial Leather: Race, Gender and Sexuality in the Colonial Contest*. New York: Routledge.

McCormack, Jo. 2008. "Memory and Exile: Contemporary France and the Algerian War (1954–1962)." In *Exile Cultures, Misplaced Identities*, edited by Paul Allatson and Jo McCormack, 117–138. Amsterdam: Brill.

McDoom, Vincent. 2014. "St. Lucia." Accessed July 27, 2017. http://envisioning-telling ourstories.blogspot.com/p/st-lucia-2.html.

McKittrick, Catherine. 2014. "Mathematics Black Life." *Black Scholar* 44 (2): 16–28.

Miguel, Corral. 2018. "The Case of Adolescents and Young People who Autonomously Engage in Selling Sex in Latin America and The Caribbean: Recognizing Their Sexual and Reproductive Health Needs and Demands." *MOJ Public Health* 7 (2): 48–52.

Mohammed, Patricia, ed. 2002. "Introduction: The Material of Gender." In *Gendered Realities: An Anthology of Essays in Caribbean Feminist Thought*, xiv-xxiii. Kingston: University of the West Indies Press.

Mohanty, Chandra Talpade. 2003. *Feminism without Borders: Decolonizing Theory, Practicing Solidarity*. Durham, NC: Duke University Press.

Moore, Carla. 2014. "Wah Eye Nuh See Heart Nuh Leap: Queer Marronage in the Jamaican Dancehall." Master's thesis, Queen's University.

Mootoo, Shani. 1996. *Cereus Blooms at Night*. Toronto: Harper Perennials.

Mullings, Beverly. 1999. "Globalization, Tourism and the International Sex Trade." In *Sun, Sex and Gold: Tourism and Sex Work in the Caribbean*, edited by Kamala Kempadoo, 55–80. Lanham, MD: Rowman and Littlefield.

Muñoz, José Esteban. 1999. *Disidentifications: Queers of Color and the Performance of Politics*. Minneapolis: University of Minnesota Press.

———. 2009. *Cruising Utopia: The Then and There of Queer Futurity*. New York: NYU Press.

Murray, David. 2002. *Opacity: Gender, Sexuality, Race, and the "Problem" of Identity in Martinique*. New York: Peter Lang.

———. 2010. "Digisex: Cell-Phones, Barbadian Queens and Circuits of Desire in the Gay Caribbean." *Anthropologica* 52 (1): 103–112.

———. 2012. *Flaming Souls: Homosexuality, Homophobia, and Social Change in Barbados*. University of Toronto Press.

———. 2016. *Real Queer? Sexual Orientation and Gender Identity Refugees in the Canadian Refugee Apparatus*. London: Rowman and Littlefield International.

Namaste, Viviane. 2011. *Sex Change, Social Change: Reflections on Identity, Institutions, and Imperialism*. Toronto: Canadian Scholars' Press.

Neptune, Harvey. 2007. *Caliban and the Yankies: Trinidad and the United States Occupation*. Chapel Hill: University of North Carolina Press.

Nicol, Nancy, Erika Gates-Gasse, and Nick Mule. 2013. "Envisioning Global LGBT Human Rights: Strategic Alliances to Advance Knowledge and Social Change." *Scholarly and Research Communication* 5 (3). http://src-online.ca/src/index.php/src /article/view/165.

———. 2014. *No Easy Walk to Freedom*. Documentary. Accessed August 14, 2018.

———. 2015. "Envisioning LGBT Refugee Rights in Canada: Is Canada a Safe Haven?" *Envisioning LGBT Human Rights.* Report. Toronto: York University.

Nixon, Angelique V. 2015. *Resisting Paradise Tourism, Diaspora, and Sexuality in Caribbean Culture.* Jackson: University Press of Mississippi.

———. 2016. "Troubling Queer Caribbeanness: Embodiment, Gender, and Sexuality in Nadia Huggins's Visual Art." *Queer Caribbean Visualities: A Small Axe Project.* Curated by David Scott, Erica Moiah James, and Nijah Cunningham. 1–16.

Nixon, Angelique V., and Rosamond S. King. 2013. "Embodied Theories: Local Knowledge(s), Community Organizing, and Feminist Methodologies in Caribbean Sexuality Studies." *Caribbean Review of Gender Studies* 7:1–15.

Oppenheim Roger. 1983. "Review." *Journal of the Polynesian Society* 92 (2): 245–257.

Parsad, Basmat Shiw. 1999. "Marital Violence within East Indian Households in Guyana: A Cultural Explanation." In *Matikor: The Politics of Identity for Indo-Caribbean Women,* edited by Rosanne Kanhai, 40–61. Saint Augustine, Trinidad and Togago: University of the West Indies.

Pascar, Lital, Gilly Hartal, and Yossi David. 2015. "Queer Safe Spaces." Conference Paper. III European Geographies of Sexuality Conference. *Crossing Boundaries: Sexualities, Media and (Urban) Spaces,* Sep 16–20, 2015. Rome, Italy.

Persadie, Ryan. 2020. "'Meh Just Realize I's Ah Coolie Bai': Indo-Caribbean Masculinities, Chutney Genealogies, and Qoolie Subjectivities." *Middle Atlantic Review of Latin American Studies* 4 (2): 56–86.

Philip, M. NourbeSe. 1999. *Genealogy of Resistance.* 1st ed. Toronto: Mercury Press.

Phillips, Anthony De V. 1995. "Emancipation Betrayed: Social Control Legislation in the British Caribbean (with Special Reference to Barbados), 1834–1876." *Freedom: Beyond the United States* 70: 1349–1372.

Placide, Kenita. 2014. "St. Lucia." Accessed July 27, 2017. http://envisioning-tellingourstories.blogspot.com/p/st-lucia-2.html.

Protopapa, Alex. 2017. "Jamaicans Invite LGBTIs to Join Them for Pride, Despite Gay Sex Being Illegal." *Gay Star News.* Accessed January 27, 2018. https://www.gaystarnews.com/article/jamaicans-pride-despite-gay-sex-illegal/#gs.MmBpPPk.

Puar, Jasbir K. 2002. "Circuits of Queer Mobility: Tourism, Travel, and Globalization." *GLQ: Journal of Lesbian and Gay Studies* 8 (1): 101–137.

———. 2007. *Terrorist Assemblages: Homonationalism in Queer Times.* Durham, NC: Duke University Press.

Quality of Citizenship Jamaica. 2018. "Press Release: Closure of QCJ." Accessed August 28, 2018. https://qcjm.weebly.com/blog/press-release-closure-of-qcj.

Quetzal, Mia. 2014. "Belize." Accessed July 27, 2017. http://envisioning-tellingourstories.blogspot.com/p/blog-page.html.

Ramoutar, Gavin. 2011. "Antiman." *Caribbean Tales International Film Festival.* Accessed August 1, 2017. http://caribbeantalesfestival.com/project/antiman/.

Ramsaran, Dave, and Linden Lewis. 2018. *Caribbean Masala: Indian Identity in Guyana and Trinidad.* Jackson: University of Mississippi Press.

Razack, Sherene. 1998. *Looking White People in the Eye: Gender, Race and Culture in Courtrooms and Classrooms.* Toronto: University of Toronto Press.

Reddock, Rhoda, ed. 2004. *Interrogating Caribbean Masculinities: Theoretical and Empirical* Kingston: UWI Press.

REFERENCES

Richards, Shirley. 2011. "Charter of Rights and the Moral Divide," *Jamaica Gleaner*, April 10, 2011. Accessed September 7, 2017. http://jamaicagleaner.com/gleaner/20110410/cleisure/cleisure6.html.

Robinson, Tracy. 2009. "Authorised Sex: Same-sex Sexuality and the Law in the Caribbean." In *From Risk to Vulnerability: Power, Culture and Gender in the Spread of HIV and AIDS in the Caribbean*, edited by Christine Barrow, Marjan de Bruin, and Robert Carr, 1–22. Kingston: Ian Randle.

———. 2011. "Our Imagined Lives." In *Sex and the Citizen: Interrogating the Caribbean*, edited by Faith Smith, 201–213. Charlottesville: University of Virginia Press.

Rositanadclemantina. 2009. "Saucy Pau Revealed." Accessed March 21, 2017. https://www.youtube.com/watch?v=wnTTgCDPK2E&index=4&list=PLj_ePdbwM3j8mS8eUC3NHlEDRfTiyRcOn.

Rowley, Michelle. 2011. *Feminist Advocacy and Gender Equity in the Anglophone Caribbean: Envisioning a Politics of Coalition*. New York: Routledge.

Samaroo, Brinsley. 1975. "The Presbyterian Canadian Mission as an Agent of Integration in Trinidad during the Nineteenth and Early Twentieth Centuries." *Caribbean Studies* 14 (4): 41–55.

Sampath, Neils. 1993. "An Evaluation of the 'Creolisation' of Trinidad East Indian Adolescent Masculinity." In *Trinidad Ethnicity*, edited by Kelvin Yelvington. Knoxville: University of Tennessee Press.

Sant, Rosemarie. 2018. "Archbishop: buggery should not be Criminalised." *Trinidad Guardian*, April 15, 2018. http://www.guardian.co.tt/news/2018-04-15/archbishop-buggery-should-not-be-criminalised.

Santos-Febres, Mayra. 2000. *Sirena Selena*. New York: Picador USA.

SASOD. 2013. "Constitutional Court Rules Cross-Dressing is Not a Crime if Not for "Improper Purpose"—Rights Groups Plan Appeal on Dubious Decision" September 27, 2013. Accessed September 7, 2017. https://www.sasod.org.gy/sasod-blog-constitutional-court-rules-cross-dressing-not-crime-if-not-"improper-purpose"-rights.

———. 2016. "Cross-Dressing Suit Set for Appeal Hearing Tomorrow Friday November 18," November 16, 2016. Accessed September 7, 2017. http://www.sasod.org.gy/sasod-blog-cross-dressing-suit-set-appeal-hearing-tomorrow-friday-november-18.

Scheim, Ayden I, et al. 2016. "HIV Epidemics Among Transgender Populations: The Importance of a Trans-inclusive Response." *Journal of the International AIDS Society* 19 (2): 1–7.

Seebaran, Desiree. 2012. "Gay in T&T: The Struggles Against Discrimination." *Trinidad Guardian*, March 31, 2012. Accessed September 5, 2017.

Sexual Culture of Justice. 2017. "The UWI and Civil Society organisations build 'A Sexual Culture of Justice' through transformative approaches to partner violence, homophobia, bullying and policing." Press Release. https://silverliningtt.com/media-release-a-sexual-culture-of-justice-project/.

Sheller, Mimi. 2003. *Consuming the Caribbean: From Arawaks to Zombies*. New York: Routledge.

———. 2012. *Citizenship from Below: Erotic Agency and Caribbean Freedom*. Durham, NC: Duke University Press.

Sidnell, Jack. 2000. "'Primus inter pares': Storytelling and Male Peer Groups in an Indo-Guyanese Rumshop." *American Ethnologist* 27 (1): 72–99.

Silvera, Makeda. 1992. "Man Royals and Sodomites: Some Thoughts on the Invisibility of Afro-Caribbean Lesbians." *Feminist Studies* 18 (3): 521.

Simpson, Joel. 2013. "SASOD at 10: Coming Full Circle." *Stabroek News*, June 10, 2013. Accessed August 28, 2018. https://www.stabroeknews.com/2013/features/in-the-diaspora/06/10/sasod-at-10-coming-full-circle/.

Smith, Frederick H. 2005. *Caribbean Rum: A Social and Economic History.* Gainesville: University Press of Florida.

Smith, Kareem. 2019. "Evangelical Christians Disgusted with LGBT Moves." *Barbados Today*, November 12, 2019. https://barbadostoday.bb/2019/11/12/evangelical-christians-disgusted-with-lgbt-moves/.

Smith, M. G. 1962. *West Indian Family Structure.* Seattle: University of Washington Press.

Smith, Miriam. 1998. "Social Movements and Equality Seeking: The Case of Gay Liberation in Canada." *Canadian Journal of Political Science* 31 (2): 285–309.

Snorton, Riley C. 2014. *Nobody's Supposed to Know: Black Sexuality on the Down Low.* Minneapolis: University of Minnesota Press.

———. 2017. *Black on Both Sides: A Racial History of Trans Identity.* Minneapolis: University of Minnesota Press.

Soomarie, David. 2018. "Now We Are Legal, I Hope to Retire to Trinidad and Tobago with My Husband." *Gay Star News*, April 20, 2018. Accessed August 28, 2018.

Stabroek News. 2009. "He Wore Blue Velvet . . . Seven Fined for Cross-dressing." February 10, 2009. https://www.stabroeknews.com/2009/news/stories/02/10/he-wore-blue-velvetseven-fined-for-cross-dressing/.

———. 2015. "2 A.M. Bar Curfew to Begin This Weekend." *Stabroek News*, July 5, 2015. https://www.stabroeknews.com/2015/news/stories/07/04/2am-bar-curfew-to-begin-this-weekend/.

———. 2017. "Guyanese man found dead in Trinidad." *Stabroek News, January 27, 2017.* https://www.stabroeknews.com/2017/01/27/news/guyana/guyanese-man-found-dead-trinidad/

Stoler, Ann Laura, ed. 2013. *Imperial Debris: On Ruins and Ruination.* Durham, NC: Duke University Press.

Summary Jurisdiction (Offences) Act, Law No. 17 of 1893 (as last amended by Law No. 10, 1998), Laws of Guyana, Ch. 8:02.

Superville, Shane. 2018. "Science, Media and Judiciary Blamed LGBTQI Agenda." *Trinidad and Tobago Newsday*, May 27, 2018. http://newsday.co.tt/2018/05/27/science-media-and-judiciary-blamed/.

Surtees, Joshua. 2018. "Homophobic Laws in Caribbean Could Roll Back in Landmark Case." *Guardia*, April 7, 2018. Accessed August 28, 2018. https://www.theguardian.com/world/2018/apr/07/caribbean-anti-gay-law-ruling-high-court-trinidad-tobago.

Tambiah, Yasmin. 2009. "Creating Immoral Citizens: Gender, Sexuality and Lawmaking in Trinidad and Tobago, 1986." *Caribbean Review of Gender Studies* 3:1–19.

Thomas, Charleston. 2010. "(Un) Clothing Maccomere Man: Female Body as Detour for New Language-Space of Male Homosexuality." *Journal of West Indian Literature* 18 (2): 115–130.

Thompson, Krista. 2007. *An Eye for the Tropics: Tourism, Photography, and Framing the Caribbean Picturesque.* Durham, NC: Duke University Press, 2007.

Tinsley, Omise'eke Natasha. 2010. *Thiefing Sugar: Eroticism between Women in Caribbean Literature.* Durham, NC: Duke University Press.

REFERENCES

———. 2018. *Ezili's Mirrors: Imagining Black Queer Genders*. Durham, NC: Duke University Press.

Tomlinson, Maurice. 2013. "Progress in Barbados despite Harsh Anti-Gay Laws." *76 Crimes*. Accessed August 5, 2017. https://76crimes.com/2013/03/06/progress-in-barbados-despite-harsh-anti-gay-laws/.

———. 2017. "Montego Bay Pride 2017: Pride Is Where I Can Be Free and Truly Express Myself without Fear." Accessed January 27, 2018. "http://www.aidslaw.ca/site/montego-bay-pride-2017-pride-is-where-i-can-be-free-and-truly-express-myself-without-fear/?lang=en.

Trotz, Alissa. 2007. "Going Global? Transnationality, Women/Gender Studies and Lessons from the Caribbean." *Caribbean Review of Gender Studies* 1:1–18.

———. 2013. "The Constitutional Challenge to the Cross-Dressing Law." *Stabroek News*, September 23, 2013. Accessed April 14, 2017. https://www.stabroeknews.com/2013/features/in-the-diaspora/09/23/the-constitutional-challenge-to-the-cross-dressing-law/.

———. 2014. "Sexual Violence and the State in Guyana: Reflecting on the Colwyn Harding Case." *Caribbean Review of Gender Studies* 8: 351–364.

Trouillot, Michel-Rolph. 1995. *Silencing the Past: Power and the Production of History*. Boston: Beacon Press.

UNAIDS. 2018. "Miles to go: The Response to HIV in The Caribbean." *Geneva: Joint United Nations Programme on HIV/AIDS*.

———. 2021. "UNAIDS Data 2021." *Geneva: Joint United Nations Programme on HIV/AIDS*.

Unwin, Rose AMC, K.S. George, I.R. Hambleton, and C. Howitt. 2015. "The Barbados Health of the Nation Survey: Core Findings." *Chronic Disease Research Centre, The University of the West Indies and the Barbados Ministry of Health*, Report, 7.

Verbeke, Ulleli. 2013. "Capturing Migration from the Caribbean to Canada." Accessed February 6, 2018. https://www.verbekeproductions.com/projects/.

VICE News. 2014. "Jamaica's Gully Queens." *Vice*. July 28, 2014. Accessed August 28, 2018. https://www.vice.com/en_ca/article/kwpn4n/young-and-gay-jamaicas-gully-queens-288.

Vivero, Maykel González. 2017. "Trinidad and Tobago: A Nation in the Closet." *Institute for War and Peace Reporting*, September 19, 2017. https://iwpr.net/global-voices/trinidad-and-tobago-nation-closet.

Wahab, Amar. 2012. "Homophobia as the State of Reason: The Case of Postcolonial Trinidad and Tobago." *GLQ: Journal of Lesbian and Gay Studies* 18 (4): 481–505.

Walcott, Rinaldo. 2009. "Queer Returns: Human Rights, the Anglo-Caribbean and Diaspora Politics." *Caribbean Review of Gender Studies* 3:1–19.

Wang, Na, Bo Huang, Yuhua Ruan, K. Rivet Amico, Sten H. Vermund, Shimin Zheng, and Han-Zhu Qian. 2020. "Association between stigma towards HIV and MSM and intimate partner violence among newly HIV-diagnosed Chinese men who have sex with men". *BMC Public Health* 20 (204): 1–8.

Wekker, Gloria. 2006. *The Politics of Passion: Women's Sexual Culture in the Afro-Surinamese Diaspora*. New York: Columbia University Press.

Westmaas, Nigel. 2008. "Reflections on Historical Guyana-US Relations in Wake of Obama's Victory." *Stabroek News*, December 27, 2008. Accessed August 29, 2018. https://www.stabroeknews.com/2008/features/12/28/reflections-on-historical-guyana-us-relations-in-wake-of-obama's-victory/.

Weston, Kath. 1991. *Families We Choose: Lesbians, Gays, Kinship*. New York: Columbia University Press.

Williams, Shariff H. 2012. "In the Heat: Toward a Phenomenology of Black Men Loving/Sexing Each Other." In *Black Genders and Sexualities*, edited by Shaka McGlotten and Dána-Ain Davis, 231–245. New York: Palgrave Macmillan.

Wills, Derwayne. 2017a. "Breaking: Guyana's Court of Appeal Dismisses 'cross Dressing' Appeal." Demerara Waves. February 27, 2017. http://demerarawaves.com/2017/02/27/guyanas-court-of-appeal-dismisses-cross-dressing-appeal/.

———. 2017b. "Transgender Assault Victim Barred from Entering Court as Magistrate Dismisses Case." Demerara Waves. March 2, 2017. http://demerarawaves.com/2017/03/02/transgender-assault-victim-barred-from-entering-court-as-magistrate-dismisses-case/.

Wilson, Peter. 1973. *Crab Antics: The Social Anthropology of English-Speaking Negro Societies of the Caribbean*. London: Yale University Press.

Winer, Lise. 2009. *Dictionary of the English/Creole of Trinidad & Tobago: On Historical Principles*. Kingston: McGill-Queen's Press.

Winner, Michael. 2010. "Michael Winner: Bother on Paradise Beach." *Telegraph*, July 10, 2010. https://www.telegraph.co.uk/news/worldnews/centralamericaandthecaribbean/barbados/7903349/Michael-Winner-Bother-on-Paradise-Beach.html.

Wynter, Sylvia. 2003. "Unsettling the Coloniality of Being/Power/Truth/Freedom: Towards the Human, After Man, Its Overrepresentation—An Argument." *New Centennial Review* 3 (3): 257–337.

Zabus, Chantal. 2013. "Cyaan Live Split: Under-Dressing and Over-Performing, Transgendering, and the Uses of Camouflage in Michelle Cliff's No Telephone to Heaven." In *The Cross-Dressed Caribbean: Writing, Politics, Sexualities*, edited by Maria Cristina Fumagalli, Bénédicte Ledent, and Roberto del Valle Alcalá, 57–73. Charlottesville: University of Virginia Press.

Index

Absence, 21, 22, 23, 27, 47, 88, 104, 108, 109, 121, 140, 166 "absented-presence", 5, 88, 91, 104, 105, 166
Agard-Jones, Vanessa, 40, 81, 173n4
Ahmed, Sara, 100, 101
AIDS, 12, 26, 36, 42, 43, 46–47, 89, 90, 96, 111, 118, 122, 129, 179n2
AIDS-Free World, 33–37, 43, 175n5
alcohol, 91, 92, 108, 136, 139, 151–152, 155, 157, 180n1, 180n8
Alexander, M. Jacqui, 8, 11, 22, 166; citizenship, 43, 81, 106, 164; erotic autonomy, 23, 140; heteropatriarchy in law, 22–23, 43, 54, 96–97; spirituality, 31; technologies of control, 150; unproductive sexuality, 54, 151
Allen, Jafari, 12, 14, 174n13
Alliance for Justice and Diversity, 56, 70, 165, 178n12, 178n14
all-inclusive hotel model, 85–86
Americanized, 66, 114, 118, 133
Amsterdam, 118
anachronistic time, 27, 42, 81, 88
anal sex/sodomy, 55, 100, 130
Anderson, Fiona, 88
anti-gay laws, 59, 63, 93; buggery, 78, 93, 162; criminality, 63, 97, 106, 150; sodomy, 78, 98
Antiman, 11, 19, 173n5
Archdiocese of Port of Spain, 57
Arima, 1, 2, 4, 140, 141
ASPIRE, 68
Astraea Lesbian Foundation for Justice, 66, 69, 176n8, 177n11
asylum, 30, 33, 37, 58, 118, 176n7

Bahamas, 55, 90, 174n10
Bailey, Marlon, 27, 90, 119, 122, 174n12
ballroom, 119, 174n12, 179n2
Barbados, and Canada, 32, 35, 80, 93, 103; labor, 86, 103; Reed Street, 47; tourism, 27, 85–87; trans activism, 47
Barbados Labor Party, 96
Barbados Tourism Investment Incorporated, 85
Barbados Underground, 84
Battyman, 11, 117, 148
Bedasse, Monique, 95
Belize, 37, 38, 55, 90, 165, 174n10, 176n7
Bermuda, 90
Bey, Marquis, 7, 15–16
Big Redz, 1, 140, 146, 147
Bishop, Matthew, 86
body: bodily fluids, 103; bodily horizons, 100; bodily orientation, 100–101; bodily pleasures, 23; bodily practices, 7; bodily rights, 69
black absented presence, 5
bullerman, 2, 11, 90, 100, 146–147
butch, 108, 137; boys, 145; queens, 119

CAISO: Sex and Gender Justice, 26, 50, 58, 65–79, 111, 165, 177n11, 178n9, 178n10, 178n14, 180n1; Homosexual Agenda, 66–67, 111; social class, 3
Canada, 29–42; author, 5, 6; banking, 31; Canadian High Commission, 71; funding, 71, 176n7; intervention, 72; migration and refugee, 5, 174n9, 176n8;

INDEX

Canada (cont.)
religious missions, 30–31; savior, 29.
See also Sexual Orientation and Gender
Identity (SOGI)
Canadian High Commission, 71, 72
Canadian HIV/ AIDS Legal Network, 35,
36, 39
Canadian Lesbian and Gay Archives
(CLGA), 38, 176n7
Candle in the Wind, 48
Caribbean Court of Justice, 60–62
"Caribbean" narratives: as diseased,
death, criminal, other, 49, 65, 81, 82, 106,
107, 112, 129, 139; colonial consumption,
87; queer (un)belonging, 53, 54, 80, 109;
social class, 51
Carnival, 13, 20, 21, 71, 118, 148, 180n11
Carrington, Michael, 98
Chaguanas, 113
Chaguaramas, 150; Boardwalk, 150;
Chaguaramas Convention Center, 118
Chang, Ian, 60, 61
Charles, Stacey, 122, 124; partner, 123
Chevannes, Barry, 18, 151
Choo King, Raymond, 118
Christmas Room, 156–158
citizenship, 10, 13, 22–23, 43, 52–55, 81, 93,
98, 105; claiming it, 8, 14, 26, 150, 164;
from below, 123–124, 161, 166, 177n13
Cliff, Michelle, 20, 114–117
CLR James, 150
coalition building, 56, 65, 66, 165
Cohabitational Relationship Bill
(1996), 121
Cohen, Cathy, 12, 135–136
common law, 121
community. *See* drag, community; queer,
community; and trans, community
conditional queerness, 14, 26, 32, 33, 42,
64, 99, 112, 162
condom, 27, 42, 47, 49, 90–92, 110–112
Crichlow, Wesley, 18, 19, 21, 151
cross-dressing, 19, 20, 26, 47, 59, 60–64,
65, 68, 108, 116, 130–131, 138, 160
See also dressing up
cruising, 88, 100; online, 132, 142, 148
Cuba, 14, 90, 174n13

dancehall, 14–15, 108, 136, 145, 161. *See also*
soca
debris, 27, 81, 88, 89, 91, 104–105;
ephemera, 89
decolonization, 10, 86
Democratic Labor Party (DLP), 96, 98

desire. *See* queer, erotic praxis; queer,
sexual desire; queer, sexual practices
de Souza, Jowelle, 149
diaspora, 6, 7, 32, 36, 59, 139
Diva World pageant, 113, 118
dizziness, 111–112
Dominica, 90, 165
Dominican Republic, 90, 131
Dougla, 1, 113, 173n1
down low, 6, 8, 36, 107, 141
drag: Butch Queens, 119; community, 119;
exploitation, 112, 119; identity, 119; king,
125–126; mothers, 110, 112–113, 119–122,
131; pageantry, 8, 109–114, 110–122
(*see also* Diva World; Queen of Queens);
performance, 1, 14, 108, 117–119, 141;
queens, 1, 16, 110–122, 131, 148; RuPaul
Drag Race, 114. *See also* Prestige House
Drag King Show, 125–128
dressing up, 110, 118, 119, 137, 141, 145–147

economies of desire, 86, 87, 97, 113. *See also*
sex work
Edmondson, Belinda, 160
Edwards, Sean, 118
Ellis, Nadia, 14
embodied theory, 24, 135, 166; disembodied
beings, 105; embodied practices, 6, 7, 16,
17, 21–24, 107, 123, 135, 151
embodiment: Queer, 22–24, 33, 107; of
fear, 57
Envisioning LGBT Human Rights, 36–39
Equal Opportunity Act, 56, 65, 70
Equal Opportunity Commission, 56
Eric Williams, 150
erotic, 121, 161; erotic autonomy, 11, 21, 135,
140, 155; eroticism, 41, 87, 139, 148; erotic
practices, 65, 122, 130, 136; erotic
subjectivity, 14, 122, 124; (*see also*
homoeroticism); intimacy, 166
Espinet, Ramabai, 31
ethnography, 9, 106
exotic, 80, 87, 131, 154, 155

family, 18, 30, 120–121, 126
Family-Faith-Freedom Barbados, 93
Family Planning Association (FPATT),
68, 129
Farrell, Daniel Trey, 126
Father Jason Gordon, archbishop of the
Archdiocese of Port of Spain, 57
femininity, 117, 119, 139, 140–148, 154, 155;
fetishizing, 154–155; hyper, 133, 142, 145,
147, 150; trangressive, 140–151

INDEX

feminist praxis and pedagogies, 6, 11, 54, 72; scholarship, 22, 121; transnational, 22

feminized labor: childcare, 143–144; domesticity, 145; sexuality, 145

Ford-Smith, Honor, 45–46; Sistren Theatre Collective, 45

Four Seasons Hotel, 80, 82, 88, 100, 104

friending, 121

Friends for Life (Trinidad and Tobago), 44, 70, 122

funding, 24, 33, 65. *See also* transnational: funding

futurity, 81, 101, 103, 112, 131, 133, 164

gatekeeper credibility, 9

gay Barbadian queens, 86

gay men, 107, 108, 145

gender, 18, 108, 126, 135; butch, 135–136, 139; fluidity, 130; fuck, 114; labor, 121; nonconforming, 114, 135; performance, 108, 110, 114–117, 126, 137; policing, 126; queer, 126. *See also* transgressive gender

Ghisyawan, Krystal, 5, 14, 107–109, 135, 137–139, 162

ghosts, 88–89

Gill, Lyndon, 14, 44, 122

Global Fund, 44

Golden Girls, 118

Gosine, Andil, 12, 25, 67, 68, 123

Gossett, Reina, 109, 149

Grenada, 91, 113, 122, 165

group of six, 122–124, 136–140

Guyana, 19, 25–26, 36–38, 42–43, 47–48, 135, 151; court of appeal, 60–61; cross-dressing, 65, 68, 138, 153; intimate partner violence, 152; police violence, 54, 72; queer space, 135, 152–163; race, 155–156, 159; state violence, 4, 60–63; trans, 151, 156

Guyana Trans United, 47

Haiti, 31, 90

Harding, Colwyn, 4, 54

Harlequin Hotel, 85

Harriet/Harry, 114–117

hegemony, 22, 23, 32, 33, 140, 155, 166; imperialism, 32, 33, 55, 72; queer liberal hegemony, 32

Help and Shelter, 151

hermeneutic, 14

heteronormativity, 12, 19, 23, 26, 52–53, 96, 99, 100–101, 103, 135; family, 120, 122; masculinity, 54, 113, 177n4; nation, 67, 98–99; personhood, 52, 80, 100; space,

145, 150; violence, 92. *See also* heteropatriarchy; heterosexuality

heteropatriarchy: of development work, masculinity, 4, 155–156; militarization, 150–151; nationalism, 23, 52–54, 95, 155, 177n1, 179n1

heterosexuality, Compulsory, 14, 23, 103, 151

HIV/AIDS, 89, 90, 93, 94, 96, 110, 112, 118, 122, 129, 149; "at risk" trans, 32, 41, 43–45, 90, 111. *See also* AIDS; trans

Hoad, Neville, 6

Hodge, Merle, 120, 122

hoe, 112, 126, 141

homoeroticism, 139, 154–156, 160

homohegemony, 32, 33

homonationalism, 25, 34, 69, 175n3

homonormativity, 29, 111, 123, 164

homophobia, 14, 33, 144, 149; internalized, 144; messages, 87; nationalism, 26, 151; othering, 32; Rasta, 96; religious, 26, 93; trauma, 45 *See also* police

hotel, 80–105, 132, 145

Hugo Graubel, 131

human rights, 5–7, 9, 32, 36, 65, 98; interventions, 32

I Am One, 3, 70, 124, 125, 127–129

identity, 12, 19, 20, 50, 96, 118; cultural, 19; gender and sexual identity, 7, 13, 17, 19, 23, 36, 39, 55, 57, 65; globalized "gay" identity, 57; national, 118; racial, 17; self-making, 5, 20, 28; SOGI, 30; and violence, 30, 45, 60, 62. *See also* drag, identity; queer, identity politics; trans, identity

IGDS (Institute for Gender and Development Studies), 68

"improper purpose", 60–62

Indian/Indo-Caribbean, 10, 21, 30, 48, 63, 108, 113, 118; class and race, 19, 155, 156, 159, 160; dance, 139; drag, 117–118; families, 145; masculinity, 19, 152; rum, 138, 152, 154, 155, 156; socialisation, 108; transgressive gender, 113, 160

internal exile, 106, 109, 114–119, 123, 127, 133, 164

intimacy, 36, 87, 91–93, 123, 126, 144, 152, 164, 176n7, 180n4

Jackson, Shona, 12

Jamaica, 6, 9, 10, 35, 90; activism, 34–35, 49, 64, 124, 174n10, 176n7; HIV, 90; homophobia, 38, 94; human rights, 33, 35; migration, 37; Pride, 39–42; queerness, 14, 15, 32; religion, 53–58

Jamaica, 32; Ministries of Labor and Health, 35; National HIV Commission, 35. *See also* TransMan

Jamaican Coalition for a Healthier Society, 56

Jamaican Forum for Lesbians Allsexuals and Gays (JFLAG), 39, 49

Jamaica Youth Support for Life (JASL), 49

jamette, 63

Jeremy, 151, 153, 154, 156, 159, 160, 161

Johnson, E. Patrick, 22

Jones, Jason, 26, 56, 57, 69, 70, 98; and CAISO, 58

Kay, 135–139

Kempadoo, Kamala, 21, 79, 86, 96

Kia Rankin Boss, 149

King, Rosamond, 11, 20, 21, 24, 80, 119, 124, 174n14

kinship, 8, 19, 59, 68, 106–134. *See also* community; family

Kitty Village, 154

Kleos, 124–125, 133

Kumar, Preity, 92, 152, 154–155

landscape, 9, 40, 155, 165; abandoned, 87; invented, 82; political, 174n10, 177n11; tourist, 87

Lazarus, Latoya, 53, 57

Lee, Phillip, 66

legitimacy, 14, 16, 32, 33, 36, 63, 65, 67, 69, 104, 135, 153, 162

lesbian, 11, 122–124, 128, 135–137, 153–154

Lewis, Linden, 18, 19, 20–21, 151, 152, 155, 160

lime, 121, 139, 140, 145, 148, 154, 173n3; beach lime, 150; liming, 1, 4, 108, 136

litigation, 51, 60–62, 175–176n6

loitering laws, 3, 26, 62, 63, 163

Lorde, Audre, 12, 106, 121, 140

Love, Heather, 7

love: community, 68, 128, 131; God's, 93–94, 99, 123; of life, 109; lover, 114, 121, 123, 126; zami, 121–122

Lucas, Bryan, 118, 129

macoumé, 2, 13, 173n4

Madivine, 121

Manhattan, 88

Marc, 136–139

Martha, 131, 146, 147

Martha Divine, 131

Mati, 121–124, 180n4

masculinity, 17–20, 147; Black male heteropatriarchy, 4, 133, 155; hypermas-

culinity, 145; Indo-Caribbean, 19; metaphors of, 18; and race, 155–156; transgressive, 136, 139

Mashramani, 159

May, Theresa, 58

McEwan, Clarke, Fraser, Persaud and SASOD vs the Attorney General of Guyana, 26, 60–63

McKittrick, Katherine, 5

men who have sex with men (MSM), 12, 15, 34, 35, 42, 44, 93

Merricks Resort, 85

Metal House, 118

Moore, Carla, 14, 32, 58

Mitchell, Kenty, 53, 155

Mohammed, Patricia, 18, 19

Mohanty, Chandra, 72, 109

Mootoo, Shani, 20

Mona, Kwesi, 72

Mottley, Mia, 98

Muñoz, Jose, 88, 101, 103, 104, 107, 164; ecstatic time, 101

Murray, David, 13, 30, 80, 86–87

Mullings, Beverly, 86

nationalism, 52, 65, 68. *See also* heteronormativity; homonationalism

natural/unnatural, 13, 23, 40, 52, 68, 100, 115

neocolonialism, 24, 27; imperialism, 81, 82, 87, 88, 105; international organizations, 25

Network of NGOs (Non-Governmental Organizations), 68

Nicol, Nancy, 38

Nixon, Angelique, 11, 13, 21, 24, 66, 86, 87

Non-governmental organizations (NGOs), 4, 12, 24, 156

"non-procreative" sex, 97, 100

Old Time Cellar Lounge, 153–154

organizations, 123

"othering", 30–31

Pablo's, 145–146

Pan American Health Organization, 91

Paradise Beach LLC, 85

Paramaribo, 121

passing, 13, 117, 141, 142

Pat, 136

Paterson, Robin, 83

Peace Corps, 156

Pemberton, Michael, 83

penis, 136, 139, 140, 180n2; cock, 11; dick, 103, 130–131; prick, 2–4, 136–137

Persadie, Ryan, 139
personhood, 16, 19, 23, 52. *See also*
  subject
Petronella, 60–61
phantoms, 100; ghost, 88, 89, 105
Philip, M. NourbeSe, 63, 111
police, 2–4, 60, 78, 156; harassment, 158;
  human rights violation, 61; Royal
  Barbados Police Force, Royal Saint
  Lucia Police Force, and the Royal Police
  Force of Antigua and Barbuda, 33–36;
  violence, 2–4, 53, 54, 117, 156
politics of escape, 5, 17, 38, 132, 176n7
pornography, 133
Port of Spain, 1, 55, 57, 63, 70, 107, 108, 110,
  113, 118, 125, 141, 143, 148
Prestige House, 119–122
Pride, 38, 118, 128; Jamaican Pride, 39–42;
  Montego Bay, 39; Pride Arts Festival,
  129; Trinidad and Tobago, 128
Princess, 113–114, 117, 130–134
Promenade (Georgetown, Guyana), 161
Puar, Jasbir, 34, 69, 117

Quality of Citizenship Jamaica (QCJ), 43
Queen of Queens, 110, 112, 113, 125
queer, 12–15, 101, 167; absented presence, 5;
  acceptance, 56; belonging, 111; community, 8, 16, 56, 107, 109–111, 118, 120,
  122–127, 144, 147, 164; conditional
  queerness, 26, 32, 64; embodiment, 41,
  107, 133, 136; erotic praxis, 80, 82, 87, 96,
  99, 100, 140; exile, 7; freedom, 37, 40, 72;
  hermeneutic, 14; history, 80; identity
  politics, 47, 103; impossibility, 107;
  kinship, 119–122; liberation, 9, 25, 27,
  79; modernity, 40, 58; parties, 108;
  performance, 14; pleasure seeking, 80,
  90–91, 100, 104, 132–133; politics, 6, 12;
  refuge, 30, 32; resistance, 37; sexual
  desire, 13, 86, 87, 88, 103, 129–134; sexual
  practices, 82, 90; subjectivity, 101, 109,
  117. *See also* drag; queer activism; trans;
  trans, activism
queer activism, 6, 25, 32, 33, 45, 57–58, 69,
  78, 140, 166. *See also* Alliance for Justice
  and Diversity; CAISO; Friends for Life;
  Guyana Trans United; Help and Shelter;
  I Am One; Jamaican Coalition for a
  Healthier Society; Jamaican Forum for
  Lesbians Allsexuals and Gays (JFLAG);
  Jamaica Youth Support for Life (JASL);
  Quality of Citizenship Jamaica; the
  Silver Lining Foundation; Transgender

Coalition of T&T; TransMan; WINAD;
  Womantra; Women's Caucus of T&T
queer international media, 58; Gay Star
  News, 38, 58, 59; Daily Xtra, 38; Pink
  News, 58

race, 21, 155, 161
Ramjattan, Khemraj, 151
Rampersad, Devindra, 55
Ramsaran, Dave, 152, 155, 160
Rastafari/an, 94–96; URIA [Universal
  Rastafari Improvement Association],
  96; sex, 96; women, 96
Razack, Sherene, 29
Rebuild TT, 56
Reddock, Rhoda, 121
red woman, 154; mixed race, 154–155,
  159–161, 173n1
relics, 27, 81, 82. *See also* debris
religion, 30–31, 53, 55–59, 61, 93; Christian,
  93–94, 123; evangelical christianity, 66,
  93; Jesus, 93; salvation, 93; sin, 93
religious nationalism, 55–59, 60, 105
resilience, 4, 5, 17, 38, 66, 105, 165–167
resistance, 38, 41, 70, 87, 128, 135, 140, 166;
  queer resistance, 38, 55–59
respectability, 65, 68, 81, 87, 111, 113, 140,
  142–143, 158–159. *See also* dizziness
Responsive Grant Mechanism, 66
Richards, Shirley, 55; Lawyers' Christian
  Fellowship, 55
Robinson, Tracy, 24, 52, 62
Robinson, Colin, 50, 58, 65, 67, 69, 78
Rudd, Amber, UK Home Secretary, 59
ruin, 81, 100, 105; structural decay, 88
ruination, 80, 87, 105
rum, 27, 31, 91, 121, 122, 138, 154, 180n1
rumshop/bar, 15, 18, 19, 21, 22, 48, 59, 80,
  122–124, 135–136, 138–141, 145–146

safety: Keep safe, 72–78; Safer Together,
  79; safe sex, 111, 132; safe space, 100, 109,
  132–133, 135–140, 145, 158; and social
  class, 158
Sally's Rum Shop, 154–156, 159–160
Samaroo, Brinsley, 30
same-sex marriage, 26, 36, 56, 58, 67,
  93, 121
Sandy, 1–5, 119, 140
Sandy Lane Resort, 83
Santos-Febres, Myra, 131
Sariah, 109–113, 117, 119–122, 129
Sasha, 154–155
Sasha and Vik, 117

198   INDEX

Saucy Pow, Kelvin Darlington, 147–151

Savannah, 2, 3, 109, 141

Savannah Bar, 141, 145, 158

savior/"save", 25, 29, 30, 36, 40, 42, 58, 93

secreto abierto, 80

sensitivity, 33–36, 66

sex, 166. *See also* queer, erotic praxis;
queer, sexual desire; queer, sexual
practices; safety, safe sex; sex work; suck
(prick)

sexual agency, 14

sexual desire, 81, 130

sexual economies, 87. *See also* economies
of desire

sexual education, 129–130, 133

Sexual Offences Act, 10

Sexual Orientation and Gender Identity
(SOGI) refugee, 30

sex work, 5, 41, 109, 112, 117, 118, 122, 130,
140, 145–146, 156, 179n3; criminality, 26,
62, 79; gully queen, 41; HIV/AIDS, 20,
44, 45, 90; street girl, 1, 113; support
services, 45–48; survival, 86, 109; and
trans identity, 16

Sheller, Mimi, 80; citizenship from below,
123, 161, 162; erotic power, 136. *See also*
landscape: invented

Shiw Parsad, Basmat, 152

Sidnell, Jack, 138

silencing, 5, 13, 17, 25, 27, 37, 117, 124,
152, 167

Silvera, Makeda, 11, 31

Sirena, Selena, 131

Sistren Theatre Collective, 45–46

skunk, 88, 89, 93

slackness, 81

Smith, Frederick H. 138

Smith, M.G. 120–121

Smokey and Bunty, 141, 148

Snorton, C. Riley, 5, 17, 36

soca, 108, 148, 159, 160, 179n1, 180n7, 180n11

social class, 108, 118, 139, 155–163

social media, 71, 119, 132, 148, 150;
community, 6, 107; hook-ups, 132;
marketing, 119, 128, 148; visibility, 148

Society Against Sexual Orientation
Discrimination (SASOD), 26, 36, 37, 47,
48, 60–63, 162, 175n6

soil, 82. *See also* debris; relic

space-making, 107, 119–122, 135–136;
co-opting space, 141, 147, 162, 166

St. Lucia, 35, 86

Stoler, Ann, 27, 81, 88, 91, 105

street girl, 1

Style Cafe, 161–163

subject. *See* personhood: subjectivity

subjective boundaries, 137

suck (prick), 2, 3, 4, 101, 130, 145

Super Grand, 118

Suriname, 90

Tambiah, Yasmin, 52

temporality: anachronistic time, 81, 103;
ecstatic time, 101–103

the Silver Lining Foundation, 70, 129

Thompson, Krista, 87

Tinsley, Omise'eke, 4, 41, 140, 177n2

Tomlinson, Maurice, 33; husband Tom
Decker, 33

Toronto, 6, 9, 10, 11; human rights work,
32, 34, 37, 38, 39, 71, 176n7, 176n9

tourism, 24, 85; employment, 86, 103;
informal, 86; overdependence, 86; sex,
86, 87

tourist imagination, 87

trans, 3, 15–17, 72, 79, 107, 161; activism,
46–51, 60–63, 70, 135; agency, 4; chick
with a dick, 130–131; community, 107,
119–122; erotic praxis, 130; family,
126–127; fetishism, 132–133, 145–146;
friendship, 107; healthcare, 125; HIV/
AIDS, 90, 112, 118, 128; identity, 125;
kinship, 107, 119–122, 131; men, 122–128,
136–140; padding, 114, 116, 136; passing,
117; performance, 117, 136, 147–151; sex
with, 130–131; social class, 64–65, 110–111,
139; women, 8, 15, 62, 107–122. *See also*
internal exile; sex work

Transgender Coalition of T&T, 70

transgressive gender, 80, 82, 117, 124–125,
133, 135, 140, 147–151. *See also* femininity;
masculinity

transgressive subject, 19, 20–22, 63, 100,
103, 104, 140

transitory spaces, 109, 135, 162

TransMan, 124–125

trans masculine, 122, 179n4

transnational, 116, 118; feminism, 22;
funding, 26–27, 33, 42–47, 50, 58, 68, 71,
90, 105, 165; gaze, 80; media, 39, 41,
57–58, 133; queer liberation politics, 5–7,
15, 57, 78, 159, 162, 165; queer organizing,
25–26, 33, 39; sexuality, 117

transphobia, 142, 144, 146

Trinidad and Tobago, 90, 118, 135. *See also*
Arima; Port of Spain

Trotz, Alissa, 4, 31, 61

Trouillot, Michel-Rolph, 166

UNAIDS, 33, 42–43, 49–50, 90
unbelonging, 111
Uncle Cyrus, 118
United Nations, 50, 176n7
United Progressive Party, 96
University of the West Indies, 91
University Rights Action Project (U-RAP), 61
unliving, 5

vice, 130
Villa Court, 159
violence, 39, 78, 139; abuse, 91; colonial violence, 80, 82, 83, 88, 90, 111, 124; domestic violence, 91, 118, 151; familial, 30; and intimacy, 91–92, 152; invisible, 92; in media, 149; murder, 72; racially motivated, 155; sexual abuse/assault, 149; trauma, 45, 117; victimhood, 37, 149. *See also* alcohol; police: violence
visibility, 54, 100; hypervisibility, 1, 161–162

Wahab, Amar, 3, 36, 54, 173n8, 177n3
Wekker, Gloria, 121, 124, 180n4
West, Wayne, Bishop D, 56
Weston, Kath, 122
white neoliberal rhetoric, 58
Williams, H. Shariff, 91
Wilson, Peter, 138
WINAD (Women's Institute for Alternative Development), 68
wining, 148, 160
Winner, Michael, 83
Womantra, 70
Women's Caucus of T&T, 70
World Health Organization, 91
World Pride Human Rights Conference, 38

Youth, 41, 45, 49, 129; trans youth, 113; youth-led organization, 176

Zabus, Chantal, 117
Zami, 121

About the Author

Nikoli A. Attai is an assistant professor of ethnic studies, focusing on Black, queer, and feminist studies. Alongside his teaching and academic work, he also collaborates with LGBTIQ+ communities in the Caribbean. He holds a master of philosophy in cultural studies from the University of the West Indies, St. Augustine, Trinidad and Tobago, and a bachelor of arts in media and communication from the University of the West Indies, Mona Jamaica. Attai's other research and scholarly interests include queer carnival tourism in Trinidad and Tobago, transgressive community making in the Caribbean, and social media visibility by gender-nonconforming people in the Caribbean.

Available titles in the Critical Caribbean Studies series:

Giselle Anatol, *The Things That Fly in the Night: Female Vampires in Literature of the Circum-Caribbean and African Diaspora*

Alaí Reyes-Santos, *Our Caribbean Kin: Race and Nation in the Neoliberal Antilles*

Milagros Ricourt, *The Dominican Racial Imaginary: Surveying the Landscape of Race and Nation in Hispaniola*

Katherine A. Zien, *Sovereign Acts: Performing Race, Space, and Belonging in Panama and the Canal Zone*

Frances R. Botkin, *Thieving Three-Fingered Jack: Transatlantic Tales of a Jamaican Outlaw, 1780–2015*

Melissa A. Johnson, *Becoming Creole: Nature and Race in Belize*

Carlos Garrido Castellano, *Beyond Representation in Contemporary Caribbean Art: Space, Politics, and the Public Sphere*

Njelle W. Hamilton, *Phonographic Memories: Popular Music and the Contemporary Caribbean Novel*

Lia T. Bascomb, *In Plenty and in Time of Need: Popular Culture and the Remapping of Barbadian Identity*

Aliyah Khan, *Far from Mecca: Globalizing the Muslim Caribbean*

Rafael Ocasio, *Race and Nation in Puerto Rican Folklore: Franz Boas and John Alden Mason in Porto Rico*

Ana-Maurine Lara, *Streetwalking: LGBTQ Lives and Protest in the Dominican Republic*

Anke Birkenmaier, ed., *Caribbean Migrations: The Legacies of Colonialism*

Sherina Feliciano-Santos, *A Contested Caribbean Indigeneity: Language, Social Practice, and Identity within Puerto Rican Taíno Activism*

H. Adlai Murdoch, ed., *The Struggle of Non-Sovereign Caribbean Territories: Neoliberalism since the French Antillean Uprisings of 2009*

Robert Fatton Jr., *The Guise of Exceptionalism: Unmasking the National Narratives of Haiti and the United States*

Rafael Ocasio, *Folk Stories from the Hills of Puerto Rico/Cuentos folklóricos de las montañas de Puerto Rico*

Yveline Alexis, *Haiti Fights Back: The Life and Legacy of Charlemagne Péralte*

Katerina Gonzalez Seligmann, *Writing the Caribbean in Magazine Time*

Jocelyn Fenton Stitt, *Dreams of Archives Unfolded: Absence and Caribbean Life Writing*

Alison Donnell, *Creolized Sexualities: Undoing Heteronormativity in the Literary Imagination of the Anglo-Caribbean*

Vincent Joos, *Urban Dwellings, Haitian Citizenships: Housing, Memory, and Daily Life in Haiti*

Krystal Nandini Ghisyawan, *Erotic Cartographies: Decolonization and the Queer Caribbean Imagination*

Yvon van der Pijl and Francio Guadeloupe, eds., *Equaliberty in the Dutch Caribbean: Ways of Being Non/Sovereign*

Patricia Joan Saunders, *Buyers Beware: Insurgency and Consumption in Caribbean Popular Culture*

Atreyee Phukan, *Contradictory Indianness: Indenture, Creolization, and Literary Imaginary*

Nikoli A. Attai, *Defiant Bodies: Making Queer Community in the Anglophone Caribbean*